T0391647

The Law of Riba in Islamic Banking

The issue of riba, that is, interest/the "excess" or "surplus," on loans is crucial for both Islamic and non-Islamic countries. Western economic systems use interest to distribute financial resources efficiently for investment and/or consumption, while Islamic economies pursue a completely different strategy for financing loans, which adheres to Islamic laws and prohibits the activities of conventional banking systems with regard to interest. This book argues that there is scope for new definitions and analysis based on alternative concepts which respect Islamic values and principles, yet pave the way for modification and debate.

The book comprises two parts. Theoretical issues are dealt with in the first section. The first two chapters examine conventional Islamic views on the prohibition of riba, while Chapters 3 and 4 contain unprecedented and alternative theoretical analysis based on concepts such as "earned" (halal–permitted–legal) vs. "unearned" (haram–impermissible–illegal) income and SUKUK, that is, Islamic interest-free bonds. The second part of the book tackles another unconventional aspect of Islamic finance, that is, the concept of NAS. The book considers whether the NAS-influenced anti-inflationary interest policy was a success or failure. Empirical data is evaluated in terms of bank incomes, inflation rate, interest rate, and the distribution of income.

This book will be a useful guide for students, scholars, and researchers of Islamic banking and finance.

Hasan Gürak is Senior Researcher in the School of Economics and Management, University of Lund, Sweden.

Neelambar Hatti is Professor Emeritus in the Department of Economic History, School of Economics and Management, University of Lund, Sweden.

Islamic Business and Finance Series

Series Editor: Ishaq Bhatti

There is an increasing need for Western politicians, financiers, bankers, and indeed the Western business community in general to have access to high-quality and authoritative texts on Islamic financial and business practices. Drawing on expertise from across the Islamic world, this new series will provide carefully chosen and focused monographs and collections, each authored/edited by an expert in their respective field all over the world.

The series will be pitched at a level to appeal to middle and senior management in both the western and the Islamic business communities. For the manager with a Western background, the series will provide detailed and up-to-date briefings on important topics; for the academics, postgraduates, business communities, manager with Western and an Islamic background the series will provide a guide to best practice in business in Islamic communities around the world, including Muslim minorities in the West and majorities in the rest of the world.

Higher Education Finance and Islamic Endowments
Nurul Adilah Hasbullah and Asmak Ab Rahman

Economic Capital and Risk Management in Islamic Finance
Abdul Ghafar Ismail and Muhamed Zulkhibri

The Global Halal Industry
A Research Companion
Hussain Mohi-ud-Din Qadri

The Law of Riba in Islamic Banking
Conventional and Unconventional Approaches to Interest-Free Financing
Edited by Hasan Gürak and Neelambar Hatti

For more information about this series, please visit: www.routledge.com/Islamic-Business-and-Finance-Series/book-series/ISLAMICFINANCE

The Law of Riba in Islamic Banking

Conventional and Unconventional Approaches
to Interest-Free Financing

**Edited by
Hasan Gürak and Neelambar Hatti**

Routledge
Taylor & Francis Group

LONDON AND NEW YORK

First published 2024
by Routledge
4 Park Square, Milton Park, Abingdon, Oxon OX14 4RN

and by Routledge
605 Third Avenue, New York, NY 10158

Routledge is an imprint of the Taylor & Francis Group, an informa business

British Library Cataloguing-in-Publication Data
A catalogue record for this book is available from the British Library

Library of Congress Cataloging-in-Publication Data
Names: Gürak, Hasan, editor. | Hatti, Neelambar, 1940– editor.
Title: The law of riba in Islamic banking : conventional and unconventional approaches to interest-free financing / edited by Hasan Gürak and Neelambar Hatti.
Description: Abingdon, Oxon ; New York, NY : Routledge, 2024. | Includes bibliographical references and index.
Identifiers: LCCN 2023047572 (print) | LCCN 2023047573 (ebook) | ISBN 9781032631516 (hardback) | ISBN 9781032631554 (paperback) | ISBN 9781032631561 (ebook)
Subjects: LCSH: Banks and banking—Religious aspects—Islam. | Interest—Religious aspects—Islam.
Classification: LCC HG3368.A6 L428 2024 (print) | LCC HG3368.A6 (ebook) | DDC 332.10917/67—dc23/eng/20240125
LC record available at https://lccn.loc.gov/2023047572
LC ebook record available at https://lccn.loc.gov/2023047573

ISBN: 978-1-032-63151-6 (hbk)
ISBN: 978-1-032-63155-4 (pbk)
ISBN: 978-1-032-63156-1 (ebk)

DOI: 10.4324/9781032631561

Typeset in Times New Roman
by codeMantra

Seek knowledge from the cradle to the grave.

Contents

Figures

Tables

Contributors

Dr. Mohammed Nurul Alam
Professor, Yorkville University, Ontario Campus, Concord, Canada

Dr. Şenol Babuşcu
Professor, Department of International Finance and Banking, Baskent University, Ankara, Türkiye

Dr. Atalay Çağlar
Associate Professor, Department of Economics, Pamukkale University, Türkiye

Dr. Haşmet Gökırmak
Associate Professor, Department of Business and Management Sciences, Sabahattin Zaim University, Istanbul, Türkiye

Dr. Hasan Gürak
Professor, Senior Researcher at the School of Economics and Management, University of Lund, Sweden

Dr. Neelambar Hatti
Department of Economic History, School of Economics and Management, University of Lund, Sweden

Dr. Adalet Hazar
Professor, Department of International Finance and Banking, Baskent University, Ankara, Türkiye

Dr. Nihat Işık
Professor, Department of Econometrics, Kirikkale University, Türkiye

Dr. Monzer Kahf
Professor, Istanbul Sabahattin Zaim University, Istanbul, Türkiye

Dr. Efe Can Kılınç
Associate Professor, Department of Econometrics, Kirikkale University, Türkiye

Dr. Handan Kumaş
Professor, Department of Labor Economics and Industrial Relations, Pamukkale University, Türkiye

Dr. Fuat Sekmen
Professor, Department of Economics, Sakarya University, Türkiye

Safa Yıldıran
Research Assistant, Istanbul Sabahattin Zaim University, Istanbul, Türkiye

Dr. Suat Serhat Yılmaz
Research Assistant, Department of Economics, Kirikkale University, Turkiye

Introduction

The issue of *riba*,[1] or interest, is crucial for both Islamic and non-Islamic countries. Western economic systems use the interest rate to efficiently distribute financial resources for investment and/or consumption. In the entire economic system outside the Islamic countries, interest rates are practically a prerequisite, for the functioning of the economic system. Islamic economies, on the contrary, pursue an entirely different strategy for financing loans, which must be in accordance with Islamic laws and do not allow the activities of conventional Western banking systems in Islamic countries.

Since the economies of Islamic and non-Islamic countries are interdependent, they have to learn how to live together for mutual benefit. In fact, many global Western financial companies seem to have adapted some of their operations to the conditions prescribed by Islamic law. Today, numerous financial companies, founded on Islamic principles, operate not only in countries ruled by Islamic law but also in many other countries around the world.

> The Banker's 2020 Top Islamic Financial Institutions ranking highlights the continued growth of the industry, which has doubled in size over the past decade and has experienced a compound annual growth rate (CAGR) of around 10.8% since 2006. Globally, there are now 47 financial institutions with more than $10bn in sharia-compliant assets, with 27 institutions recording a pre-tax profit of more than $500m in 2019.
>
> (www.thebanker.com/Markets/Top-Islamic-Financial-Institutions-2020, 2023-01-25)

Regarding riba on loans, the Holy Quran determines the principles and maintenance of life for all faithful Muslims. When Muslims cannot find the answer they are looking for in the Holy Quran, they refer to the Hadith, which comprise the words and customs of the Prophet. The Hadith, just like the verses in the Holy Quran, must be obeyed, but they deal, mainly, with *shopping or trade*, known as *commodity-riba*. Since commodity-riba is not the main issue dealt with in the present study, the Hadith will be excluded to avoid confusion between **riba on loans** and **commodity-riba**. The critical question is whether *there is a divine definition of riba and its scope for loans*.

DOI: 10.4324/9781032631561-1

Thus far, the study of a "divine" definition of riba seems to have been over-looked. It will be interesting to find out whether the question raised above is justified. If there is no divine definition, it would imply that Islamic economic rules *for loans* have been shaped and implemented *not by "divine" orders* but by the interpretations of the Ulama or Islamic scholars, who are neither "divine" nor "sacred."

If Islamic concepts and objectives are correctly interpreted and applied, avoiding riba-interest reductionism, it would facilitate the effective application of international economic transactions while preventing "unjust" or "unearned" income and minimizing exploitation.

The plan of study

The present volume consists of two sections. The theoretical issues will be dealt with in the first section comprising four chapters. The first two chapters contain the conventional "Islamic" views on the prohibition of riba, without questioning the nature of riba or its scope. The following chapters by Gürak contain unconventional analysis based on concepts such as **"earned"** (*halal*–permitted–legal) **vs. "unearned"** (*haram*–impermissible–illegal) income, which interprets riba as "unjust gain" or "unearned income."

The second section of the book starts with the chapter by Gürak and concerns the Islamic concept of *Nas*,[2] with special reference to Turkish President Erdoğan's claim that *"interest is the cause; inflation is the result."* The remaining empirical chapters take a closer look at the data for 2022, the year Türkiye was subject to President Erdoğan's Nas policy. The data is evaluated in terms of bank incomes, inflation rate, foreign exchange-rate-protected deposits, and the position of women in the Turkish labor market. These contributions aim to examine whether the Nas-influenced anti-inflationary interest policy was a success or failure.

The contributions[3]

In their essay, in Chapter 1, Prof. Kahf and Dr. Yıldıran state that financial crises are one of the most critical problems faced frequently in the recent history of humanity and that after each severe financial crisis, decision-makers are inclined to more regulations and interventions in the financial system. In response, deregulation processes are introduced, following the inadequacies initiated by the previous interventions. The authors argue that while there is a clear need for reforming the financial system, it is crucial to think about the reforms outside the box because the reforms attempted inside the box could not propose a remedy with adequate satisfaction for the financial crises and the other problems in the current financial system. This chapter focuses on the reforms outside the box and their possible implications for economic development as well as the stability and sustainability of the financial system.

The authors seek to explain the potential economic rationale behind the prohibition of interest through discussions on the reforms outside the box and their possible implications for economic development as well as the stability and sustainability of the financial system. They argue that excessive credit/indebtedness and interbank connectivity are idiosyncratic characteristics of the capitalist financial system, leading to instability and unsustainability, whereas the Islamic financial system rejects interest-based finance and proposes financing methods based on sale, lease, and venture capital (equity sharing). This feature of Islamic finance tackles the inconveniences, resulting in instability and unsustainability because of excessive credits/indebtedness and high interbank connectivity through debt sales, as shown by empirical studies on the performance of Islamic financial institutions during and after financial crises and shocks.

Prof. Alam's views in Chapter 2 discuss the role of interest in Islamic banking and provides an empirical review of Islamic financing. The "riba" or "interest" is prohibited in Islam. There are different Islamic financing techniques or modes applied by Islamic banks while conducting financial transactions with customers, details of which are discussed in the chapter. In many developing nations, small and medium enterprises (SMEs) contribute considerably to economic growth. However, due to the shortage of capital, SMEs are forced to borrow funds from local moneylenders and at a high rate of interest. Dr. Alam highlights the fact that Islamic banks in many countries like Bangladesh, Sudan, Türkiye, and Cyprus invest their funds in the SME sector without interest. Prof. Alam concludes that even though Islamic banking functions differ in different countries under different socioeconomic and environmental conditions, the lender–borrower relationship is remarkably close. Moreover, Islamic banks apparently show greater interest in investing a large proportion of their cash in the small business sector in "partnership mode."

Prof. Gürak's Chapter 3 begins with the statement that getting or paying "interest" on loans is "the" most vehemently and frequently debated subject of Islamic economics. While there is no doubt that the Holy Quran forbids riba, he raises the question of whether the Holy Quran gives a "divine" definition of riba or its scope and concludes that the Holy Quran does not offer a "divine" definition of riba or its scope. The present definitions and interpretations of riba are provided by Islamic scholars, who are mainly educated in religious issues and not infrequently have poor knowledge of actual economic issues.

Islamic scholars are not sacred people and are prone to making mistakes, like all humans. Therefore, their words cannot be considered equivalent to "divine" orders. In light of this background, Dr. Gürak attempts to provide alternative concepts and an analysis based on **"unjust"** or **"unearned" income**. He argues that by applying the alternative concepts and their analysis to the financial sector, the nature and approach of the issue of the prohibition of riba could be changed. Lastly, Dr. Gürak makes the point that the alternative concepts and analysis presented in his chapter are not meant as alternatives to the Quranic verses but as alternatives to the Islamic scholars' interpretations of these holy verses.

Prof. Gürak's second contribution, Chapter 4 deals with the question of an Islamic "interest-free" bond. He states that conventional non-Islamic financial instruments have existed for centuries, whereas Islamic financial activities are relatively recent, beginning in the 1960s. Nevertheless, the Islamic financial sector has developed its instruments rapidly since then, and a Muslim customer can get almost all the financial services supplied by a conventional Western type of financial sector through so-called participation banks in Türkiye, which are claimed to be run in compliance with Islamic values and norms. For instance, these participation banks collect funds through special methods to finance economic activities, such as interest-free Islamic bonds. Based on a detailed analysis, Prof. Gürak concludes that banking transactions on bonds, whether Islamic or non-Islamic, are remarkably similar in that they both gain excess income at predetermined rates of return. In addition, the investment procedure for external capital owners is almost identical for both traditional and Islamic bonds.

Prof. Gürak's third contribution, Chapter 5, deals with President Erdoğan's assertion that "Interest is the cause, inflation is the result." Did Erdoğan just intend to remind Muslims that if they disobey Allah's order on the prohibition of getting/paying interest and bow before evil, they will have to suffer the consequences? Prof. Gürak seeks to shed light on the nature of Erdoğan's argument and to find out whether there is indeed a Nas, i.e., words in the Holy Quran and/or Hadith with the specific aim of "**curbing inflation by using interest rate**" as an economic instrument. Dr. Gürak concludes that there is no Nas either in the Holy Quran or in Hadith with direct reference to the inflation-interest rate (riba) relationship to guide the Muslims **in the fight against inflation**. The Holy Quran has clearly forbidden riba but provided no definition of riba or its scope on loans. And there is no statement supporting the cause-result relationship considering riba and inflation. Prof. Gürak concludes that it is perhaps more appropriate to consider Erdoğan's claim as an "Erdoğan-patented anti-inflationary hypothesis with a religious flavor."

Profs. Babuşcu and Hazar in their essay, in Chapter 6, analyze the impact of the new economic model implemented in Türkiye on the banking sector's profitability in 2022 and aim to provide a forward-looking analysis. According to them, the model is based on the belief that "interest rates are the cause, and inflation is the result" of economic problems. In line with this philosophy, the Central Bank significantly lowered its interest rates despite falling behind the inflation rate, causing deterioration in the macroeconomic indicators of the country. The measures introduced to support the model primarily targeted the banking sector. According to the authors, the observed profitability of the banks in 2022 will likely decline or experience limited growth, thus increasing the risks associated with the banks' balance sheets in both the medium and the long term. They conclude that the implementation of the new economic model over the past year and a half has had serious economic consequences in Türkiye and *plunged the country on a perilous journey*.

Dr. Gökırmak and Dr. Sekmen provide an empirical analysis of President Erdoğan's interest rate policy on the economy of Türkiye, in Chapter 7. Türkiye's economy in 2022 was particularly impacted by a substantial current account deficit, a sharp depreciation of the Turkish Lira, and soaring inflation, notwithstanding a small increase in exports. The authors conclude that the Central Bank's low-interest rate policy from October 2021 worsened these conditions. This sustained low-interest environment adversely impacted various markets, including goods and services, credit, foreign exchange, and labor, thus magnifying the economic strain. The authors explore the complex relationship between inflation and exchange rates in Türkiye's economy, revealing bidirectional causality. This interaction emphasizes the significant influence of interest rates on inflation through shifts in exchange rates, further complicated by the Central Bank's interventions. In conclusion, the authors recommend a comprehensive and proactive macroeconomic strategy, including growth-fostering political and economic policies and careful monitoring of the untenable low-interest rate policy to avoid potential hyperinflation and currency crises, which are crucial for Türkiye's economic stability and future growth.

In their contribution, in Chapter 8, Prof. Işık, Dr. Kılınç and Dr. Yılmaz analyze the effects of the Foreign Exchange Rate-Protected Deposit (FXPD) Implementation, introduced toward the end of December 2021 to stabilize the Turkish lira, on the exchange rate, which is analyzed through the Granger (1969) Causality Test and Breitung and Candelon's (2006) spectral GC test using weekly data for the period between February 18, 2022, and April 14, 2023, for Türkiye. The traditional GC test suggested one-way causality from exchange rates to money supply and from FXPD to deposit interest rates. Breitung and Candelon's (2006) spectral GC analysis revealed that in the medium and long term, there is causality from the dollar exchange rate to the FXPD, in the short and medium terms toward the deposit interest rate and in the long term toward the money supply. Moreover, a medium- and long-term causal relationship between the money supply and the FXPD can be observed. The authors conclude that to achieve the desired impact on exchange rates through the exchange rate–protected deposit application and to ensure stability in exchange rates, deposit interest rates need to be maintained at a level that safeguards depositors' savings against inflation rates.

Prof. Kumaş and Dr. Çağlar examine the effects of the recently changed interest policy, and individual job-related characteristics, on women's wages, in Chapter 9. Based on the international and national labor force, wage, and poverty data, they show that "working women" are one of the most disadvantaged groups in the Turkish labor market. In this sense, the relationship between women's wages and various interest rates has been examined since the beginning of the new discourse on interest. Furthermore, the authors analyze the effect of individual and job-related characteristics on women's wages for 2022, the year after the low-interest rate policy was introduced. Based on their analysis of the 2022 Household Labor Force Statistics Micro Dataset provided by the TURKSTAT, the authors observe a significant correlation between female wages and individual characteristics other than their marital status and the characteristics of the occupation. Prof. Kumaş and Dr. Çağlar conclude that, in Türkiye during 2022, while the interest rate decreased and inflation showed an increasing trend, a *nominal* increase was observed in the average and median wages of women and in the poverty thresholds.

Notes

1 Riba means not only **interest rate** or **usury** but also **unjust gain**.
2 The concept of Nas means the word of God (Allah) and the Prophet, including his actions. The rules of Nas are not open to debate or to interpretation, according to Islamic scholars.
3 All authors are responsible for the content of their articles. The editors, H. Gürak and N. Hatti, take no responsibility for their opinions.

Part 1

Theoretical articles on riba, the "excess"

1 Why does Islamic finance reject interest?

Monzer Kahf and Safa Yıldıran

Introduction

Financial crises are one of the most critical problems in the recent history of humanity. Although we can mention different frequencies of financial crises for particular regions and periods, it can be noted that Western Europe experienced a financial crisis approximately once a decade throughout the past 400 years to give an idea of how frequent this phenomenon is (Kindleberger, 2006, p. 269). After each severe financial crisis, decision-makers are inclined to make more regulations and interventions in the financial system. However, these extensive regulations and interventions generally cause inefficiencies, as stated by Allen and Gale (2007, p. 2). In response, we observe deregulation processes following the inadequacies initiated by the previous interventions. It shows how the paradoxical loop of regulations and deregulations took root in the financial system.

It is well-known that different monetary regimes and regulations have been adopted during the course of the past two centuries while repeatedly experiencing these paradoxical loops. Bordo et al. (2001), classifying the years between 1880 and 1997 into four periods mainly based on the monetary regimes, found that the probability of financial crises in a year varies between 7% and 13%, except in the first period corresponding to years between 1880 and 1913. In addition to the increasing frequency trend, these numbers mean that the countries focused on by Bordo et al. (2001) faced a high probability of financial crisis after 1997, regardless of the monetary regime and regulations. Beyond a doubt, we cannot expect a system that does not let any financial crises happen. However, it is not peculiar to demand a system with fewer crises.

These considerations bring us to the point that there is a clear need for reforming the financial system. At this point, it is crucial to think about the reforms outside the box because the reforms attempted inside the box could not propose a remedy with adequate satisfaction for the financial crises and the other problems in the current financial system. In other words, what we are going to regulate and supervise is a more critical question, although regulation and supervision are, per se, essential. This chapter focuses on the reforms outside the box and their possible implications for economic development as well as the stability and sustainability of the financial

DOI: 10.4324/9781032631561-3

system. Through these discussions, it is aimed at explaining the potential economic rationale behind the prohibition of interest.

The chapter consists of four sections as follows: The first section, after this introduction, asserts the foundational perspective adopted while approaching finance. The second section elaborates on Islamic finance-inspired reforms. The economic rationale for the prohibition of interest, with a particular focus on the distinction between Islamic finance and interest-based finance, constitutes the context of the third section. Lastly, the fourth section presents the implications of implementing the Islamic financial system on development, stability, and sustainability. The chapter ends with concluding remarks.

A foundational perspective toward finance

This section aims to assert a foundational perspective toward finance and financial intermediation. Since finance is a subset of economics and financial intermediaries have roles and functions in economic systems, it is proper to start our discussion on finance with the goals of economic systems. Increasing efficiency and maintaining socioeconomic justice are the two aims that are common in every economic system, although they prioritize either of them over the other to different degrees. Through these aims, economic systems ultimately intend to increase human welfare. Beyond any doubt, one of the prominent determinants contributing to human welfare is the availability of goods and services produced for the people.

Financial tools and institutions, as part of economic systems, are expected to support the production of goods and services, considering the close relationship between production and human welfare. Thus, financial intermediation must be a channel between deficit and surplus economic units to allocate the financial sources to productive activities, which eventually end up improving human welfare. Although the theoretical position of financial intermediation is straightforward and can be easily justified, it has been drifting away from its essential function since the mid-1900s.

Krippner (2005, pp. 180–181), who adopts profit-making channels as the key indicator for financialization, asserts that FIRE, consisting of finance, insurance, and real estate companies, has become the dominant sector in terms of its share in corporate profits in the United States, especially after the 1980s. He also emphasizes that non-financial firms' behavior regarding their sources of profits must also be considered for a better understanding of the financialization level of an economy (Krippner, 2005, p. 182). The data indicating the portfolio income to corporate cash flow ratio, presented by Krippner (2005, p. 185), shows that most non-financial firms' revenues are generated from financial sources of income. From this perspective, it can be said that the profits derived from the US economy are mainly procured by the FIRE companies. Also, non-financial firms' focus has been diverted from production to financial activities. Among these financial activities, interest-generating transactions account for more than 50% of non-financial firms' portfolio incomes (Krippner, 2005, p. 186).

The financial tools have also been transforming in parallel to the changes in the financial sector's share in corporate profits and the involvement of non-financial firms in financial transactions. When the first organized futures exchanges were established, all the contracts were for agricultural commodities. So the claimed aim was to help farmers sell their crops. However, the composition of futures trading has changed in favor of financial instruments in terms of the number of contracts traded, according to the statistics compiled by the Commodity Futures Trading Commission (Born et al., 1997). Currently, the base commodity is not agricultural products, and future contracts are traded assuming they generate wealth. We may see similar patterns in the other financial tools and indicators. For instance, exchange currencies were needed to facilitate international trade. However, it was later thought that currencies create wealth, so we traded currencies online and bet on their price changes. Further, indices were initiated to ease our understanding of market behavior. Nevertheless, we started to trade them because of the same fallacies.

When the transformations in the financial sector's share in the economy, non-financial firms' behaviors, and the structure of the financial tools are considered together, it is obviously seen that not only has the financial sector gradually moved away from contributing to the production and exchange of goods and services and thus to welfare but also the resources of the real sector have shifted to financial instruments that are dysfunctional in terms of their contribution to human welfare. We argue that the most severe problem of the modern economic and financial system is a persistent and intensive disorientation of the finance sector by confusing its support and service functions with a wealth creation function that cannot be undertaken outside the real sector's production and exchange. Therefore, we need to go back to the basics, i.e., financial and human resources must be re-diverted out of speculation and pure financial transactions back into wealth-creating activities. The following section focuses on the Islamic finance-inspired reforms to make the finance sector supportive of the real sectors and prevent it from disturbing, distorting, distracting, and diverting resources.

Islamic finance-inspired reforms

Adapting regulations and supervisory requirements to new needs and circumstances has continuously been resorted to after each crisis cycle, but the subject matter of regulations and supervision is at least as important as the regulations and audits themselves. Regulations that ignore the inherent characteristics of their subject matter cannot deliver the desired results. As a matter of fact, the regulations introduced after each financial crisis have been questioned in terms of whether they target the true deficiencies of the existing financial system (Abojeib et al., 2018, p. 609). Dukhan (2022, p. 150), examining the financial reforms in the late 20th century, emphasizes the necessity of reforming the fundamentals of the capitalist financial system. The fundamental characteristics of the capitalist financial structure, which lead to instability, are the interest being the resource allocator, disengagement of financial transactions from real-world transactions, extreme credit/

indebtedness, excessive virtual assets, trading of risk and expectation, short-term funds roving around, inadequate consistency of regulation and information systems, and high interbank connectivity (Kahf, 2018, pp. 11–12). Since reforms of the financial system essentially aim to ensure allocation efficiency and stability, which are crucial for real-economy growth and its sustainability, the inside-box reforms which ignore the present financial system's unstable nature are unable to achieve the desired aims. Unfortunately, this is what was done after the 2007–2008 Financial Crisis. The virtual instruments enabling risk and expectation trading with a weak link to the real economy continued to be profitable after the Crisis, although they were subjected to some limitations and supervision for a while (Helvacıoğlu, 2022, p. 236). Based on these considerations, this section elaborates on Islamic-finance-inspired and out-of-the-box reforms that are required for long-term policies to ensure financial stability and sustainability.

Elimination of purely speculative zero-sum contracts

Zero-sum contracts indicate that one of the contracting parties' gains is an exact loss for the other contracting party. They transfer wealth from only one party to another without any increase in the total wealth. Poker is an obvious example of a zero-sum game. The prevailing financial system also consists of many zero-sum transactions and contracts, such as contracts for the difference (CFDs), Internet forex trades, and index trading (Kahf, 2018, p. 20). Short contracts in all commodities, currencies, and equity markets have a similar effect of transferring rather than producing wealth.

A more detailed description of one of the zero-sum contracts present in the current financial system helps understand their nature and consequences. Let us consider a CFD that enables investors to trade SPDR S&P 500 (SPY), an exchange-traded fund deriving its value from the S&P 500 index (Chen, 2020). Investors must make a down payment to the broker corresponding to 5% of the amount that will be traded. At the end of maturity, the CFD contract is cash-settled. Depending on the current price of SPY, either the so-called profit derived from the price differences between the contract date and the maturity date is credited to the investor or the so-called loss is compensated from the investor's account.

As seen, the trade through a CFD does not represent an actual trade where a valuable asset is transferred between contracting parties. Instead, it is just a contract that transfers wealth from one party to another based on the price movements of a derivative instrument. It is made up of only speculation and ends up with a cash settlement. Ultimately, one of the contracting parties' gains becomes an exact loss for the other party. As a matter of fact, the figures showing the percentage of investors who lose in trading CFDs confirm the zero-sum nature of the contracts. According to information revealed by six brokerage firms in Europe, between 58% and 85% of traders who trade CFDs end up with a loss (Quantified Strategies, 2023).

The characteristics of a CFD exist in other purely speculative zero-sum contracts, such as Internet forex trades, index trading, and short contracts in commodities, currencies, and equity markets. Considering the total trading volume of these kinds of financial instruments, we are faced with the fact that a significant amount of human and financial resources is attracted to transactions that do not carry any added value. In a different scenario where purely speculative zero-sum contracts are eliminated, these resources would be used in the real market or financial markets supporting the production of goods and services (Kahf, 2018, p. 20). That is why we argue that all purely speculative zero-sum contracts must be gradually eliminated to direct the resources to productive activities and tame the speculation (Kahf, 2016, pp. 261–265).

Restrictions on derivatives trading

Derivative contracts are designed to transfer risks from one party to another. All derivative contracts have an underlying asset from which their value is derived. The most common underlying assets for which derivative contracts are used are stocks, bonds, currencies, commodities, market indices, and interest rates (Powel, 2020). Through forwards, futures, or swap contracts, which are the primary derivative contracts, one may take a short position, meaning that they are obliged to sell the underlying asset at the price and future time specified in the contract. Against every short position, the other party involved in the derivative contract is supposed to have a long position, which stands for an obligation to buy the underlying asset based on the exact specifications in the contract. Depending on the contract, parties may be required to physically deliver the underlying assets or settle the positions in cash without a physical delivery (Powel, 2020). It is worth noting that options, the other most common type of derivative contract, do not refer to an obligation but to the right of delivery or settlement, although they are similar to forward, futures, and swap contracts in terms of the main components.

The parties involved in a derivative contract do not have to wait until the expiration date. They may square off their position by entering an equal transaction in the opposite direction of their current position. Since traders in derivative markets are generally not interested in asset delivery, they offset their position before the expiration date (Samuelsson, 2021). In addition, traders prefer contracts with cash settlement instead of physical delivery (Corporate Finance Institute, 2023). Offsetting the position before the expiration date and the dominance of the contracts with cash settlement reveal the speculative nature embedded in the derivative market.

Although common practices and types of contracts indicate that the purpose of speculation comes into prominence in the derivative markets, derivative contracts have another function: to provide hedging. Let us explain the differences between speculation and hedging through option contracts. When an investor, who bought a technology share in a stock market, wants to restrict possible losses in case of falling prices, he/she can buy a put option, which gives his/her the right to sell the share until or at the expiration date of the option contract. If the share price falls, he/she exercises the put option at a price determined in the contract and offsets the losses in his/her investment by paying the premium for the option (Downey, 2023).

On the contrary, one may buy a call option even though he/she has no investment in the stock market. In this scenario, he/she assumes or predicts that the share price will go up, and the call option he/she bought will give him a chance to sell the share at a higher price than the one determined in the contract. Thus, he/she benefits from the price differences between the strike price in the contract and the spot price in the stock market and gains profits if the stock prices increase as he/she expected (Downey, 2023). While the case mentioned in the previous paragraph shows how an option contract can hedge a real position, the second case presents purely speculative options trading without having a real position in the exchange market. Since the premium paid for the option is much lower than the share price, option contracts make speculation more cost-effective. In other words, one can buy a lot more options with the same amount, and thus gains and losses explode.

Although derivatives, when used for hedging purposes, lower the risk for traders who have an actual position in the market, their speculative trading does not contribute to the real economy. As seen in the examples above, the current structure of the derivative market does not prevent those who trade derivatives for purely speculative gains. The opportunity for cash settlements and the lack of a requirement for an existing real position in the market encourage and facilitate speculative trading. Thus, human and financial resources are attracted from productive activities and directed to purely speculative transactions that do not generate any added value.

Based on the above considerations, we argue that derivative trading must be restricted only to hedging objectives. For this purpose, buying and selling derivatives by those without an outstanding market position should be de-legalized. Only those with an existing position in the market would be able to trade derivatives to sustain the link between the derivative market and the real market. By this regulation, we expect that vast sources consumed for speculation will be re-channeled to the real market, and the instability in financial markets will be reduced.

Elimination of speculative patterns of behavior and genuinizing regulated markets

The exclusion of contracts and markets established for purely speculative purposes does not annihilate speculation in the markets altogether. In other words, speculative behaviors exist in the market and contracts other than those with a purely speculative nature, such as CFDs, forward contracts with cash settlement, and index trading. During the early stages of the financial markets, speculators were considered essential for ensuring liquidity, risk fusion, and depth of the markets. However, this argument has become irrelevant after the improvements in communication technologies that enable trading beyond political borders (Kahf, 2018, p. 22). These developments have eliminated the need for speculation in the markets.

At this point, it is crucial to distinguish between trade and speculation. While both are based on expectations with the risk of failure, the latter stands for much more volatile transactions, which are considerably less associated with real-life activities (Kahf, 2018, p. 16). This is because speculators aim to benefit from price differences in a short time span without intending to acquire real goods and invest in production. In this context, the empirical analysis conducted by Barber et al.

(2009) provides interesting results regarding the behaviors of individual investors trading on the Taiwan Stock Exchange (TSE). According to their findings, the turnover in TSE decreased by one-fourth after legalizing gambling in Taiwan (Barber et al., 2009, p. 629). It can be said that gambling in Taiwan is a direct substitute for trading stocks for a considerable number of individual traders. Thus, the intentions of these individual traders are weakly linked with investments and production.

Currently, speculation is identified in common jargon as "trade" and "investment." The ones who are doing day trading consider themselves traders or investors. However, this assumption or conceptualization does not mean their speculative transactions contribute to and facilitate real investments, productions, or activities that create added value. The percentage of annual trading activities in stock markets that provide additional capital to the listed companies is a good indicator of the difference between investment and speculation. As shown by Askari and Mirakhor (2015, p. 27), only 0.8% of the total annual trade in the stock exchange markets of the United States between 2010 and 2015 enabled capital formation in the real sector. In other words, 99.2% of the transactions were purely speculative without contributing to value-adding investments or production.

Islamic finance is committed to rulings that prevent and tame speculation (Kahf, 2018, p. 16). The requirement of full and immediate payment in transactions of gold, silver, currencies, and quasi-currency items has substantial implications for reducing speculation in foreign exchange and commodity markets. The condition of requiring ownership and physical possession before any sale transaction prevents short sales and leverages, which are facilitators of speculation. Furthermore, there is a need for legal restrictions which reduce market accessibility and lengthen trade processes. The main aim of such restrictions and additional measures is to have stock markets work for the capital needs of the real sector and design the currency markets to serve institutions that have a genuine need for foreign exchange (Kahf, 2018, p. 22).

Restrictions on debt trading

Debt trading is a common practice in the current financial system. Debt securities are issued and traded in the primary and secondary bond markets, one of the largest financial markets. The transactions in the secondary bond market are nothing but a transfer of debt from one creditor to another. The cash value of the transferred debt differs from its face value, depending on maturity and interest rates. Collateralized debt obligation (CDO) is another form of financial derivative that enables financial institutions to transfer debts in the current financial system. Similar to the debt securities traded in the secondary bond markets, CDOs also consist of already-existing debts such as mortgages, other loans, and bonds (Grapulin, 2018, pp. 3–6).

Especially after the 2007–2008 Financial Crisis, CDO-like instruments were subjected to more regulations, but their existence and circulation were not questioned, and the intrinsic characteristics of the instruments leading to problems were ignored (Helvacıoğlu, 2022, p. 246). As explained by Colan (2017), CDOs enable financial institutions to build a derivative consisting of numerous debt contracts expected to provide a certain amount of repayment within a specified maturity. Then, they are sold to the investors at a price lower than the expected repayment amount. Thus, both the initiators of the CDOs and the investors aim to generate profit from the transfers of debts.

Debt transfer allows financial institutions to avoid the liabilities and consequences of their lending. As a natural result of this ability and opportunity, they become less cautious about the risks related to credits, such as default risk, while providing finance to their customers. Thus, the risk-related reasons for limiting credits are eliminated to a great extent (Kahf, 2018, p. 23). As a matter of fact, the real estate bubble and the domino effect that occurred after the collapse of the real estate market during the 2007–2008 Financial Crisis mainly stemmed from the ability of financial institutions to avoid the consequences of their soft lending by using CDO-like instruments.

Another critical issue worth mentioning here is the problem of debt transfer for profits. Transferring debts does not generate any added value since it only transfers indebtedness between economic units. Therefore, there is no justification for transferring debts at a price other than their face value; this also means the investor's profit has no justification as the transaction does not generate any added value (Kahf, 2018, p. 14). However, genuine needs exist for transferring debts at their face value, such as liquidity adjustments, collateral liquidation, and debt collection (Kahf, 2018, p. 23). For these reasons, the debt transfers must be held without any profit, meaning at face value and by charging fees for related services if there are any.

Taking into account the points mentioned above, it can be argued that debt transfers for avoiding liabilities related to lending and generating profits must be eliminated. Such a reform will have important implications for conventional markets and instruments such as the bond markets, derivatives, and interbank debt transactions. Through this reform, financial institutions will act with the awareness that they will bear the risk of the loans they offer. Thus, they will be more careful about credit supply. This will prevent unhealthy credit expansion and possible financial bubbles.

An economic rationale for the prohibition of interest

The proposed Islamic finance-inspired reforms consist of many restrictions on and eliminations of markets, contracts, and types of behavior, which comprise intrinsic characteristics of the capitalist financial system. However, these reforms do not imply that we aim to eliminate finance entirely. As discussed in Section "A foundational perspective toward finance", finance, with its tools and institutions, is expected to support the production and exchange of goods and services, which is a crucial determinant of human welfare. Therefore, we also believe in finance and its role in the real market. However, finance must be reconsidered with regard to determining rewards for the finance provider and its position in wealth creation.

Loan-based financial activities do not produce wealth or create value per se. When a bank offers credit to an entrepreneur, the added value is generated not at the financing stage but after the entrepreneur uses the provided credit to produce goods and services. When a company sells its share in the primary stock market, the sold shares do not mean wealth production until the capital increase is transformed into productive activities by the listed company. Therefore, the financial sector is in a position to help the real sector in the activity of creating value and producing wealth. Since added value is produced in the real sector and the financial sector has a supportive role in this process of value creation, it is not peculiar to expect that the reward of the finance providers should be determined in the real sector, not remotely before the beginning of the process in the finance sector.

The way of facilitating finance is a prerequisite for understanding the finance providers' reward. The conventional financial sector can facilitate finance for the real sector mainly in two ways. The first way is to offer capital based on sharing together in the venture (Kahf, 2014, p. 179). In this case, the finance provider owns part of the venture and is entitled to get its predetermined share from the profit generated by the venture, and it must undertake the loss according to its share in the capital. In conformity with the expectation about where the reward must be determined above, the reward for the finance provider is settled as an outcome of the production activities conducted by the venture. In other words, no fixed reward is assigned to the finance provider independently from the real sector. The finance providers receive the profit generated in the real sector, corresponding to their share in the venture as an owner of its capital.

The second way of financing is by providing monetary capital and raw materials on a loan basis. When a producer borrows money or raw materials from a finance provider, ownership of these assets is transferred to the borrower. In other words, the debtor carries the ownership risk related to the borrowed assets. He/she employs the borrowed assets in producing goods and services and is entitled to get the profits generated as an outcome of the production and takes over the potential losses and risks attached to the ownership. On the contrary, the lender does not carry the ownership risk since he/she transfers ownership to the borrower through the loan. By the nature of the loan contract, the lender has a guarantee to take back the same amount lent. Therefore, the lender neither owns the assets used in production processes nor is exposed to ownership risk (Kahf, 2014, pp. 179–180).

One of the possible economic rationales for the prohibition of interest manifests itself when we approach the case in the previous paragraph from the point of view of the finance provider's reward. As presented above, the finance provider does not have ownership of the production factor because of the fact that the monetary capital or raw materials are transferred to the borrower along with the risks associated with them through a loan contract. Thus, the lender does not have a claim on a share in the profits produced. In addition, the financier does not have the right to demand a fixed return on the assets lent, as is the case for those who rent their human and physical capital in exchange for specific compensation. Although both monetary capital or raw material lent and human or physical capital rented contribute to the production of goods and services, in the latter case, the owners of human and physical capital continue to be exposed to the ownership risk for the duration of the lease while the lender has the guarantee for receiving the asset lent as it is and transfers the ownership risk to the borrower. The renter is exposed to depreciation in the capital owned and carries all responsibilities regarding ownership. Therefore, the reward of the finance provider based on a loan contract cannot be justified either in the form of a share in the profit or a fixed compensation, which stands for interest, while the renter is entitled to a wage or rent.

One may argue that the relationship between the finance provider and the client can be established in the form of a lease contract instead of a loan contract for the provision of monetary capital and raw materials. However, the lease contract's structure requires that the rented assets' lifetime must exceed the lease contract's duration. Since monetary capital and raw materials are not durable, they change forms and vanish in production processes. Therefore, the lease contract is unsuitable for providing monetary capital and raw materials, and a fixed compensation in the form of rent cannot be justified as well.

The discussion above asserts that the loan contract with interest, as one of the two financing channels of the contemporary capitalist financial system, violates economic intuitive rationale arguing that the owner of an asset must benefit from its positive outcomes and undertake the risk this asset is exposed to. This violation results in assigning an unjust reward to the finance provider in the form of interest. A noteworthy feature of interest, along with its injustice, is being determined independently from the outcomes of real sector activities, as opposed to the other way of facilitating finance by offering capital based on sharing together in the venture in the conventional framework. With such a feature, interest can be considered the starting point of the diversion of the financial sector from the real sector. The inclusion of interest in the financial system opens roads for further disengagement of financial transactions from real-world transactions through debt trading and CDO-like instruments. As a matter of fact, the difference between the face value of a debt and the amount paid in exchange for the debt is nothing but interest. Just as there is no economic justification for the so-called reward to the financial provider who offers monetary capital and raw materials through the debt contract, the profit from the transfer of debt cannot be economically justified. Transferring debts does not generate any added value since it only transfers indebtedness between the economic units. As noted by Colan (2017), Islam treats a problem in such depth that the possibility of the financial sector's divergence from the real sector is prevented at the very beginning by the prohibition of interest.

By means of the prohibition of interest and other Islamic finance-inspired reforms elaborated in Section "Islamic finance-inspired reforms", Islamic finance aims to ensure the supportive role of finance for the real sector, a strong link between the financial and real sectors and thus a reward for finance providers apportioned by the real sector (Kahf, 2018, p. 13). In this regard, Islamic finance proposes a supplementary reform, which is channeling finance through sale, lease, and venture capital (equity sharing). Since the connection of the finance provider's reward with the outcome of the production activities conducted by the venture in the real sector for the case of equity sharing mode of financing has been clarified, there is no need to repeat it. On the contrary, finance based on sale contracts (including the sale of usufruct through lease contracts) requires finance providers to own the assets that will be sold to clients with deferred payments, although the ownership risk is minimized by limiting the period in which finance providers hold the assets. The rate of return the finance provider applies in sale-based financing is expected to be transmitted from the real market to the financial market in a system that is not dominated by the financial institutions working based on interest. It is because of the fact that the return rate reflects the added value created during the sale transaction in the real market. Consequently, all forms of financing proposed by Islamic finance are highly linked to the real sector, in contrast to interest-based finance.

The Muslim-majority countries, which attempt to adopt a policy against interest, including Türkiye, can be taken into consideration from the above-mentioned perspective. Such a policy aims to eliminate financing based on debt-generating increments while preserving the intermediary role of finance and financial institutions. Hence, these countries promote Islamic/participatory finance on the basis of its strong link with the real sector. However, it is worth noting that the problem does not arise from the interest rate level but rather from the interest's existence as the resource allocator that determines the reward unjustly and independently from the real sector. In addition, some transactions, such as organized tawarruq and 'inah, adopted by some Islamic financial institutions constitute another issue that policymakers and decision-makers must approach with caution while promoting Islamic/participatory finance. These kinds of transactions mimic interest as they consist of features that lead to a divergence of finance from the real sector even though they formally appear to have legal legitimacy. Eventually, we suggest policymakers bring finance back to its essential function by eliminating interest from the financial system and applying Islamic finance-inspired reforms and channels. The possible fruits of the proposed reforms in terms of stability, sustainability, and development are briefly discussed in the following section.

Implications of Islamic finance on stability, sustainability, and development

All financial systems suffer from a set of common causes of instability and unsustainability. Many of these causes mainly arise from the nature of financial relationships, independent of the financial system adopted. The presence of uncertainty in every transaction and the high cost of financing risky projects ending up with imbalances can be listed as examples. In addition to reasons for instability and unsustainability stemming from the nature of financial relationships, balance sheet weakness, weak regulations, a lack of supervision, and macroeconomic problems may constitute impediments to the stability and sustainability of the financial systems. The issues above are valid for both the Islamic and capitalist financial systems.

There are idiosyncratic characteristics of the capitalist financial system that lead to instability. Interest being the resource allocator, disengagement of financial transactions from real-world transactions, extreme credit/indebtedness, excessive virtual assets, trading of risk and expectation, short-term funds roving around, and high interbank connectivity are the prominent ones, as noted at the beginning of the section "Islamic finance-inspired reforms.". Some of these characteristics have been partially discussed in the context of the Islamic finance–inspired reforms and economic rationale for the prohibition of interest. In this section, excessive credit/ indebtedness and interbank connectivity are primarily taken into consideration regarding their impacts on stability and sustainability in comparison with the features of Islamic finance that secure inherent and intrinsic stability and sustainability. In addition, the developmental nature of Islamic finance is explained along with the findings of empirical studies on the Islamic financial institution's performance during crises.

Excessive credit and indebtedness in the contemporary financial structure result from interest-based financing instruments and channels. It is because financing through loans with interest does not create any natural ceiling for credit expansion. Conventional financial institutions can offer credits to their clients without expecting any real transactions producing added value for the economy. The cash credits provided to households can be used for any purpose. One may purchase furniture and domestic appliances for his house, while the other uses borrowed funds to finance the working capital needs of her business. When these are the cases, it can be argued that loans end up with real transactions, although not required, even if finance is offered through loans with interest. However, this argument not only overlooks the fact that interest is economically illegitimate and unfair as it is determined remotely from the real sector outcomes as discussed in the section "An economic rationale for the prohibition of interest" but also neglects other possible non-value-adding areas where borrowers direct their acquired cash/credit to, such as payment of already-existing debts, giving further interest-based financing, or ending up hoarded in the purse of a spouse or associate.

At this point, it is worth emphasizing again the other distinctive characteristics of the capitalist financial system: the excessive presence of virtual assets, the trading of risk, and expectation. The cash credits provided by interest-based financial institutions are highly used in non-real-value-added transactions and zero-sum contracts such as CFD, Internet forex trades, and index trading to derive so-called financial revenues. In addition, speculative patterns of behavior spreading in most societies because of the current financial architecture give rise to the speculative usage of borrowed money in derivative and stock exchange markets, as noted in the subsections "Elimination of speculative patterns of behavior and genuinizing regulated markets" and "Restrictions on debt trading." As a matter of fact, the three tendencies of financialization identified by Lapavitsas (2013) show how all economic agents go toward financial transactions, most of which do not generate added value economically. According to Lapavitsas (2013), the activities of non-financial enterprises have been financialized, and the share of financial profits in their total profits has been dramatically raised. Furthermore, he notes that banks and financial institutions mainly seek profits through transactions in the financial markets and lending to households. On the side of households, it is observed that they borrow more and have more financial assets (Lapavitsas, 2013). The three tendencies of financialization give serious clues as to the extent to which resources are diverted from the real economy and directed to non-real-value-adding transactions and speculation in the interest-based financial system.

A finance structure based on interest, which does not require real transactions at the financing stage as well as the usage of the borrowed funds for other than real transactions producing added value in the economy, causes excessive credit expansion and high indebtedness among economic agents, including non-financial enterprises and households. In an environment where credits expand limitlessly, credit-fueled asset price bubbles are inevitable. When the bubbles explode, the sustainability of the current level of indebtedness and repaying debts becomes impossible, as experienced in the 2007–2008 Financial Crisis. In addition, credit expansion independently from the real sector's dynamics constitutes a weakness in terms of the stability of the financial and real sectors because of the business cycles caused by the volatile credit movements.

The Islamic financial system, which rejects interest-based finance, proposes financing methods based on sale, lease, and venture capital (equity sharing). As a substitute for loans with interest, finance based on sale contracts necessitates real market transactions by definition. The finance providers, who purchase the goods and services upon demand and promise to buy them from the customer, sell the same to the client based on agreed-upon deferred prices and conditions. Therefore, its structure rules out cash financing. No doubt, loans without interest may exist, but they are rendered non-economically and based on criteria that are aloof from the expected return. They would have a minor share in institutional fund disbursements. A first implication of rejecting interest-based finance and adopting finance based on sale, lease, and venture capital (equity sharing) is structuring finance strictly tied to real market transactions. In other words, the signals always come from the real market to the financial sector through demands for goods and services and for establishing or expanding ventures. Accordingly, credit expansion becomes limited by real market activities, meaning there becomes an intrinsic natural cap on debt creation and debt size. This feature of Islamic finance tackles the inconveniences, resulting in instability and unsustainability because of the excessive credits/ indebtedness caused by finance based on interest since the fund needs of the clients who plan to "invest" in non-real-value-added transactions and zero-sum contracts cannot be met by Islamic financial products. This goes along with Minsky (2008, p. 365), who considers financing trade and production a prerequisite for a more stable financial system. Furthermore, this same idea of capping credit by the volume of real market transactions is further enhanced by the fact that the elimination of interest renders non-economical all pure debt exchanges, e.g., discounting and packaging for sale.

Islamic finance is developmental by its nature, even when consumption is financed. It is because consuming a good is a positive signal for its producer and means more job opportunities to increase production. In other words, financing the real sector is itself a valuable contribution to growth, employment creation, and stimulating technological advancement.

Apart from the developmental nature of Islamic finance, the structure of financing methods requiring real transactions at the financing stage enables Islamic financial institutions to check the goods and services' purchase requests of clients in terms of moral aspects. This ability is where a second implication of the finance based on sale, lease, and venture capital (equity sharing) manifests itself. Anything that is not moral according to the rulings of Islam cannot be considered property and thus must not be the object of financing contracts. Therefore, Islamic finance does not offer credit for the production and sales of alcohol, narcotics, pork, tobacco, or tobacco products. Also, businesses dealing with gambling, interest-based finance, future contracts for money and money-equivalent assets, porno publishing, and dirty entertainment, which violate Islamic moral rulings and principles, cannot be funded through Islamic financial institutions. Abstaining from financing harmful goods and services by Islamic finance reduces their adverse impacts on the moral and economic development of both societies and the environment. It also helps communities save on repair, medical, or other expenses. Such a control mechanism does not exist in the loan-based financial structure unless additional precautions and regulations are taken, while Islamic finance inherently possesses it by virtue of its financing methods.

A third implication of Islamic finance on stability and sustainability is derived from its principle regarding debt transfers. As noted in the section "An economic rationale for the prohibition of interest," the difference between the face value of a debt and the amount paid in exchange for the debt is nothing but interest. Thus, the Islamic finance system, which rejects interest, does not allow transferring debts unless they are at face value. Rejecting interest and for-profit debt transfers by the Islamic finance system minimizes the connectivity between financial institutions that takes its way through sales and discounting of debts, which caused domino effects during the 2007–2008 Financial Crisis in the interest-loan-based financial architecture where banks and insurance companies are highly inter-linked to each other through transfers of debts and debt derivatives such as CDOs. In addition, by virtue of the elimination of debt sales, financial institutions cannot evade the potential liability resulting from the credits they provide. This feature introduces a subsidiary stability-enhancement mechanism of credit expansion since financial institutions become more conscientious at the stage of facilitating finance when they know from the beginning that they bear the consequences of the credits offered without any potentiality of passing the buck to others, such as wholesale financial institutions or open market risk\return hungry investors.

We would like to conclude this section by referring to some empirical studies on the performance of Islamic financial institutions in terms of stability and sustainability. The literature on Islamic banks' performance during and after financial crises in comparison with conventional banks helps deduce the comparative stability and sustainability of Islamic finance and interest-based finance. In this regard, studies obtain various results, meaning that the estimates of some studies acknowledge the better performance of Islamic banks, while some other studies suggest the opposite, as presented by Hassan and Aliyu (2018). The difference in the conclusions may stem from the sample (selected banks and countries), periods, methodology, reliability of the data, and other reasons. Even the size of the banks can be a source of variation in banking performance, as demonstrated by Chakroun and Gallali (2015). However, by referring to the survey of Hassan and Aliyu (2018), it can be stated that the majority of the studies on this matter affirm the relatively better performance of Islamic banks and their resilience to financial crises compared to their interest-based counterparts (Al-Khouri & Arouri, 2016; Chazi & Syed, 2010; Čihák & Hesse, 2010; Fakhfekh et al., 2016; Hasan & Dridi, 2011).

Several studies in the literature reveal a noteworthy finding, asserting that the comparative performance of Islamic and loan-based banks differs depending on the time elapsed after the crises. Khan (1986) and Alqahtani et al. (2016) share the same opinion that the better performance of Islamic banks as against interest-based banks is valid only for a short period immediately after crises and shocks. Belanès et al. (2015), who reach a similar conclusion for the countries in the Gulf Cooperation Council, assert that Islamic banks experienced a considerable decline in efficiency two years after the 2007–2008 Financial Crisis. Olson and Zoubi (2017) and Beck et al. (2013) argue that the reason for the declining performance of Islamic banks when the time elapsed after crises was the negative effects of the financial crisis started to be seen in the real economy after a lapse of time. Since Islamic finance adopts methods ensuring its strong link with the real sector, despite some malpractices in implementation, such as tawarruq and 'inah, the findings of the studies above are not surprising and support the theoretical framework suggested in this chapter.

Conclusion

This chapter aimed to propose a potential economic rationale for the prohibition of interest through discussions on the reforms outside the box and their possible implications for economic development as well as the stability and sustainability of the financial system. In line with this purpose, we have first presented the paradoxical loop of regulations and deregulations that took root in the contemporary financial system and pointed out a clear need for Islamic finance-inspired from outside the box because the reforms attempted inside the box could not propose a remedy with adequate satisfaction for the financial crises and the other problems in the current financial system.

Second, we have asserted the foundational perspective adopted while approaching finance in the first section. When the transformations in the financial sector's share in the economy, non-financial firms' behaviors, and the structure of the financial tools are considered together, it is obviously seen that not only has the financial sector gradually moved away from contributing to the production and exchange of real goods and services and thus to welfare but also the resources of the real sector have shifted to financial instruments that are dysfunctional in terms of their contribution to human welfare. We argue that the most severe problem of the modern economic and financial system is a persistent and intensive misorientation of the finance sector by confusing its support and service functions with a wealth creation function that cannot be undertaken outside the real sector's production and exchange.

The discussion on the misorientation of the finance sector by referring to the parameters of financialization in the first section reveals the necessity of re-diverting financial and human resources out of speculation and pure financial transactions back into wealth-creating activities. In this regard, the second section introduces and elaborates on Islamic finance-inspired reforms with the approach that what we are going to regulate and supervise is a more critical question, although regulation and supervision are, per se, essential. Through these outside-the-box reforms, it is aimed to eliminate and minimize the inherent deficiencies of the capitalist financial system, such as interest being the resource allocator, disengagement of financial transactions from real-world transactions, extreme credit/indebtedness, excessive virtual assets, and trading of risk and expectation.

The third section first considers two main financing methods, namely, equity sharing and loans with interest, in the current financial system from the perspective of the financial sector's position in wealth creation and the finance provider's reward. We present how interest violates economic intuitive rationale arguing that the owner of an asset must benefit from its positive outcomes and undertake the risk this asset is exposed to. This violation results in assigning an unjust reward to the finance provider in the form of interest, which is determined independently from the outcomes of the real sector's activities. Another important conclusion derived in the third section is that interest is the starting point of the diversion of the financial sector from the real sector. The inclusion of interest in the financial system opens roads for further disengagement of financial transactions from real-world transactions through debt trading and CDO-like instruments. This conclusion shows that the Islamic economic-cum-financial system treats this problem in such depth that the possibility of the financial sector's divergence from the real sector is eliminated at the very beginning by the prohibition of interest. The third section ends with a supplementary reform, which involves channeling finance through sale, lease, and venture capital (equity sharing).

The implications of rejecting interest-based finance and adopting financing methods based on sale, lease, and venture capital (equity sharing) on development, stability, and sustainability constitute the subject matter of the fourth section. Discussion in this section discloses that financial structures based on interest, which do not require real transactions at the financing stage, as well as the usage of borrowed funds for other than real transactions producing added value in the economy, cause excessive credit expansion and high indebtedness of the economic agents, including non-financial enterprises and households. Also, it is noted that debt transfers for profit caused domino effects during the 2007–2008 Financial Crisis in the capitalist financial architecture, where banks and insurance companies are highly linked to each other through the transfer of debt and debt derivatives such as CDOs. As a matter of fact, excessive credit/indebtedness and interbank connectivity are idiosyncratic characteristics of the capitalist financial system, leading to instability and unsustainability. On the other hand, the Islamic financial system rejects interest-based finance and proposes financing methods based on sale, lease, and venture capital (equity sharing). As a substitute for loan-with-interest contracts, finance based on sale contracts, by definition, necessitates real market transactions and restricts credit expansion by the extent of real market activities, meaning a cap on debt creation and debt size. This feature of Islamic finance tackles the inconveniences resulting in instability and unsustainability because of excessive credits/ indebtedness and high interbank connectivity through debt sales, as shown by empirical studies on the performance of Islamic financial institutions during and after financial crises and shocks.

References

Abojeib, M., Haneef, M. A., & Mohammed, M. O. (Eds.). (2018). *Islamic Economics: Principles & Analysis*. International Shari'ah Research Academy for Islamic Finance (ISRA).

Allen, F., & Gale, D. (2007). *Understanding Financial Crises*. Oxford, UK: Oxford University Press.

Al-Khouri, R., & Arouri, H. (2016). The Simultaneous Estimation of Credit Growth, Valuation, and Stability of the Gulf Cooperation Council Banking Industry. *Economic Systems*, *40*(3), 499–518. https://doi.org/10.1016/j.ecosys.2015.12.005

Alqahtani, F., Mayes, D. G., & Brown, K. (2016). Economic Turmoil and Islamic Banking: Evidence from the Gulf Cooperation Council. *Pacific-Basin Finance Journal*, *39*, 44–56. https://doi.org/10.1016/j.pacfin.2016.05.017

Askari, H., & Mirakhor, A. (2015). *Next Financial Crisis and How to Save Capitalism* (1st ed.). New York: Palgrave Macmillan.

Barber, B. M., Lee, Y.-T., Liu, Y.-J., & Odean, T. (2009). Just How Much Do Individual Investors Lose by Trading? *Review of Financial Studies*, *22*(2), 609–632. https://doi.org/10.1093/rfs/hhn046

Beck, T., Demirgüç-Kunt, A., & Merrouche, O. (2013). Islamic vs. Conventional Banking: Business Model, Efficiency and Stability. *Journal of Banking & Finance*, *37*(2), 433–447. https://doi.org/10.1016/j.jbankfin.2012.09.016

Belanès, A., Ftiti, Z., & Regaïeg, R. (2015). What Can We Learn about Islamic Banks Efficiency under the Subprime Crisis? Evidence from GCC Region. *Pacific-Basin Finance Journal*, *33*, 81–92. https://doi.org/10.1016/j.pacfin.2015.02.012

Bordo, M., Eichengreen, B., Klingebiel, D., & Martinez-Peria, M. S. (2001). Is the Crisis Problem Growing More Severe? *Economic Policy*, *16*(32), 52–82. https://doi.org/10.1111/1468-0327.00070

Chakroun, M. A., & Gallali, M. I. (2015). Islamic Banks and Financial Stability: An Empirical Analysis of the Gulf Countries. *International Journal of Business and Commerce*, *5*(3), 64–87.

Chazi, A., & Syed, L. A. M. (2010). Risk Exposure during the Global Financial Crisis: The Case of Islamic Banks. *International Journal of Islamic and Middle Eastern Finance and Management*, *3*(4), 321–333. https://doi.org/10.1108/17538391011093261

Chen, J. (2020, November 24). *Contract for Differences (CFD) Definition: Uses and Examples*. Investopedia. https://www.investopedia.com/terms/c/contractfordifferences.asp

Čihák, M., & Hesse, H. (2010). Islamic Banks and Financial Stability: An Empirical Analysis. *Journal of Financial Services Research*, *38*(2–3), 95–113. https://doi.org/10.1007/s10693-010-0089-0

Colan, A. (2017, November 27). *Wisdom behind Prohibition of Riba (Interest)—Case Study GFC*. https://www.youtube.com/watch?v=CCb6uFBjkYY

Corporate Finance Institute. (2023, January 8). *Commodities: Cash Settlement vs Physical Delivery*. Corporate Finance Institute. https://corporatefinanceinstitute.com/resources/commodities/commodities-cash-settlement-vs-physical-delivery/

Downey, L. (2023, March 31). *An Essential Options Trading Guide*. Investopedia. https://www.investopedia.com/options-basics-tutorial-4583012

Dukhan, B. (2022). Financial Reforms in the Late 20th Century. In M. Kahf (Ed.), *Towards a New Theory of Finance: Can Islamic Finance be It?* (pp. 127–153). Istanbul, Türkiye: Istanbul Sabahattin Zaim University.

Fakhfekh, M., Hachicha, N., Jawadi, F., Selmi, N., & Idi Cheffou, A. (2016). Measuring Volatility Persistence for Conventional and Islamic Banks: An FI-EGARCH Approach. *Emerging Markets Review, 27*, 84–99. https://doi.org/10.1016/j.ememar.2016.03.004

Grapulin, A. (2018). *Role of CDOs in the Financial Crisis 2007–2008* [Master's Thesis, Repozitorij Univerze v Ljubljani]. http://www.cek.ef.uni-lj.si/magister/grapulin3152-B.pdf

Hasan, M., & Dridi, J. (2011). The Effects of the Global Crisis on Islamic and Conventional Banks: A Comparative Study. *Journal of International Commerce, Economics and Policy, 02*(02), 163–200. https://doi.org/10.1142/S1793993311000270

Hassan, M. K., & Aliyu, S. (2018). A Contemporary Survey of Islamic Banking Literature. *Journal of Financial Stability, 34*, 12–43. https://doi.org/10.1016/j.jfs.2017.11.006

Helvacıoğlu, M. (2022). Inside-the-Box Reforms. In M. Kahf (Ed.), *Towards a New Theory of Finance: Can Islamic Finance Be It?* (pp. 221–253). Istanbul, Türkiye: Istanbul Sabahattin Zaim University.

Kahf, M. (2014). *Notes on Islamic Economics: Theories and Institutions* (1st ed.). North Charleston, SC: CreateSpace Independent Publishing Platform.

Kahf, M. (2016). Ethical Values in Conventional and Islamic Finance with Reference to Recent Financial Crises. *International Journal of Pluralism and Economics Education, 7*(3), 254–267. https://doi.org/10.1504/IJPEE.2016.079697

Kahf, M. (2018). *Financial Policy and Stability: Islamic Finance Perspective* [Public Lecture]. IFSB 10th Public Lecture on Financial Policy and Stability, Islamic Financial Services Board.

Khan, M. S. (1986). Islamic Interest-Free Banking: A Theoretical Analysis. *International Monetary Fund, 33*(1), 1. https://doi.org/10.2307/3866920

Kindleberger, C. P. (2006). *A Financial History of Western Europe* (Reprinted). London, UK: Routledge.

Lapavitsas, C. (2013). *Profiting without Producing: How Finance Exploits Us All*. London, UK: Verso.

Minsky, H. P. (2008). *Stabilizing an Unstable Economy*. Boston, MA: McGraw Hill.

Olson, D., & Zoubi, T. (2017). Convergence in Bank Performance for Commercial and Islamic Banks during and after the Global Financial Crisis. *The Quarterly Review of Economics and Finance, 65*, 71–87. https://doi.org/10.1016/j.qref.2016.06.013

Powel, S. (2020, May 20). *Derivative Contracts: Introduction to Derivatives*. https://learn.corporatefinanceinstitute.com/courses/take/derivatives-fundamentals/10917

Quantified Strategies. (2023, April 18). *Is the Stock Market a Zero Sum Game? (What about Trading?)*. https://www.quantifiedstrategies.com/is-the-stock-market-a-zero-sum-game/

Samuelsson, H. (2021, September 10). What Happens If You Hold a Futures Contract Until Expiration? *The Robust Trader*. https://therobusttrader.com/what-happens-if-you-hold-a-futures-contract-until-expiration/

2 The prohibition of "riba" in Islam and its elimination through "Islamic financing technics"

Mohammed Nurul Alam

Introduction: riba and its prohibition in Islam

"Riba" is an Arabic word that means to increase or exceed and is prohibited in Islam. The word "riba" is commonly translated in English as usury of interest and is a charge for using the client money. It is commonly used in reference to unequal exchanges or charges and fees for borrowing. Interest is deemed riba, or an unjust, exploitative gain, and such practice is prohibited in Islam. As it is said in the Islamic Holy Scripture Quran: as Allah has permitted trading and prohibited riba. Ahmad [1] in his observation opines that in Islamic Fiqh the term "riba" has a special meaning. The author argues riba as an unjustified increment in borrowing or lending money, paid in kind or in money above the amount of loan, as a condition imposed by the lender or voluntarily by the borrower. Riba defined in this way is called in Fiqh [2] riba al-duyun (debt usury). Riba also is an unjustified increment gained by the seller or the buyer if they exchanged goods of the same kind in different quantities. This is called "riba al-fadl" or "riba-al-buyu" (trade usury). Ahmad (1994), in his studies, observed the definition of riba as published in the IMF Staff Paper:

> Riba is the Arabic word for the predetermined return on the use of money. In the past, there has been a dispute about whether riba refers to interest or usury but there is now consensus among Muslim scholars that the term covers all forms of interest and not only "excessive" interest. Thus, in the ensuing discussion, the terms riba and interest will be used interchangeably, and an Islamic banking system will be one in which a payment or receipt of interest is forbidden.[1]

There are few places in the Holy Quran where "riba" and its prohibitions are mentioned. In Chapter 3, Allah says, "O you who have believed, do not consume usury, doubled and multiplied, but fear Allah that you may be successful" (Al-Quran 3:130). The verse warns the believers never to take riba at compound rates. In Chapter 2, there are three verses (verses 275, 276, and 279) about "riba": but Allah has permitted trade and has forbidden interest. So, whoever has received an admonition from his Lord and desists may have what is past, and his affair rests with Allah. But whoever returns to [dealing in interest or usury]- those are the companions of the Fire; they will abide eternally therein (2: 275). Allah destroys interest and gives an increase to charities. And Allah does not like every sinning disbeliever (2: 276). O you who have believed, fear Allah and give up what remains [due to you] of interest if you should be believers (2: 278). It is known from these verses that the riba in all forms is extremely condemned for the believers. Allah warns those who do not care for its prohibition. They are bound to get severe punishment hereafter. In Chapter 4 verse 161, it is said: "And for (their) taking of usury while they had been forbidden from it, and their consuming of the people's wealth unjustly. And we have prepared for the disbelievers among them a painful punishment" (Al-Quran 4:161).

Prohibition of riba from the viewpoint of different religions

Alam (2000) observed that the interest is prohibited in Islamic Law known as "Sharia." A similar prohibition is also observed by other religions. The Mosaic Law limited the extraction of interest, and the Old Testament states,

> And if you lend money to any of my people with you who is poor, you shall not be to him as a creditor, and you shall not exact interest from him. If ever you take your neighbour's garment in pledge, you shall restore it to him before the sun goes down; for that is his only covering, it is his mantle for his body; in what else shall he sleep? And if he cries to me, I shall hear, for I am compassionate.
>
> (Exodus 22: 25–27)

Ancient philosophers such as Aristotle and Plato condemned interest in their day. In the early ages, the Roman Empire also prohibited the charging of interest. Usury was regarded as an illegal and punishable offense throughout the Medieval Ages. It has also been observed that up to 13th century, the church rule was supreme and that the charging of interest was strictly forbidden. Till today, usury is prohibited in Western law, as it is a practice of lending money, at exorbitant interest especially at a higher interest than is allowed by law. In the Islamic Law, both usury and interest are equally prohibited and are punishable offenses. Interest on loan was also prohibited by medieval churches, but gradually it became acceptable and by the 19th century the church was itself lending and borrowing at interest (Zineldin, 1990). As it is prohibited by the Islamic law to accept and to give interest, Islamic economy is free of interest.

Economic drawbacks of riba or interest

Many authors[2] in their discussion argued that riba benefits individuals at the cost of the community. Commercial banks portray that riba or interest benefits the community. In fact, the masses have been made accomplices in the crime of usury for the meager chunk of interest to serve the financial interests of the influential minority.

Shafi (1954) in his book *Ma'ariful-Qur'an* (*The Wisdom of the Holy Qur'an*)[3] observes that the tiny amounts of interest are insufficient for the subsistence of the majority of small clients, and they are compelled to earn their living even through menial jobs. Due to insufficient capital, personal business is suicidal for them. Large capitals get the largest loans, and their businesses, are extended. Small capitals are deprived of the bigger loan, resulting in squeezed businesses, and marginalized profit scopes. Thus, small capitalists seek refuge in big capitalists who have already monopolized the market. Resultantly market crashes in the interest of greedy minority to the disaster of most small capitalists.

Ahmad (1994) observes that all efforts to finance budgetary deficit by the interest-based borrowing have been a failure. Even the richest counties of the West are overwhelmed by a mountain of debts and are not finding easy solutions. The author argued in his discussion that the US is the most indebted nation whose domestic debt crossed the limit of $3 trillion with annual interest payments to the amount of $290 billion. The author opines that resources can be contracted based on venture capital and risk-sharing deals, which is the objectives and principles of the riba free banking system. While giving an example relating to this issue the author highlighted on Türkiye, being a secular country, has promoted the entire Bosphorus Bridge Project (around $1 billion) based on participatory capital against interest-based loans. The World Bank, IFC, and other financial institutions are found in favor of an equity-based model of financing. The author (ibid.) quoted form a few paragraphs in his discussion which are based on a study by the Development Centre of the Organisation for Economic Cooperation and Development of the European Countries (Paris).[4] The study observed as "Interest-free banking is a novel form of finance. Even sceptics have accepted that Islamic banks are not merely trying to give interest another name and that legal instruments within the framework of Shari'ah[5] exist which permits profitability on a different, albeit Koranically acceptable, basis."

Islamic bank: a bank without interest

Regarding Islamic banking in the modern world, Alam (2000, 2002, 2003, 2009) in his studies observed that an Islamic bank is a financial intermediary whose objectives and operations as well as principles and practices must conform to the principles of Islamic Law (Shariah) and, consequently, it is conditioned to operate all its activities without interest. The idea of modern interest-free financing systems (FSs) based on Islamic Sharia (Law) started in the period when Muslims around the world began their exchange functions at the international level. However, due to a lack of proper research on this subject, the introduction of Islamic banking systems could not come to the forefront of the modern financial market in an institutional form until mid-1940, when the first attempt to establish an interest-free bank was made in Malaysia. The early history of Islam shows that the development of Islamic economics began when Islam started dispersing to various parts of the world. The dawn of Islam brought remarkable change among the people of the East and the West who were guided by the same faith.

During the 7th century, Islam extended to various parts of Asia and Europe, which favoring the establishment of a strong commercial relationship among the businessmen in these areas. To describe the impact of Islam during the 7th century, Wilson (1965, pp. 40–53) narrated:

> The sudden eruption of the Arab (Muslim) people in the 7th Century is something unique in history. In three generations a collection of scattered tribes, some settled, some nomadic, living by trade and subsistence farming, had transformed itself into a rich and powerful empire dominating the whole of the southern Mediterranean and the Near East from Afghanistan to Spain. ... They had succeeded in welding together peoples of diverse beliefs and languages into a unified society based on a common language and common institutions.

With the growth of Islamic communities around the world, their trade and commerce started to develop in a unique and positive manner. Lieber (1968, p. 230) also argued that, from the 7th century AD onward, Muslims succeeded in developing long-distance trade and international commerce. This was because, during that time, in the Islamic religion, merchants were greatly honored in society. At that time, the development of trade and commerce was also influenced by the religious obligation of pilgrimage that used to take place in the Arab land where people from all over the world gather once every year. As reported by Leiber (ibid., p. 230):

> Among Muslims international trade was particularly stimulated by the pilgrimage to the holy places of Arabia. Each year from all over the world, many of these pilgrims used to fulfil their religious obligations and at the same time, market their local products along the route. While returning home with foreign goods on which they hoped to make a handsome profit.

Aims of an Islamic bank

The aim of Islamic economics, as observed by Molla et al. (1988), is not only the elimination of interest-based transactions but also the establishment of just and balanced social order free from all forms of exploitation. An Islamic bank is not only a financier but also a partner in the business. The system essentially involves sharing of risks between the owner of capital and the entrepreneurs as well as sharing the result of the collective efforts. Thus, it differs from an interest-based system, in which the risks are mainly borne by the entrepreneur or by the user of capital. Sharing of profits might lead Islamic banks to keep close contact with customers. As it requires efficient supervision and control over the whole project, sometimes the bank may find it difficult to administer their lent fund, especially while financing small businesses and small and cottage industries. In this regard, World Bank Development Report (1989, box 6.3) observes:

> Several Islamic countries have recently introduced banking on Islamic principles. They include Iran, Malaysia, Pakistan, and Saudi Arabia. Islamic

principles permit profit but do not allow fixed interest on deposits or loans. Nevertheless, Islamic banking can be made to work quite well and provides an interesting contrast to commercial banking practice elsewhere.

Scharf (1983, pp. 94–95) in his study titled "Arab and Islamic Bank" conducted by the Development Centre, OECD, highlighted the Islamic banking principles and prospects as

> Islamic banking is trying to develop the relationship between finance on one hand and industry and commerce on the other. This new relationship is the basis of the Islamic economic system being set up. Though Islamic principles have yet to be put to the test in the competition of international finance, the two systems are similar in that they both strive for closer ties between financial intermediation and economic asset creation. Islamic banks could make a useful contribution to economic growth and development, particularly in a situation of recession, stagflation, and low-growth level because the core of their operation is oriented toward productive investment.
>
> (Alam, 2002)

Main features of Islamic banking

The main characteristic of an Islamic bank is that the bank operates its financial transitions according to the principle of Islamic Shariah (jurisprudence). The bank operates entirely differently from a commercial bank. An Islamic bank implies a zero rate of interest but not a zero rate of return. The bank shares in the profit and loss of the enterprise as per agreement with those who take funds from them for trade or investment. An Islamic bank does not operate like a commercial bank in lending funds as it deals in kind rather than cash. The bank is to pay the Zakat Fund,[6] which is a fund that accumulates money for the poorer section of society. The amount to be contributed is 2.5% of its total capital and profit.

The bank is committed to operating according to the principle of Islamic Shariah (Jurisprudence). In other words, their objectives, operating principles, and working procedures must conform to Islamic Law. The bank has a provision for "Qard Hasan"[7] or beneficent loans, in deserving cases without any consideration of profits or returns on the same. The beneficiary back pays these sorts of loans if they can repay the same (Ahsan Fakhrul, 1979, 1989; Alam, 2000; Huq, 1990; Zineldin, 1990).

Modes of Islamic banks with regard to accepting deposits and investment of funds

Like commercial banks, an Islamic bank accepts deposits under different deposit accounts.

These are mentioned below.

Current accounts Like other commercial banks, an Islamic bank accepts deposits from customers on current accounts. Under this account, a customer is allowed to withdraw any amount of money without any notice. From that perspective, this account is also known as a Demand Deposit Account.

Even though an Islamic bank deals with a customer on a profit-sharing basis, under this account, a customer deposits their funds at their own risk. They do not receive any share of the profit normally earned by the bank.

Savings accounts An Islamic bank accepts deposits from a customer under-saving accounts as other commercial banks do. However, since Islamic banks under this account share profits or losses with depositors, the bank accepts saving deposits from customers under two different Shariah principles, namely, Al-Wadia and Al-Mudaraba Shariah principles. A brief description of these two accounts is given below:

Al-Wadia Shariah principles The word "Al-Wadia" denotes "trusteeship." Under Al-Wadia Shariah principles, the Islamic banks act as a trustee for their customers. Under this principle, a depositor gives the Islamic bank authority to use the fund at the bank's own risk. This type of deposit is similar to a "Current Account" or "Demand Deposit," with the exception that the bank guarantees depositors a full return of the deposit.

Al-Mudaraba Shariah principles Al-Mudaraba Shariah principle is also known as the Profit and Loss Sharing (PLS) Savings principle. The word "Mudarab" means "the manager" of the fund, and it originated from the Arabic word "Al-Mudaraba." In this type of saving, Islamic banks act as a manager of customers' deposited funds. The depositors are owners of funds and known as "Sahab-Al-Mal." Under this principle there are two different types of savings accounts:

1 Savings under the PLS Agreement, and
2 Savings under the Investment Account.

The Savings under the PLS Agreement are featured by accepting deposits from customers that are invested by the bank at its own risk. Depositors authorize the bank to invest their deposited funds and share profit or loss on agreed proportions.

On the contrary, Islamic banks accept deposits from customers under the Investment Account on a PLS basis. A savings account of such a nature in an Islamic banking system is also known as a participatory account or a PLS account. Depositors of this type of account receive a share of profit to the agreed ratio from their funds invested by the bank. The profit and loss sharing also depends on the total amount deposited and the length of period the bank holds the money.

Investment accounts under the PLS Savings are again subdivided into the following various categories:

1 Joint or General Investment Account,
2 Investment Deposit on Limited-Period,
3 Unlimited-Period Investment Deposit, and
4 Specified Investment Deposit.

An Islamic bank under the "Joint or General Investment Account" bank pools together investment deposits of different maturity, which are not invested in any specified project but utilized for different financing operations of the bank. Depositors of this type of account receive profits at the end of the period that is accounted for and distributed on a pro-rata basis. Under the "Investment Deposits on Limited Period," the bank accepts deposits from customers for a specified period. Once the time has expired, the bank refunds the money to depositors. The profit generated from such funds is distributed at the end of the financial year. The bank also accepts deposits from its customers under "Unlimited-Period Investment Deposit," where investment deposits are automatically renewable without specifying the period. Depositors of this type of account may withdraw their funds within three months' notice to the bank. Profits are distributed to depositors at the end of the financial year. Certain Islamic banks accept "Specified Investment Deposit." In such a case, the bank and the customer agree to invest this fund in a specific project or trade. Profits accrued from this type of investment are shared by the bank and the customer. The bank in this regard works as an agent for the customer and may charge an agreed fee for the investment function or may share the profit at an agreed proportion (Alam, 2002, 2009).

Profit and Loss Sharing Term Deposit Receipt accounts

In the case of a PLS-Term Deposit Receipt (TDR) account, the bank accepts deposits for a period of 6, 12, 24, and 36 months. The amount of the deposit may be withdrawn after the completion of the term or within the time in case of need of the customers on surrendering the receipt of the bank. Customers who withdraw their funds before six months are not entitled to receive any benefit on their deposited amount. In case one can withdraw the deposited funds before the completion of the term but after six months he is entitled to get profit on the amount, which was kept as a deposit for a minimum of six months period. The amount of profit is credited to the respective deposit account on maturity.

Profit and loss sharing short-notice demand deposit account

This type of deposit account may be opened by any individual, institution, government institution, or corporation with any amount of money. It required at least seven days' prior notice to withdraw money from this account. Profit and loss are calculated on a daily minimum balance.

Pilgrimage (Hajj) deposit account

Muslims who have enough funds perform a pilgrimage (which is one of the five pillars of Islam) once a year and visit the holy place Mecca in Saudi Arabia. Customers who want to save money for pilgrimage at a future date open this type of savings account. The operational procedures of this type of account are similar to a PLSTDR Account.

In addition to the above functions, Islamic banks, like other commercial banks, render different transactional services to customers, which include:

– remittances through demand draft (DD),
– telegraphic transfer (TT),
– pay order (PO) clearing,
– safekeeping of personal valuables and securities,
– collection of bills, agency services, etc.

(Alam, 2002, 2009; Kazarian, 1991; Khoja and Guddah, 1997; Siddiqi, 1988; Zineldin, 1990)

Various investment modes of Islamic banks

Islamic banks, due to their profit and loss sharing and a participatory nature principle, take great care while investing their funds in any project. The bank, before giving loans to customers, thoroughly studies its project proposal and investigates the prospects and outcome of the project. To invest funds profitably, Islamic banks use the following different modes of investment.

1 Capital financing or "Mudaraba,"
2 Investment under a partnership or "Musharaka,"
3 Cost Plus Sales on a cash basis or "Murabaha,"
4 Cost Plus Sales under deferred payment "Bai-Muazal,"
5 Advance Purchase or "Bai-Salam,"
6 Hire Purchase under "Shirkatul Milk,"
7 Leasing or "Ijara," and
8 Quard E Hasan.

Capital financing or Mudaraba

Under this category of investment, Islamic banks supply the entire capital of the business. The customer normally participates by giving time and expertise. Thus, a relationship between the supplier of capital and the user of capital begins. Regarding Mudaraba mode of investment, Khoja and Guddah (1997, chap 4–2, p. 1) opine that the

> Mudaraba, in essence, is based on the concurrence of those who have capital with those who have the expertise, where the first party provides capital, and the other party provide the expertise with the purpose of earning Halal profit (lawful) which will be divided between them in ratios agreed upon.

Under this type of financing, the investor is known as "Rab-Al-Mal," meaning the owner of the property, and the entrepreneur is called "Mudarab," meaning the manager of the capital. When the venture ends, the manager of the capital, i.e., the entrepreneur, returns the entire capital to the bank, along with an agreed proportion of profit. The main future of this investment mode is that if there is any loss, it is born by the bank. The main advantage of this type of partnership is that it combines the efforts of human beings and their skills with capital, which contributes greatly toward the development activities in a society and assists to solve unemployment problems by utilizing manpower resources in a productive way.

The main feature of the Capital Financing Investment mode is that profits are shared between the customer and the bank on a predetermined ratio, and it is the bank that bears all losses if any. However, losses due to the negligence of the entrepreneur are not borne by the bank.

Partnership or "Musharaka" financing

Under Musharaka or partnership mode of investment, the Islamic bank and the customer contribute capital jointly. It is like a profit-sharing joint venture, designed to limit production or commercial activities of long duration. Besides capital, both parties contribute managerial expertise and other essential services at agreed proportions. Profit or losses are shared according to agreed-upon contract. An individual partner does not become liable for the losses caused by others. Due to this joint venture, the Musharaka mode of investment of Islamic banks is also known as the Equity Participation mode of investment. Profit is distributed according to a predetermined ratio, and loss, if any, is also shared according to the capital ratio. Both the bank and the customer take part in the management and control of the entrepreneurial activities.

In addition to the above two financial arrangements, Islamic banks currently in existence are engaging in or actively considering several other financial practices usually acceptable in Islamic Law:

Cost plus sales on a cash basis or "Murabaha,"
Cost plus sales under deferred payment "Bai-Muajjal,"
Advance purchase or "Bai-Salam,"
Hire-purchase under "Shirkatul Milk,"
Leasing or "Ijara,"
Quard E Hasan.

Cost plus sales on a cash basis or "Murabaha"

Murabaha means mark-up or costs-plus-profit-based financing. In this regard, Khoja and Guddah (1997, chap. 1, p. 2) observed that the mode of Murabaha sale connected to a promise is used by the Islamic banks which undertake the purchaser of commodities according to the specification requested by the customer and then resell them on Murabaha to the one who promised to buy for its cost price plus a margin of profit agreed upon previously by the two parties.

In this system of financing the bank agrees to purchase for a client who will then reimburse the bank in a stated time at an agreed-upon profit margin. The markup price that the bank and the buyer agree to is mainly based on the market price of the commodity. Thus, the bank earns a profit without bearing any risk.

Murabaha sales may also be defined as one kind of absolute sale (asset for price), which may be divided into four kinds with respect to price. These are:

Bargain sale,
Tawlia (respective sale),
Discount sale, and
Murabaha sale.

Bargain sale indicates the selling of commodities for an agreed-upon price irrespective of their purchase price. Tawlia or respective sale is a sale of commodities by the bank in the purchase price, i.e., a sale without any addition or discount. Discount sale is the selling of commodities for their purchase price with a certain discount. Murabaha sale, as mentioned earlier, is selling the commodity for the purchase price plus a certain agreed-upon profit margin. The margin of profit may be determined as a percentage of the purchase price or a lump sum figure. The Tawila (respective sale), discount, and Murabaha sales are regarded as "Amana (honest) sales" (Alam, 2002, 2009; Khoja & Guddah, 1997).

In this type of financing, no cash payment is made by the bank to the client; instead, the bank itself purchases goods selected by the client from respective sources, i.e., producers/suppliers/whole-sellers, etc., and sells the same to the client.

As a security, the bank takes 25–30% of the sale price from the clients. Depending on the agreement, the security may be given by cash or goods. The amount of the security is refunded or adjusted at the close of the transaction. The bank can also demand collateral securities to ensure the completion of the transaction as per the agreement. In case a client fails to take delivery of goods in full, the bank retains the right to sell the stock at the highest available price and adjust the investment account.

The bank, under no circumstances, is allowed to realize more than the amount of cost plus declared profit. In case of any loss caused by the willful default of the client, the bank can impose and recover compensation. It is the bank that retains the ownership of the goods until the agreed sale price is paid by the client.

Cost plus sale under deferred payment or Bai-Muajjal

This mode of investment is like the Murabaha mode of investment discussed above, with the exception that the sale under the Bai-Muajjal mode of investment is made on a credit basis rather than cash. The main feature of this technique consists of procurement of goods at the request of the client and selling them to him on credit. This mode follows the same conditions as the Murabaha mode of investment, except the following:

- The bank transfers the possession of goods to the client before payment.
- To cover the sale price of the goods, the bank obtains collateral securities from the client.

- The bank normally takes the property of the municipal area as a mortgage. In case the client fails to repay the sale price, the bank realizes the amount by selling the mortgaged property.

Bai-Salam or advance purchase

Under Bai-Salam or Advance Purchase mode of investment, the bank purchases industrial and agricultural products in advance from their customers. The main features of this mode are as follows:

- The price is normally paid with the execution of an agreement.
- According to the terms of the agreement, the bank receives the goods in due time.

The agreement includes the following facts into consideration:

- Description of goods,
- Quality and quantity of goods,
- Time of delivery, and
- Place of delivery.

To ensure the timely delivery of the goods, the bank can obtain collateral security. The goods can also be received in installments.

Hire-purchase investment under Shirkatul Meelk

Islamic banks also invest funds under the hire-purchase mode. Under this mode of investment, the bank sells buildings, transport, and other valuable items to the client. The value of the hire-purchase amount is payable in installments. When the client pays back the value of the goods including rent, the ownership is transferred to him.

The following are the salient features of the hire-purchase mode of investment.

- Before the purchase of the item, the bank determines its actual price, monthly rent, schedule of payment, cash security, additional security, etc.
- The ownership of the item remains with the bank till the entire amount of installment is paid by the client.
- The rent is received based on actual income.

Ijara or leasing

The word "Ijara" indicates leasing. The leasing purchase is another technique followed by Islamic banks in financing customers. This system is almost similar to the leasing activity provided in traditional banking. Leasing is a contract between the bank and the customer to use particular assets. In this case, the bank is called the lessor and the customer is called the lessee who wants to use the assets and pays rent. Zineldin (1990, p. 83), in this regard, argued that

> the leasing agreement is based on profit sharing in which the bank buys the movable or immovable property and lease it to one of its clients for an agreed sum by installments and for a limited period of time into a saving account held with the same bank. These installments are invested in Mudaraba investment (Venture) for the customer's account. The accumulated profit generated from the payments, and the payments themselves are invested in the bank's investment ventures over the time period of the lease, contributing to the eventual purchase of the leased assets.

Quard E Hasan

Islamic banks sometimes give interest-free loans to needy people in society. This sort of investment is known as Quard E Hasan. The practice of dealing with this sort of investment differs from bank to bank. Quard E Hasan is normally given to needy students, small producers, farmers, entrepreneurs, and economically weaker sections of society, who are not able to obtain loans or any financial assistance from any other institutional sources. The main aim of this loan is to help needy people in society to make them self-sufficient (Alam, 2002, 2009; Kazarian, 1991; Khoja and Guddah, 1997; Siddiqi, 1988; Zineldin, 1990).

Financing small entrepreneurs by Islamic banks: an empirical review (a case of Türkiye–Cyprus–Sudan and Bangladesh)

This section includes a brief description of empirical studies conducted during the end of the 1990s in different nations like Sudan, Bangladesh, Türkiye, and Cyprus. The study is based on an Institutional Network theoretical approach. A brief discussion of the prospect and barriers of small entrepreneurs around the globe is done at the initial stage. The theoretical and methodological aspects and the research processes used in the study are also explained in detail in this section. The main aim of this section is to give readers an in-depth idea of how Islamic banks carry on their financing activities in various countries under different environmental and economic situations by implementing financing modes discussed in the previous section. Data was collected through direct interviews with senior Islamic banks staffs in different countries under review.

Small entrepreneurs and their impacts on a nation's economy

Small entrepreneurs play a predominant role in the elimination of the unemployment problem that remains as a serious barrier to a nation's economic growth in most least developed and developing nations of the world. Small entrepreneurs in many nations succeeded not only in solving the unemployment problem of rural people but also played a significant role in increasing their standard of living (Anderson & Khambata 1982; Macuja, 1981). Many researchers (Ashe & Cosslett, 1989; Little, 1988; Little et al., 1987). The authors in their studies highlighted the issue as to how and to what extent this sector of economy contributes towards the development of a nation's economy. In this regard, the authors Ashe and Cosslett (1989, p. 17) observes:

> In rural areas, in addition to the legion of subsistence and small farmers, there is a growing percentage of individuals whose primary source of income is trading, cottage industries and a wide range of services, generally categorized as off-farm activities: the figure ranges from 19 to 23 per cent in countries like India, Sierra Leone and Colombia, from 28 to 38 per cent in Indonesia, Pakistan, Kenya and Philippines, and as high as 49 per cent in Malaysia.

The main contribution of this sector of the economy is that it creates job facilities for many unemployed people in the rural areas of a country. Thus, skilled but unemployed rural workers can contribute greatly toward the economic growth of a country (Alam, 2002).

Impediments of small enterprises

Myrdal (1968, p. 527) in his study observed that the rapid destruction of small entrepreneurs in the form of cottage industry would not only eliminate a source of supplementary rural income but also accentuate the push toward urbanization and further aggravate congestion in urban areas.

Almost all previous studies carried out by various authors have analyzed the problems of small entrepreneurs within various national contexts. Further to these studies on this sector economy, it may be noted that under the auspices of the United Nations Economic Commission for Asia and the Far East (ECAFE), UNIDO, and Asian Development Bank (ADB), many studies were conducted on small-scale industry in the ECAFE region. Alam (2002) in his study observes that these studies[8] highlight the root causes of the impediments to the development of small entrepreneurs and proposes various suggestions for solving these problems.

Islamic banking finances for small entrepreneurs

Since the early 1960s, Islamic banks with their profit-sharing principles have started financing various sectors of economies in different countries. To study how and to what extent Islamic banks finance small entrepreneurs, an empirical study was carried out in different nations like Bangladesh, Türkiye, Cyprus, and Sudan. To study this phenomenon, I used the "institutional network" theoretical framework (Alam, 2002, 2009). The aim of the study was to study the lender–borrower network relationships between different Islamic banks and small entrepreneurs.

Theoretical and methodological approach used in the study

To study this phenomenon, I used the "institutional network" theoretical approach. The theoretical model is applied to study and analyze the exchange functions between Islamic banks and borrowers, especially rural-based small entrepreneurs in different nations. The model is designed in such a way that different small entrepreneurs and financing organizations of similar nature studied are grouped and institutionalized into different entrepreneurs systems (ESs) and different FSs. To achieve the objectives of the study, the concept of four components of different ESs and FSs is developed in the theoretical model:

Nature of organization,
Market organization,
Employment systems, and
authority and control systems.

Like Whitley's (1992b) business systems (BSs), the Islamic financing system (IFS) is seen as an Islamic Financing Business System of its own, with a foundation based on religion, having its own rules governed by the Islamic Shariah (laws). These rules differ from those of other financial systems. Other financial systems, for example, the Market-Based Financing System such as conventional banks both public and private, the Cooperative Financing System, and the Traditional Money Lending System, are viewed as arrangements of hierarchy-market relations that become institutionalized and relatively successful in a particular context.

A similar arrangement in the theoretical model is also made to institutionalize different rural-based small entrepreneurs. Similarly, different small entrepreneurs of similar nature studied are thus grouped into three different small entrepreneurs systems (SESs). These are, for example, the grass-roots level, the season-based, and the semi-mechanized SES systems. Since the network relationships as an important part of the hierarchy-market relationships are poorly developed in Whitley's (1992b) BSs, the concepts of Jansson (2002), the network institutional model, were also taken into consideration. In this network institutional model, Jansson (2002) highlights network relationships between the multinational corporations in India and major external parties in the product/services market like customers, intermediaries, competitors, and suppliers. It also gives some examples of external institutional factors that affect the networks.

The theoretical model also includes the concept of Jansson's (2002) societal sector institutional influences like country culture, legal systems, religion, family/ clan, and government that have direct or indirect influences on lending and borrowing activities between different financing organizations and the rural-based small entrepreneur owners. Since one of the main objects of the study is to see as to how and to what extent various societal sector institutions influence the network relations between financial organizations and other major external parties in the financial market, especially the SEs, regarding the use of the network approach among many others (for example, Aldrich & Whetten, 1981; Anderson & Carlos, 1976;

Easton, 1992; Easton & Araujo, 1991; Elg & Johansson, 1992; Emerson & Cook, 1984; Håkansson, 1993; Kuklinski & Knoke, 1988; Rasmussen, 1988), I found the concept of Jansson's (2002) model appropriate for the study (Alam, 2002, 2009).

Based on the above discussion the "institutional network farmwork" used in the study is shown in Figure 2.1.

The above-mentioned institutional network model, which was developed to study the present phenomenon, consists of three major fields. Since the relationships between the internal networks of the SES and MFS are mainly financial, the financial exchange network is focused on these two institutions. The second box consists of the product and service exchange network as another organizational field influencing the organizational field in the first rectangle. As the activities and the network relationships of network actors of various institutions in these two organizational fields, shown in both the first and the second rectangles, are influenced by societal factors like country culture, religion, family/clan, political system, legal system, and government, these institutions are placed in the outer rectangle to study their influences on the network institutions within and between the organizational fields (Alam 2002, 2009).

Methodological approach of the study

The methodological approach used in the study is a combination of both "deductive and inductive" (Glaser, 1978; Jansson et al., 1995; Strauss & Corbin, 1990). Initially, the research design was based mainly on Whitley's BSs institutional theory (1987, 1990, 1992a,b) and Jansson's (2002) "Network Institutional" theory and network theories of Kuklinski and Knoke (1988), Johanisson and Nowicki (1992), and Håkansson (1993). Based on the above theoretical model, data collected from the field is analyzed. The research methodology applied in the study is of a qualitative nature (Jick, 1979; Merriam, 1998; Patton, 1985; Sherman and Webb, 1988). A qualitative type of research is characterized by collection of data directly from respondents in the field. This is because the entire research program is based on facts acquired from the material world, that is, the practical field of study. An in-depth interview was conducted with senior officials from Islamic banks in Türkiye, Cyprus, and Bangladesh. A case study (Yin, 1994) method was adopted as a research strategy to focus on contemporary phenomenon within the real-life context of different Islamic banks and their network relationships with their customers, especially the small entrepreneurs (Alam, 2002, 2009).

Research process

The following research process was followed to accomplish the study:

- Data was collected from Islamic banks through direct interviews. The entire data collection procedure consists of three different phases.
- The data collection process in different nations varies from 1994 to 1999. Visited different countries to conduct direct interviews with Islamic bank officials in the countries under review.

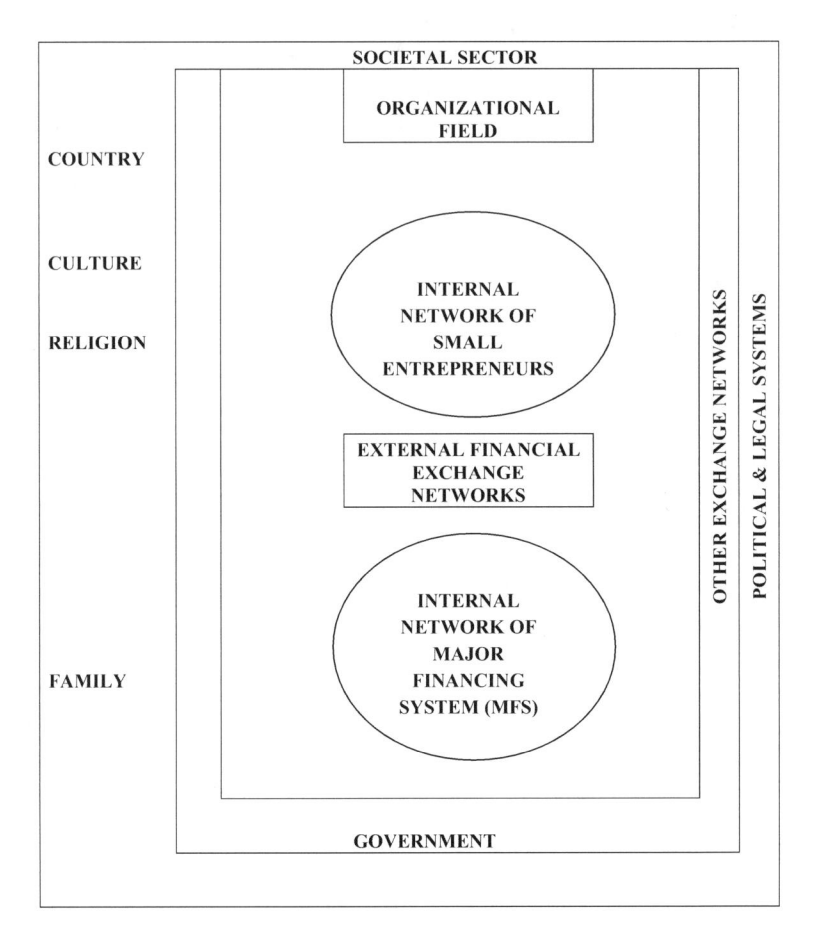

Figure 2.1 The "Institutional Network Framework".

Source: Adapted from Alam (2002).

- The second and third phases of data collection were conducted through correspondence and communication over the telephone.
- As a follow-up procedure, the final data collection was done in the year 2002.
- Questions were asked to respondents based on questionnaires depending on the circumstances and the qualifications of the respondents.
- Different banks in different nations are taken as an individual case while interviewing respondents.
- Used tape recorder to record respondents' answers.
- Subsequent to the interview data recorded in the spreadsheet.
- All respondents interviewed are senior officials of the banks (a brief description of all banks is given in the Appendix) (Alam, 2002).

Characteristics of the components of IFS

The institutional concept of the theoretical approach specifically characteristics of the component of the IFS is discussed in detail in this section. Data collected from field studies in different nations is analyzed to see how and to what extent the activities of Islamic banks under IFS and their relationship with clientele differ from country to county.

It is mentioned in the above section that like Whitley's (1992b) BSs' IFS is outlined as distinct ways of organizing economic activities in a market society and identified the major characteristics, according to which FSs vary between institutional contexts. The characteristics of the components of Whitley's (1992b) BS are developed while structuring the institutional network framework to study differences in the economic activities between organizations under IFSs and small entrepreneur systems. The components or major characteristics of these FSs are the nature of dominant economic activities and resources, the structure of market relations, the nature of authoritative coordination and control systems, and employment systems. These components of the FSs are again analyzed in terms of a number of sub-characteristics that form the basis for comparison across institutional contexts. The first component is the "Nature of organization" with sub-characteristics like managerial discretion from owners, managerial homogeneity, growth focus, risk management, and ownership. The second component is "Market organization" with sub-characteristics like information process interdependence of lender-borrower, commitment to exchange partners, and incentive to employees. The third component is "Employment systems" with sub-characteristics, like recruitment procedures, boss–subordinate relationships, job training, and seniority-based rewards. The fourth component is "Authority and control systems" with sub-characteristics like centralization of decision-making, the delegation of authority, reliance on formal coordination and control, and managerial involvement in the workgroup (Alam, 2002, 2009).

Configuration of the hierarchy-market relations

Field studies were conducted in Sudan, Bangladesh, Sudan, Türkiye, and Cyprus on the financing organizations within the parameters of the IFS (see Appendix where different Islamic bank officials were interviewed in countries under review) to gain practical knowledge about the configuration of the hierarchy-market relations of economic actors within IFS. Data collected from the field was analyzed in accordance with their conformity to the institutional network theoretical frame of reference. A configuration of various characteristics under four components of the IFS in different countries under review is shown in Table 2.1.

Analysis of differences in hierarchy-market relation and institutional influences

The results of the field study as reflected in the above table are analyzed briefly in the following paragraph.

Table 2.1 Configuration of the Hierarchy-Market Relations of IFS in Bangladesh, Sudan, Türkiye, and Cyprus

Market Organization

	Bangladesh	Sudan	Türkiye	Cyprus
Information process	Formal/ Informal	Formal/ Informal	Formal	Formal
Interdependence of lender-borrower	High	High	Medium	Low
Commitment to a particular exchange partner	High	High	Medium	Low
Exchange relations with partners	High	High	Medium	Medium
Reliance on personal ties and trust	High	High	Medium	High

Employment systems

	Bangladesh	Sudan	Türkiye	Cyprus
Boss subordinate relationship	Formal/ informal	Mixed	Formal	Mixed
Job training for staff	High	Medium	High	Low
Importance of seniority-based rewards	High	Low	Low	Low
Incentives to employees	High	Medium	High	Low

Authority and control systems

	Bangladesh	Sudan	Türkiye	Cyprus
Centralization of decision making	Medium	Low	High	High
Reliance on formal co-ordination and control procedures	Medium	Low	High	Medium
Delegation of power and authority system	High	High	Medium	Medium
Importance of managerial involvement	Medium	Medium	Low	Low
Importance to staff morale	High	High	Medium	Medium

Influences of societal sector

Characteristic	Bangladesh	Sudan	Türkiye	Cyprus
Religious faith	High effect	High effect	Low effect	Low effect
Political systems	Medium effect	Low effect	High effect	High effect
Legal system	Medium effect	Low effect	High effect	High effect
Country culture	High effect	High effect	Medium effect	Low effect

Source: Adapted from Alam (2022, 2029).

Contact with customers

It is observed that Islamic banks in Sudan, Cyprus, and Bangladesh maintain direct contact with their customers. However, in Türkiye, apart from direct contact, the bank uses various media to reach the ultimate customers.

Bank–customer relationship

In Türkiye and Cyprus, the bank–customer relationships are more formal than those in Sudan and Bangladesh. Islamic banks in Türkiye and Cyprus, like other conventional banks in the country, follow various formal rules and regulations of the bank and observe all formalities strictly while lending funds to their customers. In Bangladesh and Sudan, Islamic banks, besides their formal procedures in some special cases, maintain informal relationships with customers. This is mostly happening when the banks deal with rural- and urban-based small entrepreneurs. Like Bangladesh, Islamic banks in Sudan also think that if rural customers are developed with regard to their moral behavior and habits, etc., it might help accumulate public savings make proper use of their borrowed funds. In Türkiye and Cyprus, Islamic banks do not consider much on the aspects of moral teaching; rather these banks are mostly concerned with customers' economic conditions and the ability to give collateral securities for borrowing funds from the bank. It is also observed that the loan administration tendency of the Islamic banks in Cyprus and Sudan is much more intense than those in the other two countries. It is reported by senior staff of the banks interviewed that, at the initial stage, customers misused the partnership ("Musharaka") system of lending funds. Due to that the bank stopped lending funds based on this mode of investment. In Sudan, the Islamic bank lends funds to customers on the "Musharaka" or the partnership mode finance. In comparison to Sudan and Bangladesh, reliance on bank–customer personal networks is not as high as in the case of Islamic banks in Türkiye and Cyprus.

Findings of the study in brief

Islamic bank in Sudan practices "Musharaka" (PLS) mode of financing. The study showed that in Sudan, the Sudanese Islamic Bank (SIB) follows "Musharaka" (PLS) mode of financing while lending funds to rural-based small entrepreneurs. The bank and the clienteles determine the amount of capital they require to start the business. The borrowers contribute a certain percentage of the capital and the bank pays the remaining. Thus, the lender and borrowers establish a relationship as partners. This method of lending stipulates that financing organizations and borrowers together contribute capital and share profit and losses according to the agreed proportions. On the contrary, in Türkiye, Cyprus, and Bangladesh, the Islamic financing organizations follow the "Murabaha" (cost plus profit) mode of finance. The only Islamic bank in Cyprus, Bangladesh, and a few other Islamic banks in Türkiye initially tried to introduce the "Musharaka" or PLS mode of financing, but they could not realize the desired objectives since they had an environment that could not sustain business potentials for partnership systems.

Lender–borrower relationships through "Musharaka" financing activities in Sudan

The "Musharaka" mode of financing that the SIB in Sudan is almost like a supervisory FS. The study showed that, according to the policies of the Musharaka financing in SIB, a staff of the bank known as the "Musharaka Manager" pays regular visits to customers' premises to supervise their activities. Apart from that the manager helps clients in maintaining books of accounts and prepares a periodical income statement for determining the profit or loss of the business. The SIB also assists small entrepreneurs in creating marketing facilities for their products.[9] This arrangement builds a close network relationship between the exchange partners and strengthens the exchange partners' commitment and trust in one another. It also provides opportunities for the bank to get to know their customers and their behavior well. Since the credit policies of the financing organizations in IFS in Sudan are characterized by long-term lender–borrower relationships, the levels of interdependency and commitment to one's exchange partners in these countries were found to be higher than those in Türkiye and Cyprus.

An informal way of processing information in Sudan

It is understood from the study that the SIB in Sudan contacts various interest groups and local leaders in the locality to collect information about potential small entrepreneurs before they lend funds to them. The financing organization uses more informal means of collecting information about borrowers. It is observed that the same practice of the informal way of collecting information about prospective customers is also observed in Bangladesh before lending funds by Islamic banks to their rural-based small entrepreneurs in the country.

In Türkiye and Cyprus, the financing organizations in the IFS collect information about their borrowers, following the same principles as the other conventional financing organizations do. However, in many cases, they go beyond formal procedures to collect information about their customers. The study then concluded that although the Islamic financing organizations in Türkiye and Cyprus mostly follow formal lender–borrower network relationships, the process of collecting information about customers consists of both formal and informal types.

Use of media to promote Islamic banks

In Türkiye and Cyprus, Islamic financing organizations spend huge amounts of money to inform the public about the newly developed FS in these countries. It was known from the study that almost all Islamic financing organizations in Türkiye and Cyprus use several methods to do this. They arrange interviews with TV personalities, advertise in special newspapers, and publicize in various national news media, economic magazines, and television and on the radio to inform about the Islamic banks' activities in the country. The banks also host conferences in various hotels and public places and seminars and lectures where leading businessmen, members of parliament, leading personalities, well-known scholars, bankers, and journalists attend. Thus, it was concluded from the study that the information technology used by financing organizations in Türkiye and Cyprus differs from methods used in Bangladesh and Sudan.

Correspondence banks are an exception to the Islamic banks in Türkiye

It was found from the study that, in Türkiye, Islamic banks assist customers by providing necessary services through the correspondence banks. These services were not found in any other countries under review. This sort of arrangement is done mainly for people who are interested in Islamic finance where there are no branches of Islamic banks. In such cases, Islamic banks arrange with the country's different conventional banks in those areas to assist their customers in carrying out their lending and borrowing activities. These conventional banks work as "correspondence banks" for Islamic banks and charge fees for their services.

Use of subsidiary companies for different Islamic banks in Türkiye

According to the laws of the state, the financial systems in Türkiye and Cyprus do not allow any financing organization to lend funds to customers other than in cash. The country's financial systems prohibit the exchange transactions between lenders and borrowers in-kind or materials-based. The lending and borrowing of funds must be conducted with cash. It is known from the study that the "Murabaha" and the "Bai-Muajjal" modes of lending funds by Islamic banks do not give loans to customers in the form of cash; rather, the bank uses the loan amount to buy the raw materials or products for customers. Due to the restrictions placed on them by the government, Islamic banks in Türkiye have their own subsidiary companies. Customers of these banks who borrow funds on either the "Murabaha" or "Bai-Muajjal" mode are required to bring pro-forma invoices for goods from a supplier. In a such situation, the subsidiary companies of the lending organizations function as suppliers of materials or products for the customers. To accomplish this exchange function legally, the Islamic bank pays its subsidiary company cash and the customers' accounts are debited with the amount paid based on the pro-forma invoice.

Control over Islamic banks by the government in Türkiye

In Türkiye, although Islamic financing organizations are privately owned organizations, the government has indirect control over their activities. For example, Islamic banks in Türkiye are not formed in accordance with the country's normal financial regulations. Rather, these are established with the nation's Special

Decree. Even though these financing houses are rendering services according to the Islamic Sharia (Law), these financing organizations are not allowed to call themselves interest-free banks. They are called "OZEL FINANS KURUMLARI," meaning "Special Finance House." These Finance Houses have been established in accordance with the Special Decree of the government, dated December 16, 1983 (No. 83/7506) for the formation of a Special Finance House and are commonly referred to as "interest-free banks."

The legal systems in Türkiye and Cyprus are lengthy and costly. It is thus concluded that the financing organizations in the Islamic banks in Türkiye and Cyprus experience limitations from legal and political systems while conducting the exchange functions.

Personal trust is not a prime requirement in Türkiye and Cyprus

The study revealed that neither Islamic banks nor the small entrepreneurs in Türkiye and Cyprus relied much on personal trust and ties between each other. As mentioned earlier, Islamic banks in Türkiye contact customers in a formal way and the lender–borrower relations are mostly of formal types. The bank does not rely on the personal ties and the trust of their customers in the exchange functions. Since the SIB in Sudan uses the "Musharaka" mode of financing while lending funds to small entrepreneurs, more importance is given to the personal trust of their customers because it intensifies the lender–borrower relationships.

Small loans for women customers in SIB in Sudan

In Sudan it was also observed that the SIB encourages rural-based poor women to start small businesses of their own and the bank gives loans for the same. There are special arrangements in the bank for women customers. Normally women in the locality feel very shy to go to a man officer and to discuss anything about their family affairs. To facilitate women customers, the bank employed many women staff, and they take care of the women's section. Almost two-thirds of the small entrepreneurs interviewed under the Productive Family Project in Omdruman are women. The bank officer reported that women are found more organized and active than male customers. However, in other countries under review, Islamic banks do not have any demarcations among their customers.

Working environment differences in different nations: It is found from the study that hierarchical working relationships within the SIB consists of both formal and informal types. It was noted that, in many cases, senior staff members maintained close and informal relationships with their juniors. It is observed that in Cyprus, the number of staff at Faisal Islamic Bank Kibris is not many both in the head office and the branch office, facilitating better contact between staff members within the bank. On the contrary, Islamic banks in Türkiye maintain a formal supervisor–staff relationship. However, they possess unique methods of meeting each other informally. They like to meet at lunch organized within bank premises. With the leadership of the CEO of the Islamic bank, all staff perform their obligatory prayers together in congregation on the bank premises.

Concerns about the religious faith of customers: It was known from the study that the SIB in Sudan is more concerned about religious faith and the dedication to the work of its customers than other countries under review. This results in the promotion of trustful relationships between the lender and the borrowers. It was also found that many people in Türkiye are also conscientious of their religious faith since they refuse to save money or carry out any financial transactions with any interest-bearing conventional banks. In one incident it was known from a senior official of one of the Islamic banks in Türkiye that the bank accepted huge idle finds as deposits from the public soon after they started their exchange functions.

Influences of social culture

A country's social culture, like its religious systems, norms, and habits, influences the exchange activities of Islamic banks differently in different societies. The study demonstrated that in Sudan the rural people were fond of passing time without work and used to enjoy time by gossiping with friends. They love to spend hour after hour in marriage ceremonies and other cultural activities. It is part of their cultural beliefs to entertain guests by spending a great deal of time with the person. As a host, it is considered wise to make the guests happy by giving them time. The officials of Islamic banks in Sudan started teaching their customers to make proper use of their time and advised them to devote themselves to productive activities.

Conclusions

It may be concluded from the above analysis that even though Islamic banking functions differ in different countries under different environmental and socioeconomic conditions, the lender–borrower relationship between the bank and the customers is remarkably high. Islamic banks, with their principle of lending funds in kind rather than cash, develop close supervision of borrowed funds, and the banks make sure that the customers use their borrowed funds in a proper and productive way. From the study, it may also be concluded that once Islamic banks show their interest in investing a larger portion of their savings in the small entrepreneur sector in "partnership mode," it will not only eliminate rural poverty but also be successful in establishing just and balanced social order free from all kinds of exploitations in the society.

Appendix

A brief description of different interest-free banks interviewed in Bangladesh, Sudan, Türkiye, and Cyprus

Islami Bank Bangladesh Limited (IBBL)

Based on Islamic principles and Shariah (Islamic law) with an authorized capital of TK. 500 million (12.5 US million dollars) the Interest-free bank in Bangladesh, called Islami Bank Bangladesh Limited (IBBL) was incorporated on March 13,

1983, as a Public Limited Company under the companies Act. 1913. The bank started its financial activities with effect from March 30, 1983. This is one of the Islamic banks in South Asia and Southeast Asia (Annual Report IBBL, 1994, 1995, 1996).

Al-Baraka Bank Bangladesh Limited (AL-BARAKA)

Four years after the establishment of the Islami Bank Bangladesh Limited the Al-Baraka Bank Bangladesh Limited (ABBBL), commenced its banking business as a scheduled bank in the country in May 1987. This bank is the second largest Interest-free bank in the country. It is a joint venture enterprise of Al Baraka Investment and Development (ABID) Company, a renowned financial and business house of Saudi Arabia, Islamic Development Bank (IDB), a group of eminent Bangladesh industrialists and the Government of Bangladesh (Annual Report ABBBL, 1995).

Social Investment Bank Limited (SIBL)

The Social Investment Bank Limited (SIBL), is one of the Islamic banks in Bangladesh, with its three sectors unique model joint venture bank working together for a caring society in Bangladesh. The three sectors of the bank activities are consisting in formal, non-formal and voluntary sector. The bank was incorporated in Bangladesh in the year 1995 as a banking company under the Companies Act. 1994 (Annual Report SIBL, 1995, 1996).

Islamic banks in Türkiye

It was known from one of the managing directors of an Islamic bank during a field tour that although Islamic principles dominate the entire activities of financing organizations in the IFS in Türkiye, it is constitutionally prohibited to use the word "Islam" before any financial organization. Due to this reason all IFSs that are rendering financial services based on Islamic Shariah (Law) are called "OZEL FINANS KURUMLARI," meaning "Special Finance House." These finance houses have been established in accordance with the Special Decree of the government, dated December 16, 1983 (No. 83/7506), for the formation of a Special Finance House and are commonly referred to as "interest-free banks."

There are five such financing organizations in Türkiye. A brief description of these financing organizations is given below.

Ihlas Finance House (IFH)

In Türkiye, *Ihlas Finance House (IFH)* is very popular as a group of companies in the industry, trade, media, and finance sectors. The Ihlas Finance Kurumu A.S, also known as an interest-free financial organization, belongs to the IHLAS group. Shareholders and percentage of shares of shares of Ihlas Holding, in 1996, was Ihlas holding A.S 64.77%, public 15%, Türkiye Diyanet Vakfı 8%, others 2.23%.

Ali (2007), in his article, informed that "Ihlas Finance House is closed and no more operating its financial activities"[10] (Annual Report IFH, 1997).

Faisal Finance Institution (FFI)

Faisal Finance Institution (FFI) was incorporated by the Decree of the Turkish Council of Ministers, dated June 11, 1984, which is based on an earlier decree of the Council of Ministers in December 1983. On receipt of the Operation License from the Central Bank of Türkiye FFI commenced its financial activities on April 2, 1985 (Annual Report FFI, 1996).

Al Baraka Turkish Finance House (ABTFH)

Al Baraka Turkish Finance House (ABTFH), known as "Al Baraka Turk" started rendering banking services to the public in June 1988, after the bank was registered in the Istanbul Stock Exchange. This is the first interest-free bank in Türkiye. The bank was established in the year 1983, with a special decree of the government of Türkiye (Annual Report ABTFH, 1996).

Kuwait Turkish Evkaf Finance House

Kuwait Turkish Evkaf Finance House ("the Institution") (KTEFH) was formed on December 16, 1983, in accordance with the provision of a special decree from the Government of Türkiye, relating to the establishment of Special Finance House in the country. In February 1989, the institution obtained permission from the Central Bank of Türkiye and started its financial activities in March 1989 (Annual Report KTFH, 1996).

Anadolu Finance Institution (AFI)

Anadolu Finance Institution (AFI) was established in November 1991. AFI is the first special financial institution founded with 100% domestic capital (Annual Report AFI, 1996).

ASYA Finance House (AFH)

Besides the above, FH *Asiya Finance House (AFH)* is one of the newly started interest-free banks, which started its activities a few months before my visit to Türkiye in the year 1997. Although I interviewed a few senior officials of the bank, no detailed data was available, and hence this bank is not included in the present discussion (Annual Report AFH, 1996).

Faisal Interest free bank Kibris (FIBK)

In T.R.N. Cyprus, the *Faisal Interest free bank of Kibris (FIBK)* was established in late 1982 (under the name of "Interest free bank of Kibris"). The bank started its operation in March 1983 in Lefkosa (Nicosia) with an authorized capital of USD 350,000. Arab subscribers paid the entire amount of capital. During my field trip, the bank had three branches including the principal branch located in the head office building, in Lefkosa. One branch is in Gazi Magusa (Famagusta), and the other is in Girne (Kyrenia) (Annual Report FIBK, 1996).

Islamic bank in Sudan

Sudanese Islamic Bank (SIB) started giving credit in early 1988 to small farmers and rural-based small entrepreneurs on a "Musharaka" (partnership financing) mode of investment. To assist rural-based small entrepreneurs, SIB started many pilot projects based on "Musharaka" financing, and one of these projects is called "The productive family project." While highlighting the role of conventional banks in Sudan, Khalifa and Shazali (1988), Khalifa (1992) argues that the formal financial market failed to function efficiently and to reach the small farmers in the agrarian sector. It is basically due to the failure to accommodate the risk aversion attitude of the small farmers in their finance model. To overcome this problem, the SIB started giving loans to agricultural and other small manufacturers on a "Musharaka" mode of Islamic financing system.

Notes

1 IMF Staff Papers, Vol. 33. No. 1, March 1986, pp. 4–5.
2 Ahmad et al. (2014), Badr (1989), Chapra, (2001), Farooq (2005, 2009), Khan (2015) Muhammad Akram (2013), Kuran (2004, 2011), Nomani (2002), Al-Qaradawi (2016), Saeed (1999), Siddiqi (2004, 2007), and Usmani (1998, 1999).
3 Marifu Quran Tafsir' Internet edition in eight volumes: https://archive.org/details/ English-MaarifulQuran/English-MaarifulQuran-MuftiShafiUsmaniRA-Vol-1/page/ n21/mode/2up (Mufti Muhammad Shafi).
4 Arab and Islamic Banks, Trante Wohlus Scharf, OECD, Paris, 1983, p. 90.
5 Sharia is an Islamic religious law that governs the day-to-day life of its Muslim followers. *Sharia establishes guidelines for investment and banking.*
6 "Zakat" is an Islamic finance term referring to the obligation that an individual must donate a certain proportion of wealth each year to charitable causes.
7 Qard hassan is a loan extended on a goodwill basis, mainly for welfare purposes. The borrower need only pay back the amount they borrowed, with no interest.
8 For example, in Bangladesh, Nepal and India (ESCAP Secretariat, 1984), Bangladesh (Siddiqi, 1992), China (Sit, 1991; Wang, 1992), China, Japan, India (Vepa, 1982, 1984), Ceylon (Abeyasingha, 1982), Hong Kong (Tam, 1984), Korea (Ouh, 1984; UNIDO, 1988), India (Agrawal, 1988; Bhattachryya, 1988; Bhende, 1974; Brodribb, 1982, 1991; Ganguly, 1988; Kundra, 1991; Rooseboom, 1972; Solanki & Qureshi, 1991; Singh, 1982; Sury, 1987; Venkataraman, 1986; Vepa, 1982, 1984), Indonesia, Philippines, Malaysia (ESCAP/UNIDO, 1984), Suhardi, 1991), India, Pakistan, and Sri Lanka (Subramanian, 1992), Japan (Aburtani, 1964), Malaysia (Hoong, 1989; Jordon, 1972), Pakistan (Syed, 1984), Philippines (Alonzo et al., 1992; Macuja, 1981; Rosario, 1964; Salazar, 1986; Tan 1987), Philippines and Thailand (UNIDO, 1988), and Singapore (Keng, 1987; Yue, 1992).
9 During the field study in Sudan while I visited some small entrepreneurs in "Omdurman," a suburb of Khartoum, it was noted that the SIB preserves various types of products of their customers within a showroom on the bank premises that is reserved for and

belongs to their customers. This arrangement was as the bank manager said "an attempt to market customers" products. Thus, the bank creates marketing facilities for their different customers who borrow funds from the bank under "Musharaka" financing mode.

10 Ali Salman Syed, Financial Distress and Bank Failure: Lesson from Closer of Ihlas Finance in Turkey (January 1 2007). *Islamic Economic Studies*, Volume 14, No 1 & 2, 2007.

References

Abeyasingha, A. I. G. (1982), "Role of Appropriate Technology and Marketing in Modernization and Improvement of Efficiency of Small-Scale Industries." *Small Industry Bulletin for Asia and Pacific*, No. 18, United Nations, New York.

Aburtani, S. (1964), "Marketing of Small Industry Products in Asian Countries: A Re-Appraisal of the Role of Markets." *Small Industry Bulletin for Asia and Pacific*, No. 4, United Nations, New York, pp. 27–29.

Agrawal, C. (1988), "Human Resources Development for Small Industries Promotion." *Small Industry Bulletin for Asia and Pacific*, No. 23, United Nations, New York, pp. 100–104.

Ahmad, A. Y. (2011), "Prohibition of Riba (Interest) in Islam: Its Economic Rationale and Implications." https://www.academia.edu/723631/PROHIBITION_OF_RIBA_INTEREST_IN_ISLAM_ITS_ECONOMIC_RATIONALE_AND_IMPLICATIONS

Ahmad, K. (1994), "Elimination of Riba: Concepts and Problems." In Ahmad, K. (ed.), *Elimination of Riba from the Economy*, Institute of Policy Studies, Islamabad, pp. 33–53.

Ahsan Fakhrul, A. S. M. (1979), "Performance of Rural Financial Market in Bangladesh." In *Problems and Issues of Agricultural Credit and Rural Finance*, Bangladesh Bank, Dhaka.

Ahsan Fakhrul, A. S. M. (1989), *Islamic Banking in Perspective*, Islamic Bank Bangladesh Limited, Dhaka.

Alam, M. N. (2000), "Islamic Banking Systems: A Challenge in the Modern Financial Market." (A case study on IBBL Bangladesh). *International Journal of Islamic Financial Services*, 1 (4 Jan–March), pp. 10–27. ISSN 0972-138X.

Alam, M. N. (2002), *Financing Small and Cottage Industries in Bangladesh by Islamic Banks: An Institutional-Network Approach*, Institute of Economic Research, Lund Studies in Economics and Management 72, Lund Business Press, Lund, Sweden. ISBN 91-971179-2-7.

Alam, M. N. (2003), "Institutionalization and Promotion of Saving Habit Through Bai-Muajjal Mode of Financing (A Unique Means of Mobilizing Rural Savings towards Productive Sources)." *Managerial Finance*, 29 (2/3), Selected Financial Institutional Structures and Policy Perspectives. pp. 3–22.

Alam, M. N. (2009), "Empowering Small Entrepreneurs by Islamic Banks: A Study of Lender-Borrowers Network Relationships between Small Entrepreneurs and Different Financing Organizations." ISBN 13 978-3-8383-1241-5. LAP Lambert Academic Publishing AG & Co KG, December 2009.

Aldrich, H. and Whetten D. A. (1981), "Organisation Set, Action-Sets and Network; Making the Most of Simplicity." In P. C. Nystrom and W. H. Starbuck (eds.), *Handbook of Organizational Design*, Volume 1, Oxford University Press, Oxford, pp. 385–408.

Ali, S. S. (2007), "Financial Distress and Bank Failure: Lesson from Closer of Ihlas Finance in Türkiye." *Islamic Economic Studies*, 14 (1), 2.

Alonzo, R. P., De Dios, E. S., and Tecson, G. R. (1992), "Role of Small and Medium Scale Enterprises in Industrial Restructuring in the Philippines." *Small Industry Bulletin for Asia and Pacific*, No. 26/27, United Nations, New York, pp. 33–40.

Anderson B. O. and Carlos M. L. (1976), "What Is Social Network? Power and Control, Social Structures and Their Transformation." *SAGE Studies in International Sociology*.

Anderson, D. and Khambata, F. (1982), "Financing Small-Scale Industries and Agriculture in Developing Countries, the Merits and Limitations Of Commercial Policies." *World Bank Staff Working Paper*, No. 519.

Annual Report, ABBBL. (1995), *Al-Baraka Bangladesh Bank Limited*, ABBL, Dhaka.

Annual Report, ABTFH. (1996), *The Al Baraka Turkish Finance House (ABTFH)*, ABTFH, Istanbul.

Annual Report. AFH. (1996), *Asia Finance House (AFH)*, AFH, Istanbul.

Annual Report, AFI. (1996), *The Anadolu Finance Institution (AFI)*, AFI, Ankara.

Annual Report, FFI. (1996), *The Faisal Finance Institution (FFI)*, FFI, Istanbul.

Annual Report, FIBK. (1996), *The Faisal Islamic Bank Kibris (FIBK)*, FIBK, Lefkosa (Nicosia).

Annual Report, IBBL. (1994, 1995, 1996), *Islami Bank Bangladesh Limited*, IBBL, Dhaka.

Annual Report, IFH. (1997), *The Ihlas Finance Kurumu A.S (IFH)*, IFH, Istanbul.

Annual Report, KTFH. (1996), *The Kuwait Turkish Evkaf Finance House (KTFH)*, KTFH, Istanbul.

Annual Report, SIBL. (1995, 1996), *Social Investment Bank Limited*, SIBL, Dhaka.

Ashe, J. and Cosslett, C. E- (1989), "Credit for the Poor." *Past Activities and Future Directions for the United Nations Development Program*, UNDP Policy Discussion Paper, United Nations Publications, New York.

Bhattachryya, M. (1988), "Planning and Development of Small-Scale Industries in India." *Small Industry Bulletin for Asia and Pacific*, No. 23, United Nations, New York.

Bhende, N. M. (1974), "Small Industries Development a Tool for Social Transformation." *Small Industry Bulletin for Asia and Pacific*, No. 15, United Nations, New York, pp. 75–79.

Brodribb, M. (1982), "Modernization and Improvement of Efficiency of Small-Scale Industries." *Small Industry Bulletin for Asia and Pacific*, United Nations, No. 18, New York, pp. 1–3.

Brodribb, L. (1991), "Financing for Small Business." *Small Industry Bulletin for Asia and Pacific*, No. 25, United Nations, New York, pp. 12–15.

Easton, G. (1992), "Industrial Networks: A Review." In Axelsson, B. and Easton, G. (eds.), *Industrial Networks. A New View of Reality*, Routledge, London, pp. 1–36.

Easton, G. and Araujo, L. (1991), "Language, Metaphors and Networks." *Paper Presented at the 7th I.M.P. Conference, International Business Networks, Evaluation, Structure, and Management*, Uppsala, Sweden.

Elg, U. and Johansson, U. (1992), *Dagligföretags Strategiska Agerande -En Analysis or ett Interorganisatoriskt Nätverkperspective*, Lund University Press, Lund.

Emerson R. M. and Cook K. S. (1984), "Exchange Network and the Analysis of Complex Organisation." *Research in the Sociology of Organisation*, 3, 1–30.

ESCAP. (1984), "On Some Aspects of the Strategies, Policies and Measures for the Development of Small-Scale Industries in Bangladesh, Nepal, and India." *Small Industry Bulletin for Asia and Pacific*, No. 19, United Nations, New York, pp. 37–40.

ESCAP/UNIDO. (1984), Policies for Development Small and Medium-Scale Industries in Four Large Asean Countries, *Small Industry Bulletin for Asia and Pacific*, No 19, United Nations, New York.

Ganguly, A. K. (1988), "Export Promotion in the Small-Scale Industry: India." *Small Industry Bulletin for Asia and Pacific*, No. 23, United Nations, New York, pp. 3–14.

Glaser, B. G. (1978), *Theoretical Sensitivity*, Sociology Press, San Francisco, CA.

Håkansson, H. (1993), "Industrial Network and Technological Innovation." Uppsala University, Anders Lundgren, Stockholm School of Economics.

Hoong, S. S. (1989), "Action Plan for the Development of Small and Medium-Scale Industries-Malaysia." *Small Industry Bulletin for Asia and Pacific*, No. 24, United Nations, New York. pp. 65–67.

Huq, M. A. (1990), "Islamic Banking in Bangladesh, Manpower Development and Establishment of a Regional Training and Research Institute." *Proceedings and Papers of International Seminar on Islamic Banking and Insurance Held in Dhaka*, October 27, pp. 33–53.

Jansson, H. (2000), *International Strategic Management in Emerging Markets: Global Institutions and Networks*.

Jansson, H. (2002), *International Business Management in Emerging Markets. Global Institutions and Networks*, Book Manuscript, Baltic Business School, University of Kalmar.

Jansson, H., Saqib, M., and Sharma, D. (1995), *The State and Transnational*.

Jick, T. D. (1979), "Mixing Qualitative and Quantitative Methods, Triangulation in Action." *Administrative Science Quarterly*, 24, 602–611.

Johanisson, B, Nowicki K. (1992), "Using Networks to Organize Support for Entrepreneurs…. a Graph Analysis of Swedish Contexts." *Paper Presented at the Babson College Entrepreneurship Research Conference*, Fontainebleau, Franch.

Jordon, D. (1972), "Small-Scale Production – Which Way? *Small Industry Bulletin for Asia and Pacific*, No. 9, United Nations, New York, pp. 39–42.

Kazarian, E. (1991), "Finance and Economic Development, Islamic Banking in Egypt." *Lund Economic Studies*, No. 45.

Keng, K. A. (1987), "Business Practices of Small and Medium Enterprises in Singapore." *Small Industry Bulletin for Asia and Pacific*, No.22, United Nations, New York, pp. 97–102.

Khalifa, M. U. (1992), Musharaka Finance: An Optimum Risk Management Approach to Small Farmers: A Paper Prepared for the Risk Management Workshop held in Damascus, 24–27 May.

Khalifa, M. U. and Shazali, S. (1988), *The Experience of Sudanese Islamic Bank in Musharaka Financing*, SIB Publication, Khartoum.

Khoja, E. M. and Guddah, A. S. A. (1997), "Instrument of Islamic Investment." *Research & Development Department.* Al-Baraka Investment & Development Co. Islamic Banking & Finance. http://www.albaraka.com/Islamicinfo/IslamicBooks/Instrument.

Kuklinski, J. H. and Knoke D. (1988), *Network Analysis Series, Qualitative Application in the Social Sciences*, volume 28, SAGE University Press.

Kundra, J. P. (1991), "Financing Small-Scale Industries in India." *Small Industry Bulletin for Asia and Pacific*, No. 25, United Nations, New York, pp. 3–8.

Lieber, A. E. (1968), "Eastern Business Practices and Mediaeval European Commerce." *Economic History Review*, 21, 230–243.

Little, I. M. D. (1988), "Small Manufacturing Enterprises and Employment in Developing Countries." *Asian Development Review*, 6 (2).

Little, I. M. D., Mazumdar, D., and Page, J. M. (Jr) (1987), *Small Manufacturing Enterprise*, Oxford University Press, New York.

Macuja, P. C. (1981), "Small Scale Industry Development in the Philippines." *Small Industry Bulletin for Asia and Pacific*, No. 21, United Nations, New York, pp. 182–189.

Merriam, S. B. (1998), *Qualitative Research and Case Study Applications in Education, Revised and Expanded from Case Study Research*, Jossey-Bass publishers, San Francisco, CA.

Molla, R. I., Moten R. A., Gusau, S. A., and Gwandu A. A. (1988), *Frontiers and Mechanics of Islamic Economics*, University of Sokoto, Nigeria.

Myrdal, G. (1968), *Asian Drama. An Inquiry into the Poverty of Nations*. Pantheon, A Division of Random House, New York.

Nassief, N. (1989), "Islamic Banking around the World." *Islamic Banking and Insurance: Proceedings and Papers of International Seminar Held in Dhaka in October*.

Ouh, Y. B. (1984), "Major Policies and Measures for Promotion of Export by Small-Scale enterprises in The Republic of Korea." *Small Industry Bulletin for Asia and Pacific*, No. 19, United Nations, New York.

Patton, M. Q. (1985), *Quality in Qualitative Research: Methodological Principles and Recent Development*, Invited addresses to Division J of the American Educational Research Association, Chicago.

Rasmussen, J. (1988), "Goodbye Theory – Hello Reality? Recent Trend in Social and Regional Theory Its Consequences for Network Studies in Africa." *Centre for Development Research (CDR) Working Paper 88.3*. Jan–Mar. Vol. 8, No. 2.

Rooseboom, H. J. B. (1972), "Role of Government in Promotion of Employment in Small Scale Industries." *Small Industry Bulletin for Asia and Pacific*, No. 9, United Nations, New York, pp. 70–72.

Rosario, A. T. D. (1964), "Problems of Marketing in the Cottage Industries." *Small Industry Bulletin for Asia and Pacific*, No. 4, United Nations, New York, pp. 35–40.

Salazar, M. S. (1986), "Small Scale Industry Development in the Philippines." *Small Industry Bulletin for Asia and Pacific*, No. 21, United Nations, New York.

Scharf, T. W. (1983), Arab and Islamic Banks: New Business Partners for Developing Countries, OECD, Paris, pp. 79–80.

Shafi, M. (1954), Marifu Quran Tafsir internet edition in eight volumes. https://archive.org/details/English-MaarifulQuran/English-MaarifulQuran-MuftiShafiUsmani-Vol-1/page/n21/mode/2up (Mufti Muhammad Shafi).

Sherman, R. R. and Webb, R. B. (1988), "Qualitative Research in Education: A Focus." In I. R. R. Sherman and R. B. Webb (eds.), *Qualitative Research in Education: Focus and Methods*, Falmer Press, Bristol, PA.

Siddiqi, G. A. H. (1992), "Role of Small and Medium-Scale Enterprises in Industrial Restructuring in Bangladesh." *Small Industry Bulletin for Asia and Pacific*, No. 26/27, United Nations, New York.

Siddiqi, M. N. (1988), *Banking without Interest, Islamic Economic Series No 5*, Islamic Foundation, Leicester.

Singh, B. N. (1982), "Standardization and Development of Small-Scale Industries." *Small Industry Bulletin for Asia and Pacific*, No.18, United Nations, New York, pp. 11–13.

Sit, V. F. S. (1991), "Export-Oriented Industrialization of Macau and the Role of Small and Medium Size Industries." *Small Industry Bulletin for Asia and Pacific*, No. 25, United Nations, New York, pp. 41–50.

Solanki, S. S. and Qureshi, M. A. (1991), "Promotion of Commercialization of Indigenous Technology by Small Entrepreneurs: Role of Financial Institutions in India." *Bulletin for Asia and Pacific*, No. 25, United Nations, New York.

Strauss, A. L., and Corbin J. (1990), *Basics of Qualitative Research, Grounded Theory Procedures and Techniques*, SAGE Publication, Thousand Oaks, California, USA.

Subramanian, S. K. (1992), "Role of Small and Medium-Scale Enterprises in Industrial Restructuring in South Asia." *Small Industry Bulletin for Asia and Pacific*, No. 26/27, United Nations, New York, pp. 59–65.

Suhardi, T. (1991), "Financing Small and Medium-Scale Industries in Indonesia." *Small Industry Bulletin for Asia and Pacific*, No. 25, United Nations, New York, pp. 9–11.

Sury, M. M. (1987), "Excise Concessions to Small-Scale Industries in India: Some Issues." *Small Industry Bulletin for Asia and Pacific*, No. 22, United Nations, New York.

Syed, H. R. (1984), "Development of Small-Scale Industries Sector in Pakistan." *Small Industry Bulletin for Asia and Pacific*, No. 19, United Nations, New York, pp. 10–12.

Tam, E. (1984), "The Role of Joint-Venture in the Development of Small Industries in Hong Kong." *Small Industry Bulletin for Asia and Pacific*, No. 19, United Nations, New York.

Tan, Q. G. (1987), "Success Stories in Small Industries: Case Studies." *Small Industry Bulletin for Asia and Pacific*, No. 22, United Nations, New York, pp. 85–91.

UNIDO (1988), "Promotion of Small and Medium-Scale Industries in the Republic of Korea." *Small Industry Bulletin for Asia and Pacific*, No. 23, United Nations, New York, pp. 18–30.

Venkataraman, G. 1986. "Development of Small Industries in India: Policies, Programs and Perspectives." *Small Industry Bulletin for Asia and Pacific*, No. 21, United Nations, New York, pp. 40–49.

Vepa, R. K. (1982), "Modernization of Small Industry with Special Reference to India." *Small Industry Bulletin for Asia and Pacific*, No. 18, United Nations, New York, pp. 6–7.

Vepa, R. K. (1984), "Strategies for Small Industry Development in Japan, China, and India. A Comparative study." *Small Industry Bulletin for Asia and Pacific*, No. 19, United Nations, New York.

Wang, H. (1992), "Role of Small and Medium-Scale Enterprises in Industrial Restructuring in China." *Small Industry Bulletin for Asia and Pacific*, No. 26/27, United Nations, New York.

Whitley, R. D. (1987), "Taking Firms Seriously as Economic Actors: Towards a Sociology of Firm Behaviour." *Organization Studies*, 8, 125–147.

Whitley, R. D. (1990), *Eastern Asian Enterprise Structure and the Comparative Analysis Forms of Business Organization*, Organization Studies, EGOS.

Whitley, R. D. (1992a), *The Comparative Analysis of Business Systems*, SAGE Publication Ltd., London.

Whitley. R. D. (1992b), *Business System in Asia*, SAGE Publications Ltd., London.

Wilson, R. (1965), "The Empire of the Prophet: Islam and the Tide of Arab Conquest." In D. Talbot (ed.), *The Dark Ages*, Thomas and Hudson, London.

World Bank. (1989), *World Bank Development Report*, World Bank, Washington, DC, p. 120.

Yue, C. S. (1992), "Role of Small and Medium-Scale Enterprises in Industrial Restructuring in Singapore." *Small Industry Bulletin for Asia and Pacific*, No. 26/27, United Nations, New York, pp. 55–58.

Zineldin, M. (1990), *The Economics of Money and Banking, A Theoretical and Empirical Study of Islamic Interest-Banking,* Stockholm University, Stockholm.

3 Is there a "divine" definition of riba and its scope in the Holy Quran?

Hasan Gürak

An 'Alternative' Approach to Analysis of Riba Based on 'Earned' (Halal) vs 'Unearned' (Haram) Income
Islam always welcomes and promotes scientific works and praises scholars.

Introduction[1]

First, there was the Western type of interest-bearing banking system. As an alternative, modern Islamic banking emerged in the 1970s with the purpose of creating an interest-free banking system. Because, according to Islamic law, it is haram (forbidden) for Muslims to get and/or pay interest on loans. Since then, getting or paying "riba" on loans has probably been the most vehemently and frequently debated concept of Islamic economics.

The Holy Book of Islam is the primary source of reference for Muslims regarding the prohibition of riba on loans. There is no doubt that the Holy Quran forbids receiving and paying riba. But the question is, does the Holy Quran give a "divine" definition of riba and its scope? Unfortunately, the answer is no![2]

Since there are no Quranic definitions, an attempt will be made to formulate and present a purely "scientific" definition of riba about loans and its scope from an economist's standpoint, as we consider that the issue of riba is a subject of economic science, not of theology.[3] All due respect will be given to all Islamic values.[4]

The word used in the Arabic language when referring to Western-style interest is "riba." That's why today when the word "riba" is mentioned, the first concept in English that comes to mind is the Western-style economic concept of "interest." Literally, the word riba implies "**additional**," "**excess**," or "**surplus**." However, it also has other meanings than "interest," which are rarely used. For instance, riba also implies "**unjust income**," "**exploitative gain**," "**unjustified excess**," or "**unearned income**."

Throughout this chapter, the concepts of "**earned vs. unearned**" **income** will be used as alternatives to Western-style "interest" in financial sector analysis. In addition, the alternative concepts will be used to prove a hypothesis asserting that alternative concepts provide a more rational and fruitful ground in the financial analysis to understand and explain the reason behind the **prohibition of riba**.

Since the Holy Quran is the only source of reference regarding financial transactions, let us begin with what the Holy Book of the Quran says about riba.

DOI: 10.4324/9781032631561-5

Riba in the Holy Quran

We have selected eight verses belonging to four Surahs in the Holy Quran that refer to the issue of riba. The Suras, in accordance with the date of Revelation, are as follows:

1 **The Romans**; 39
2 **Women**; 160–161
3 **The Family of Imrân**; 130
4 **Baqara**; 275–276–278

Now let us take a closer look at what the relevant Suras and verses say about riba.

Suras/verses on riba (according to their date of revelation)

The Romans

> **39.** That which you give in usury for **increase through the property** of (other) people, will have no increase with Allah, but that which you give for charity, seeking the Countenance of Allah, (will increase): it is these who will get a recompense multiplied.

There is no clear prohibition of riba in this verse. However, it states that it "will have no increase with Allah." The verse suggests **giving charity** for the **Countenance of Allah**. Certain scholars interpret the expression "will have no increase with Allah" as if it implies a prohibition, though others consider this perception an exaggeration. Anyway, there is no definition of riba or its scope to identify and measure the "increase" or "surplus."

Women (Nisa)

> **160.** For the iniquity of the Jews We made unlawful for them certain (foods) good and wholesome which had been lawful for them;- in that they hindered many from Allah's Way.
> **161.** That they took usury, though they were forbidden; and that they devoured men's substance wrongfully;- We have prepared for those among them who reject faith a grievous punishment.

Verses 160 and 161 criticize the Jews for getting riba though they were forbidden to get any by Allah. But at this time, there was no prohibition on riba for Muslims. A wider interpretation that includes Muslims would be a mistake. As we see again, there is neither any definition of riba nor any criteria by which to measure the "increase" or "surplus" prohibited.

The Family of Imrân

> **130.** O ye who believe! Devour not usury, doubled, and multiplied, but fear Allah; that ye may (really) prosper.

This is the first verse that prohibits riba in plain language. The emphasis is on "doubled and multiplied usury." The details of "doubled and multiplied" are open to debate and in need of clarification. According to Islamic historians, in the Era of Ignorance before Islam, when the Arab debtor could not repay his debt with riba on time, the repayment period was extended, but an added and often excessive amount was requested, i.e., interest on the loan. That is probably the critical issue referred to in this verse.

However, we cannot define the type of riba at issue with any certainty. That is because there is also riba to be paid at the end of the "initial" period of the loan, which is also prohibited. It is not definite in the Surah which type of riba is meant: the one for the "extended" period of time, including additional payment, or the riba paid for all periods, including the initial one.

Thereby, we learn specifically that getting riba is prohibited for Muslims as well, but, again, there is still no definition of it, its scope, or any criteria on how to measure the "increase."

Baqara

With the revelation of Baqara, we get detailed information on interest:

> **275.** Those who devour usury will not stand except as stand one whom the Satan by his touch Hath driven to madness. That is because they say: "Trade is like usury," but Allah hath permitted trade and forbidden usury. Those who after receiving direction from their Lord, desist, shall be pardoned for the past; their case is for Allah (to judge); but those who repeat (the offense) are companions of the Fire: They will abide therein (forever).
>
> **276.** Allah will deprive usury of all blessing but will give increase for deeds of charity: For He loveth not any ungrateful and wicked.
>
> **278.** O ye who believe! Fear Allah and give up what remains of your demand for usury, if ye are indeed believers.
>
> **279.** If ye do it not, take notice of war from Allah and His Messenger. But if ye repent, ye shall have your capital sums: Deal not unjustly, and ye shall not be dealt with unjustly.

The message is clear and needs no interpretation: receiving and/or paying riba is forbidden. If riba cannot be avoided or abstained from, one would be considered "at war with Allah and his Messenger."

However, the verses still lack a definition of riba or its scope.

To summarize, there are four Suras and eight verses related to the issue of forbidden riba as a kind of "increase," "excess," or "surplus" payment. This is not surprising because the Holy Quran is not an economics textbook.

Definitions of riba by some Islamic sources

Before going on, let us look at what the word "riba" literally means. Riba, like almost all Arabic words, has more than one meaning. There is considerable disagreement about what constitutes riba. In an economic context, it refers to an "excess," "surplus," or "increase."

No doubt Allah forbade interest in the Holy Quran, but, as we can see, the Holy Quran provides no definition of it or its scope. Given this fact, related critical questions arise that need to be clarified:

- Where can I find a simple definition of riba?
- Where can I find a simple definition of its scope?
- Where can I find simple criteria to measure riba and its scope?

The known definitions of riba about loans are made by Islamic scholars, that is, by people who interpret Islamic values.[5] The definitions and their scope, as well as the criteria to identify and measure them, can be found in their books, articles, and Internet websites. Let's take a look at some of them.

Islam Ansiklopedisi, a publication of the Turkish Diyanet (Religious Affairs) Foundation in Türkiye, defines riba as:

Real or legal surplus that has no equivalent in borrowing transactions and shopping.[6]

According to *Islam – World's Greatest Religion*:

The literal meaning of interest or Al-RIBA as it is used in the Arabic language means to **excess or increase** ... Hazrat Shah Waliullah Dehlvi a great scholar and leader has given a very concise and precise definition of interest. He says, "Riba" is a loan with the condition that the borrower will return to the lender more than and better than the quantity borrowed.[7]

The website "Islam Question & Answer" states:

Riba means an increase in a particular item. The word is derived from a root meaning **increase or growth**.[8]

For "*Islam, All About Islam*":

Riba is an Islamic term that applies generally to the concepts of **growth, rising, and beyond**, ... The term "riba" can also be loosely defined as the pursuit of illicit, exploitative gains in commerce or trade under Islamic law, which is comparable to the practice of analogous to robbery.[9]

According to "Islamic Markets" definition:

The word "Riba" means **excess, increase or addition**, which correctly interpreted according to Shariah terminology, implies any excess compensation without due consideration (consideration does not include time value of money).[10]

For Neccar (1978)

All kinds of loan transactions with interest are definitely forbidden by Islam. Whether for production or consumption, all kinds of loan and credit systems are forbidden as well. ... Small or large quantity, all kinds of interest are equally forbidden.

According to Ghazali, quoted by S. Orman, riba is considered a "surplus" as well.

Literally, riba implies **increase and excess**. As a term, it is defined as the difference between "two" financial values, an uncovered financial advantage in favor of one of the parties in an agreement.

(Orman, 2007: 102)

All definitions seem to have one aspect in common: riba is an **increase, excess, surplus,** or **addition**. None of them is a "divine" definition; they are just interpretations introduced by Faqih[11] or Islamic scholars who are not sacred. Being human, their definitions, or interpretations are the rational conclusions of their knowledgeable minds, but they are **subject to debate and prone to making mistakes**.

We, as human beings and as Allah's servants blessed with knowledge, are obliged to find a universally applicable definition that does not contradict the values of Islam. Since Islam is a universal religion, the definition of riba and its scope must be such as to separate the **halal** (legal) income from the **haram** (illegal) income applicable to both Muslim and non-Muslim economies.

In addition, we need specific criteria to separate the **halal** (legal) **"excess" income** from the **haram** (illegal) **"excess" income**, known in different forms such as profit, riba, or rent.

Searching for an "appropriate" definition of riba[12]

In this section, we shall continue the analysis of riba by introducing definitions of key terms like *earned* (halal or legal) *income* and *unearned* (haram or illegal) *income.*

In addition, we will present definitions of earned (halal or legal) as well as unearned (haram or illegal) "excess," "surplus," or "additional" income applicable not only in Islamic but also in non-Islamic countries to prove a hypothesis.

Assumptions

Given the absence of a "divine" definition of riba and its scope, in the light of our analysis in terms of **earned and unearned income**, the **excess incomes** of both Islamic and non-Islamic financial firms seem to be "earned" (legal) if they meet three criteria:

1 Employing laborer(s),
2 Assuming risks under competition, and
3 Supplying **legal** products.

"Earned" (halal–legal) vs. "unearned" (haram–illegal) income

Before proceeding with the analysis of interest and its scope, let us provide a definition of the *earned (halal–legal) income of commercial firms* in accordance not only with Islamic values but also with conventional standards, under two headings:

1 **Earned, halal**, or **legal** income, and
2 **Unearned**,[13] **haram**, or **illegal** income.

Earned (halal) commercial income

Three conditions must be met for the earnings of a commercial firm to be categorized as "**earned (halal) income**." They are described below:

1 *Employing laborer(s)*: The sine qua non input of any production is the laborer(s), who receive a wage in return for their labor effort put into production. Neither any good nor any service can be supplied by the firm without the laborer(s).

According to Diyanet,[14] "the main and natural way of earning in Islam is labor, … working and earning in a legitimate way, has been described as a sacred and valuable act in the scale of worship and jihad."[15]
2 *Assuming risk in a competitive environment*: The driving force motivating the owner of any "legal" commercial firm to supply various goods and/or services is the expectation of obtaining a **legal (halal)** "**excess**," "**surplus**," or "**additional income**" over the cost of production, which is commonly known as "**profit**." To put it differently, to make a profit, the firm(s) must not only employ worker(s) but also assume the "**risk**," given a competitive economy.
3 *Supplying legal (halal) product(s), i.e., good(s) and/or service*: The goods and/or service supplied must be **legal (halal)**, i.e., in accordance with law, whether Islamic or non-Islamic. All revenues accruing from legal (halal) business transactions are categorized as **earned income**.

Unearned (haram) income

If one of the three above-mentioned conditions of legal (halal) income is not met, then the income of the firm will be categorized as **unearned (haram–illegal)**, i.e., not in compliance with the laws, whether Islamic or non-Islamic.

For example, if a firm gets income through illegal activities, the accrued income is categorized as "**unearned**." Similarly, income accruing from the sale of alcoholic beverages or pork meat in Islamic countries is also categorized as "**unearned**." Slave-trading or selling drugs are illegal activities in all countries, and thus the income accruing from such activities is unearned, illegal, or haram in all countries, whether Islamic or non-Islamic.

In terms of ethical standards, there appears to be no significant difference between "earned" incomes and "unearned" incomes, regardless of whether the country has Islamic or non-Islamic laws.

Profit, e.g., earned "excess" income

The term "profit" is an "excess" or "surplus" over the costs of production of a product in all countries. The **profit** is not a payment for a value transmitted to the product by the owner or investor but just an "excess" over the costs of production paid for the risk assumed. It is a necessary and indispensable ingredient of production for the capitalist system to function.

If profit is obtained through legal activities, then it is an **earned** (legal or halal) "**excess or surplus**" **income**.

To put it differently, if the business activity is engaged in producing legal products by employing laborers and assuming risk in competitive markets, the "**excess**" income (profit) is "**earned.**"

"Excess" income in the financial sector: earned or unearned?

Having defined **earned income** and **earned excess income** (profit) for firms producing legal products, we can now proceed with the main subject of our analysis, the definition of "*excess income in the financial sector*" *accruing from conventional financial transactions known as "interest.*"

As we saw in the previous section, if commercial firms supplying legal (halal) products had:

1 employed laborer(s),
2 assumed risks under competition, and
3 supplied legal products,

their income would have been considered "earned" (halal) and, accordingly, the "excess" obtained known as profit would also have been considered "earned" (halal), in the real and service sectors in both Islamic and non-Islamic countries.

The related critical question is: What are the similarities or differences between excesses (additional incomes) accruing from the service supplied in the conventional financial sector and the service supplied in the education sector or the service supplied in the tourism sector?

In all conventional service-supplying firms, except the financial sector, if the firm is legally founded and the business activities are legal, then the income is also legal, earned, or halal. However, there is one exception where the "excess" income is cursed as "haram" (unearned); the return or excess income accruing from conventional banking transactions is called "interest."

From an economist's point of view, there is, in principle, no difference in the nature and essence of the services supplied, as long as the three conditions to qualify a service income as "earned income" are met. Similarly, the "excess" income of conventional financial firms can also be considered "earned" or halal.

Nevertheless, the Holy Quran clearly states that any kind of riba accruing from conventional financial activities is prohibited. Can even the most skeptical-minded scholar ignore or overlook this fact?

This critical problem with riba arises because there is no divine definition of prohibited excess income (riba) or its scope.

Recall that the Arabic word riba, like almost all Arabic words, has more than just one meaning. In an economic context, it refers to an "excess," "surplus," or "increase," which is unjust income, exploitative gain, or unjustified excess.

If we replace the predominant concept "riba," i.e., "prohibited excess income," with the concepts we used in the previous sections, i.e., earned and unearned income as well as earned and unearned "excess" incomes, i.e., profit, we would not be ignoring the prohibition while providing a definition given due respect to Islamic values. The new definitions of these old concepts would not be any different from Western conventional values and norms in the financial sector.

Is there any rational, logical, or scientific obstacle to using the concept of unearned income instead of prohibited interest income, unjust gain, unjust income, exploitative gain, or unjustified excess, except the limits imposed on our minds by ourselves[16]?

The alternative concepts and analysis used so far appear to be "compliant" with Islamic values and economic principles, as well as with Western values and norms.

Concluding remarks

Throughout this chapter, we focused our analysis on the Quranic prohibition of riba, and the only source of reference was the Holy Quran.

According to Islamic scholars, the conventional rationale for the prohibition of riba is based, in principle, on the claim that getting or paying riba is interpreted as "excess income at a predetermined rate," which, among other negative impacts, deteriorates the income distribution and harms the weak, i.e., the borrower. However, in reality, this has not always been true because the borrower can increase her/his income by investing the borrowed money in profitable areas and obtaining income far exceeding the amount borrowed. Alternatively, the borrower can improve her/his well-being by buying a safer car for the family. In addition, the argument that the bank paying interest represents the "weak one" while the bank receiving interest from customers represents the "strong one" is difficult to defend.

Interpreting the riba as **"unjust"** or **"unearned income"** instead of "**interest**" would change the whole logic of prohibition, along with the nature of the analysis and its conclusions.

Unfortunately, the Holy Quran does not offer a "divine" definition of riba or its scope. The definitions and interpretations of riba are provided by Islamic scholars, who are educated/trained people in religious issues who are, not infrequently, not thoroughly knowledgeable on actual economic issues. Islamic scholars are not sacred people and are prone to making mistakes, like all humans. Therefore, their words cannot be considered equivalent to "divine" orders.

Given these facts, we tried to provide alternative concepts and an analysis based on "**unjust**" or "**unearned**" **income**. By showing due respect to all Islamic values, the prohibited riba was re-considered in terms of:

1 earned (halal) income and "earned excess" income, and
2 unearned (haram) income and "unearned excess" income.

The critical question related to riba is: What if we translate the concept "riba" as "**unjust**" or "**unearned**" **income** instead of "interest"? By applying the alternative concepts and their analysis to the financial sector, as presented in this chapter, we could change the nature and approach of the issue of the prohibition of riba.

A final and important note: The alternative concepts and analysis presented in this chapter are not meant as alternatives to the Quranic verses but as alternatives to the Islamic scholars' definitions and interpretations of these holy verses.

Notes

1 I am grateful to Kubilay Koş who contributed by proofreading the chapter.
2 To make the point clearer, let's use an analogy. In all civilized countries, there is a "speed limit" for vehicles. If a driver exceeds the limit, she or he will have to pay a fine. But what is the scope of the speed limit for fines: 30 or 50 or 90 km per hour? What would be the fine for a violation of the limit at various speeds? Does it cover all kinds of vehicles, cars only, or heavy trucks? Is it valid all days of week, weekends only, or after 18:00?
As we see, there are clear and unambiguous traffic rules and amounts of fines that are not subject to bargaining or interpretation. Unfortunately, there is no clear definition or other criteria for riba regarding loans.
3 For a comprehensive evaluation of riba and interest relationship, see Farooq (2012).
4 The views/comments of the author should in no way be perceived or interpreted as a criticism of the Holy Quran or Islam. They are simply the logical and rational thoughts of an economist.
5 In Islam, there are no clergymen equivalent to the priesthood in Christianity.
6 "*Ödünç işlemlerinde ve alışverişte karşılığı bulunmayan hakiki veya hükmî fazlalık.*" Türkiye Diyanet Vakfı Islam Ansiklopedisi, https://islamansiklopedisi.org.tr/riba, 2023-01-31.
7 Islam—World's Greatest Religion. https://islamgreatreligion.wordpress.com/2012/03/05/interest-riba/, 2022-05-08.
8 Islam: Question & Answer. https://islamqa.info/en/answers/129458/what-is-riba, 2022-05-08.
9 Islam. https://islamicline.com/blog/what-is-riba-in-islam.html, 2022-05-08.
10 Islamic Markets. https://islamicmarkets.com/education/types-of-riba, 2022-05-08.
11 Islamic jurist.
12 Definitions of *riba* include:

- Unjustified increment in borrowing or lending money.
- Non-equality in an exchange.
- All forms of interest, "any excess on the principal sum of the loan", i.e., any and all interest, irrespective of how much is lent, whether the borrower is rich or poor, using the loan for productive investment or consumption.
- Historically, Islamic legal scholars have interpreted the Quran as "prohibiting any loan contract that specifies a fixed return to the lender."

- The above definition has been observed in a few Muslim-majority countries, which instead define riba as excessive interest or compound interest (John Esposito) or exclude from the category of *riba* interest-like charges with euphemisms such as "commission" (Cyril Glasse) and/or charges using legal subterfuges (known as ḥiyal) where (e.g.), a moneylender buys something and later sells it back for a greater amount (Ludwig Adamec).
- A contract of loan or debt for any additional amount over the principal.
- An exchange of money "of the same denomination where the quantity" exchanged is not equal, whether it is in a spot transaction or with deferred payment.
- "A barter exchange between two weighable or measurable commodities of the same kind, where either the quantity" exchanged is not equal or delivery of one side is deferred (*riba al-fadl*).
- "A barter exchange between two different weighable or measurable commodities where the delivery of one side is deferred."
- **Exploitive" loans.** https://en.wikipedia.org/wiki/Riba, 2023-02-03.

13 From now on, we will prefer to use the terms "earned" and "unearned."
14 Presidency of Religious Affairs, Turkiye, Ilmihal, Vol. 2, 409.
15 Jihad: "In Arabic, the meaning of Jihad is "**to struggle**," "**to fight**," or "**to strive**." Contextual meaning of Jihad varies from context to context. In West it is inaccurately translated as the "**Holy War**"; also in most of the places in West, it is used as synonymous with "**terrorism**" and "**militant**." However, in Islam, Jihad refers to the struggles with the praiseworthy aim, such as to promote the right and to prevent the wrong." https://www.quranexplorer.com/blog/Education-In-The-Light-Of-Sunnah-And-Qura%27an/What-Is-Jihad, 2023-01-19.
16 "Islamic scholars reject, in principle, getting/paying all kinds of interest. However, there are few dissidents who consider receiving interest from banks as permissible on the ground that: "A bank cannot be conceived as an exploiting institution." www.dawn.com/news/473771/bank-interest-is-not-ae%CB%9Cribaae. According to A. Abdurrasul the interest on bonds issued by the state or private firms is not haram. He asserts the following as a justification: The wisdom of interest (riba) being haram is to protect the weak from the strong. In the bond-issuing relationship, the interest payer (state or company) is strong, and the interest recipient (the public) is weak. Therefore, a payment is made to the weak. It is not possible to think that the weak one is the usurer (see Tabakoğlu 2008: 299–300).

These kinds of arguments are different from the ones presented above based on "earned" vs. "unearned" incomes and "excess incomes," i.e., profits.

Bibliography

Internet Sources on Islam

Quran – The Holy Book of Islam
http://www.islamicity.com/mosque/SURAI.HTM, 2013-10-01.
http://unitedamericanmuslim.org/english/2.html, 2013-11-29.
https://quran.com/53, 2022-07-09.

Answers. www.answers.com
Encyclopaedia of Islam. http://referenceworks.brillonline.com/browse/encyclopaedia-of-islam-2/alphaRange/Rh%20-%20Rn/R, 2013-12-01.
Encyclopaedia of Islam, Second Edition. https://referenceworks.brillonline.com/browse/encyclopaedia-of-islam-2/alpha/f?s.start=180, 2022-07-29.

Ilmihâl. (A summary of the principles of Islam) – publ. by Diyanet.

Islam. https://islamicline.com/blog/what-is-riba-in-islam.html, 2022-05-08.

Islamic Economics. https://islamiceconomics.net/, 2022-08-07.

Islamic Encyclopeadia. Diyanet. http://www.tdvia.org/index.php, 2014-01-28.

Islamic Financial Services Industry Stability Report. 2021. Islamic Financial Services Board (IFSB), 2023-01-30.

Islamic Markets. https://islamicmarkets.com/education/types-of-riba, 2022-05-08.

Islam: Question & Answer. https://islamqa.info/en/answers/129458/what-is-riba, 2022-05-08.

Islam–World's Greatest Religion. https://islamgreatreligion.wordpress.com/2012/03/05/interest-riba/, 2022-05-08.

Questions on Islam. www.questionsonislam.com/article/what-interest-and-why-it-forbidden, 2013-11-08.

Riba. http://errahman.de/modules.php?name=Encyclopedia&op=content&tid=1158, 2013-11-09.

The Banker. Top-Islamic-Financial-Institutions-2020. www.thebanker.com/Markets/Top-Islamic-Financial-Institutions-2020, 2023-01-26.

Watchtower. Online Library – Interest. https://wol.jw.org/en/wol/d/r1/lp-e/1200002183, 2022-06-16.

Wikipedia. https://en.wikipedia.org/wiki/Riba, 2023-02-03.

Other Sources

Abozaid, A. 2013. "Role of Fiqh in Islamic Finance", Islam Iktisadı Atölyesi-1, 2-3 Mart-2013, Istanbul.

Ahmad, A.U.F. and Hassan, M.K. 2007. "Riba and Islamic Banking", *Journal of Islamic Economics, Banking and Finance*, Vol.2007, 1–33.

Ahmed, H. (Ed.). 2002. *Theoretical Foundations of Islamic Economics*, Islamic Research & Training Inst., Islamic Dev. Bank, Jeddah.

Akın, C. 1986. *Faizsiz Bankacılık ve Kalkınma*, Kayıhan Yayınları, Ankara.

Ariff, M. 1989. "Islamic Banking in Malaysia", *Journal of Islamic Economics*, Vol.2, No.1, 67, www.iium.edu.my/enmjournal/vol2no1.pdf, 2012-11-15.

Bayındır, A. 2007. "Ticaret ve Faiz" "Trade and Interest", *Süleymaniye Vakfı Yayınları*, Istanbul. www.suleymaniyevakfi.org, 2012-12-26.

———. 2009. "İslam Fıkhı Açısından Borçlanmalarda Enflasyon Farkı". www.suleymaniyevakfi.org/arastirmalar/islam-fikhi-acisindan-borclanmalarda-enflasyon-farki.html, 2013-11-17.

Caliskan, S. 2019. Banka Faizi Haram mı? banka-faizi-haram-mc4b1-1.pdf (wordpress.com), 2023-01-08.

Central Bank of Turkiye. https://www.tcmb.gov.tr/wps/wcm/connect/060e026b-d4e7-4987-8a20-e7e1bc6e4bbe/dibs1.txt?MOD=AJPERES&CACHEID= ROOTWORKSPACE-06 0e026b-d4e7-4987-8a20- e7e1bc6e4bbe-o7plj3M, 2022-07-09.

Chapra, M.U. 2001. *What Is Islamic Economics?* Prize Winners' Lecture Serie 9, Islamic Research & Training Inst., Islamic Dev. Bank, Jeddah.

Eskicioğlu, O. 1983. İslam Açısından Enflasyon ve Çözüm Yolları. www.enfal.de/enflasyon.pdf, 2013-04-09.

Euronews. 2022. "Cumhurbaşkanı Erdoğan: Faiz sebeptir, enslasyon neticedir, kusura bakmasınlar". https://tr.euronews.com/2021/11/17/cumhurbaskan-erdogan-faiz-sebeptir-enflasyon-neticedir-kusura-bakmas-nlar, 2022-05-07.

European Central Bank. 2013. Islamic Finance in Europe Occational Paper Serious. No. 146 / June 2013.

Farooq, M.O. 2012. "Exploitation, Profit and the Riba-Interest Reductionism", *International Journal of Islamic & Middle Eastern Finance & Management*. Exploitation Profit and the Riba-Interest Reductionism. PDF (mbri.ac.ir)

Görmüş, S., Albayrak, A., and Yabanlı, A. (Eds). 2021. *Yaşayan ve Gelişen Katılım Bankacılığı*, Türkiye Katılım Bankaları Birliği Yayını, Istanbul.

Gözübenli, B. 1992. "Islam'da Faiz Yasağı ve Paralı Ekonomi", in: Heyet (Ed.). *Islam Ekonomisinde Finansman Meseleleri*, pp. 77–96, Ensar Neşriyat, Istanbul.

Gündoğdu, A. 2021. *Katılım Bankacılığında Kar Dağıtım Sisteminin Analizi ve Türkiye Uygulaması için Yeni bir Öneri Doktora Tezi*, Istanbul S. Zaim Üniversity, Istanbul.

Gürak, H. 2014. *Islam and Scientific Economics*, PL Academic Publishers, Frankfurt.

Haneef, M.A. and Furqani, H. 2008. "Theory of Profit from Islamic Perspective". http://mpra.ub.uni-muenchen.de/8129/, 2012-10-25.

Hassan, A. 2013. "What Is the Current Situation of Islamic Economics Studies Today and What Is the Future of Them", İslam İktisadı Atölyesi-1, 2–3 Mart-2013, Istanbul.

Hyder, A. 2013. "Interest-free Banking in Sweden: How Much Is it Islamic?" Paper presented at *Emerging Research Paradigms in Business & Social Research*, 26–28 November, 2013, Dubai.

Iqbal, M., Ali, S.S., and Muljawan, D. (Eds). 2007. *Advances in Islamic Economics and Finance* (Vol.1), Islamic Development Bank, IRTI, Jeddah. www.irtipms.org/PubText/230. pdf, 2013-10-22.

Karaman, H. 2012."Answer to the Question about Interest". www.hayrettinkaraman.net/sc/00144.htm, 2012-09-19.

Karar (Newspaper). 2022. https://www.karar.com/guncel-haberler/son-dakika-erdogan-dan-grup-toplantisinda-kritik-aciklamalar-1639765, 2022-05-07.

Kuran, T. 1995. "Islamic Economics and the Islamic Subeconomy". http://econ.duke.edu/uploads/assets/People/Kuran/Islamic%20economics%20and%20Islamic%20subeconomy.pdf, 2012-11-15.

———. 1997. "The Genesis of Islamic Economics", *Social Research*, Vol.64, No.2. EBSCO Database, 2012-10-31.

Mushtaq. S. and Siddiqui, D.A. 2016. "Effect of Interest Rate on Economic Performance: Evidence from Islamic and Non-Islamic Economies". https://jfin-swufe.springeropen.com/articles/10.1186/s40854-016-0028-7, 2022-10-05.

Neccar, A. 1978. İslam Ekonomisine Giriş, Hilal Yayınları, Istanbul. Çev. R. Nazlı.

Nienhaus, V. 1983. "Profitability of Islamic PLS Banks Cempeting with Interest Banks: Problems and Prospects", *Journal of Research in Islamic Economics*, Vol.1, No. 1, 31–39. https://iei.kau.edu.sa/Pages-OVOL-01-01.aspx, 2022-10-05.

Ökte, M.K.S. 2010. "Fundamentals of Islamic Ec. & Finance: Th. & Practice", *Electronic Journal of Social Sciences*, 2010. C. 9, 31. EBSCO Database, 2012-10-31.

Orman, S. 2007. *Gazali'nin İktisat Felsefesi, İnsan*, yayınları, Istanbul.

Özsoy, I. 1994. *Faiz ve Problemleri*, Nil Yayinlari, Izmir.

Prime Ministry – Undersecretariat of Treasury. "Kira Sertifikası Yatırımcı Kılavuzu". https://ms.hmb.gov.tr/uploads/2018/11/Sabit-Kira-%C3%96demeli-Kira-Sertifikas%C4%B1-Yat%C4%B1r%C4%B1mc%C4%B1-K%C4%B1lavuzu.pdf, 2023-02-14.

Sadr, M.B. 1980. *Islam Ekonomi Doktrini* (Iqtisaduna – Our [Islamic] Economics), Hicret Yayınları, Bursa.

Şeriati, A. 2004. *Islam Ekonomisi*, Dünya Yayınları, Istanbul.

Shahid, E.M. 2013. "Frontiers in Islamic Finance: A Critical Perspective". www.bisav.org. tr/yayinlar.aspx?module=makale&yayinid=116&menuID=3_3&yayintipid=3&makal eid=884, 2013-11-09.

Tabakoğlu, A. 2008. *Islam Iktisadına Giriş*, Dergah Yayınları, Istanbul.

TC Merkez Bankası (Central Bank of Turkiye). 2022. https://www.tcmb.gov.tr/wps/wcm/co nnect/060e026b-d4e7-4987-8a20-7e1bc6e4bbe/dibs1.txt?MOD=AJPERES& CACHEID= ROOTWORKSPACE-060e026b-d4e7-4987-8a20-e7e1bc6e4bbe-o7plj3M

Thomas, A. 2017. *Ribâyı Anlamak*, İktisat Yayinlari, Istanbul.

Tok, A. 2009. "*İslami Finans Sistemi Çerçevesinde Sukuk (İslami Tahvil)* Uygulamaları, Katılım Bankaları ve Türkiue Açısından Değerlendirmeler". https://spk.gov.tr/SiteApps/ Yayin/YayinGoster/992, 2022-08-13. SPK, Ankara.

Usmani, M. T.1998. *An Introduction to Islamic Finance*. file:///C:/Users/PC/Documents/ Belgeler-1/2%20-%20Yay%C4%B1nlanacak%20makaleler/Islamic%20Interest%20 Rate/Z%20-%20Usmani%20-%20An%20Introduction%20To %20Islamic%20Finance. pdf, 2023-03-28.

Yasmin, S., Hafidhuddin, D., and Najib, M. 2018. "The Impacts of Sharia Bank Customers' Awareness and Attitudes towards Islamic Working Capital Financing Use in Indonesia", *Journal of Islamic Financial Studies*, Vol.4, No.1, 15–27.

Yeni Akit (Newspaper). 2021. www.yeniakit.com.tr/haber/nas-nedir-nas-anlami-ne-1596932. html, 2022-05-28.

Yılmaz, E. 2014. "Yeni Bir Finansal Araç Olarak Sukuk: Çeşitleri, Türkiye Uygulaması ve Vergilendirilmesi", *Muhasebe ve Finansman Dergisi*, Ocak/2014.

Ziraat Katilim-1. *Katılım katılım nedir?* https://sucte.com/ziraat-katilim-nedir/, 2022-07-09.

Ziraat Katilim-2. *Lease Certificates* (Sukuk). https://www.ziraatkatilim.com.tr/en/pri vate-banking/investment-and-treasury-products/sukuk, 2022-08-12.

4 Islamic "interest-free" bonds—how Islamic are they?

Hasan Gürak

Introduction[1]

Conventional non-Islamic financial instruments have been with us for centuries and have become more sophisticated in our age. Islamic financial activities, on the contrary, are relatively new, beginning in the 1960s. Nevertheless, the Islamic financial sector has developed its instruments rapidly since then, and a Muslim customer can get almost all the financial services supplied by a conventional Western type of financial sector through so-called participation banks in Türkiye, which are run, it is said, in compliance with Islamic values and norms. For instance, they collect funds by special methods to finance economic activities, such as interest-free Islamic bonds. However

> there are no significant differences compared to the normal banking understanding. In other words, you will not see serious differences between an account with interest-bearing banking and an account at a participation bank. You'll do almost the same things on both at the same level. Therefore, it is not possible to say that (Islamic) participation banking has extra advantages for someone who is not particularly obsessed with the interest part.[2]
>
> (Ziraat Katilim-1)

An interesting feature of so-called Islamic interest-free bonds is that they gain a "predetermined" rate of return called "rental payment."

Is this return indeed compliant with Islamic values?

If so, what is the distinctive difference(s) between a prohibited riba gaining a predetermined rate of return and an Islamic permissible "rental payment," which is also a predetermined rate of return?

First, we take a look at the nature and process of **sukuk** or **lease certificates**, in general. Then we will focus our analysis on lease certificates of US dollars, euros, and gold issued by the Ministry of Treasury and Finance and then distributed or sold to external capital-owners through an "asset rental company," a special purpose company,[3] i.e., **HMVKŞ** with the sole purpose of buying and selling lease certificates on behalf of Treasury. The main purpose of this chapter is to reveal if

DOI: 10.4324/9781032631561-6

there is any essential difference between the **interest** on a conventional bond and the **rental payment** on an Islamic bond.

Sukuk or interest-free (!) Islamic bonds

Initially, there were conventional bonds with a predetermined rate of interest issued through the Western Banking System to meet the financial needs of state organs, enterprises, and institutions.

Until recently, the Islamic finance system was unable to benefit from such a financial instrument. However, the "creative" Islamic economists of Malaysia "invented" in 2001 a similar financial instrument and named it "**sukuk**." The Islamic Financial Services Board (IFSB) defines sukuk as: "Certificates that represent a proportional undivided ownership right in tangible assets, or a pool of tangible assets and other types of assets" (IFSB Report, 2021, ix) similar to conventional bonds, the income from which is impermissible (against Islamic law).

The outstanding feature of the sukuk certificate is that the rental income, i.e., ijarah,[4] from it is interest free and thus compliant with Islamic values or at least Islamic economists and scholars claim it to be so.

The critical question is: Which criteria qualify "rental income" as compliant with Islamic law and values if both conventional bonds and Islamic bonds gain income at a predetermined rate?

There is no reference in the Holy Quran to such rental transactions. Hadiths are excluded by assumption, but we can say that, as far as we know, there are no Hadiths that refer to sukuk with "rental incomes." In retrospect, there is only one source that could have inspired Islamic economists to issue Islamic bonds, and that is the conventional, fixed-rate interest-bearing bonds of the West. In fact, a closer look at the issue would show that the rules governing the listing of Islamic bonds are almost identical to the rules governing the listing of conventional interest-bearing bonds.

Let us take a closer look at the types of sukuk instruments and the extent of global Islamic financial transactions.

Types of sukuk instruments

There are diverse types of sukuk instruments.[5]

As stated, in essence, the nature and marketing process of interest-free Islamic bonds and interest-bearing conventional bonds are remarkably similar. In both cases, bonds are issued to collect external capital in return for a "**predetermined**" **rate of return** payable, normally every six months or a year. At the end of the maturity period, the original supplier of bonds buys back the bonds. The only difference that makes the Islamic bond permissible is that it is sold first to an intermediary firm owned by the original issuer of assets before the so-called lease certificates are distributed to external investors. In both cases, the external investors, whether Islamic lease certificate holders or Western-type bondholders, get a "**predetermined**" **rate of return.**

As an example, let's consider the process of a sukuk issuance for the purchase of an asset, say, a ferryboat:

1 Suppose an enterprise-TR wants to buy a ferryboat worth USD 10,000,000, but its capital is insufficient.
2 Enterprise-TR establishes an asset leasing company called special purpose vehicle (**SPV**), owned, and controlled by itself. **SPV** divides the total value of the ferry into equal shares, say, USD 1,000 each, and converts them into tangible assets called lease certificates.
3 The **SPV** sells to the public (investors) the certificates divided into equal shares, a process called **sukuk issuance**.
4 Enterprise-TR pays **rental payments at a predetermined rate** to the public, i.e., individual investors, for a certain period of time, usually semiannually or once a year.
5 Enterprise-TR buys back the certificate at a future date at par value.
6 At maturity, the individual investor's total revenue is the initial amount invested plus the sum of periodic rental payments.
7 Rental payments to the public, i.e., individual investors, are similar to the interest paid on traditional bonds, as the ratio of the "rental payment" is predetermined. However, while the interest payment is considered impermissible, the rental payment for lease certificates is considered permissible.
8 The owner of the Enterprise-TR and the asset leasing **SPV** is the same.

Let us see the periodic payment schedule for a hypothetical conventional bond. Assume that a money holder buys a bond with a fixed interest rate, say, 10%, issued by the Turkish Treasury in January 2022, amounting to USD 10,000 with a term of five years and a coupon payment every six months. Coupon payments every six months will be as follows:

June 30, 2022	:	USD 500
December 31, 2022	:	USD 500
June 30, 2023		USD 500
December 31, 2023		USD 500 and so on

Global sukuk issuances

According to **Islamic Financial Services Industry Stability (IFSI)** Report 2021, the growth of Islamic financial activities increased in 2020 despite the global pandemic, marking a growth of 10.7% year-on-year (y-o-y) in assets in USD terms. Sukuk outstanding was USD 686.5 billion or 25.6% of total assets by 2020 (see Table 4.1) (Figure 4.1).

The sukuk market proved to be fairly resilient in 2020 despite the unprecedented and wide-ranging impact of a global pandemic sukuk outstanding continued its growth trend to reach USD 703 billion in 2020. Notwithstanding

Table 4.1 Breakdown of the Global IFSI by 2020[a]

	Islamic Banking Assets	*Sukuk Outstanding*	*Islamic Funds Assets*
Total (USD billion)	1,841.8	686.5	143.8
Share (%)	68.3	25.6	5.3

Source: IFSB Secretariat Workings, Table 1.1.1, p. 6 www.ifsb.org, January 30, 2023.

[a] Data for ṣukuk outstanding and Islamic funds are for the full year 2020; for Islamic banking, they are as of 3Q20.

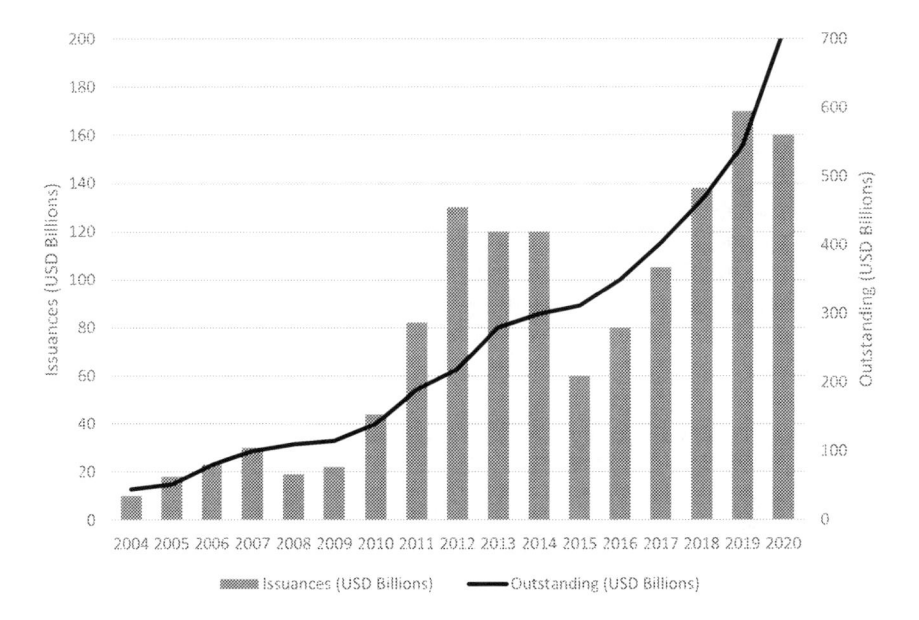

Figure 4.1 Global Sukuk Issuances and Sukuk Outstanding Trends (2004–2020).

Source: IFSB Estimates Based on Data from Refinitiv and Regulatory Authorities. Chart: 1.3.1.1 p. 18, www.ifsb.org, January 30, 2023.

the initial shock of the pandemic on financial markets early in the year, sukuk markets recovered quickly, with the impact of the crisis manifesting unevenly across countries. The overall sukuk issuances by the end of 2020 proved to be relatively strong, with total issuances worth USD 163.4 billion. While this represents a 4% drop from the USD 171.1 billion of issuances in the previous year, the sukuk market has remained relatively robust, with higher total annual issuances than in the years prior to 2019.

(IFSB;18)

Malaysia continues to be the largest issuer in terms of total sukuk issuances by domicile, followed by Saudi Arabia, Indonesia, and Turkey (see Figure 4.2).

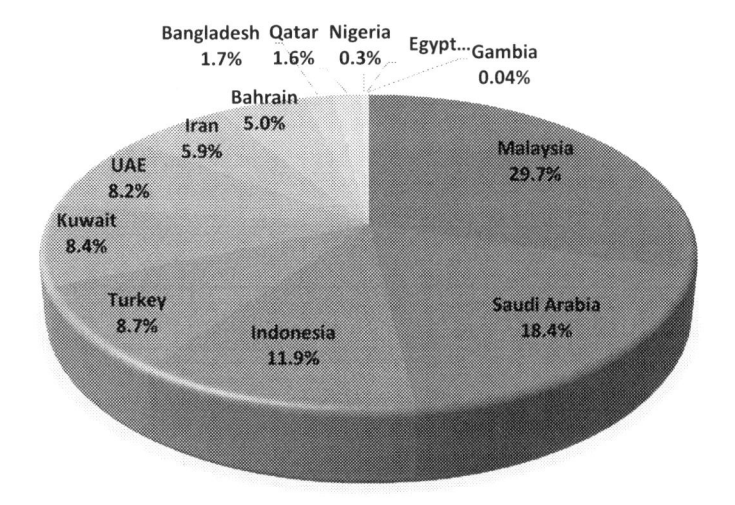

Figure 4.2 Total Sukuk Issuance by Domicile[a] 2020.

Source: IFSB Estimates Based on Data from Refinitiv and Regulatory Authorities. Chart: 1.3.1.4 p. 21, www.ifsb.org, January 30, 2023.

Note: [a]Excludes issuances by multilaterals.

"Lease certificates" in Türkiye

Let us recall that "creative" economists in the Malaysian Islamic banking system "invented" the financial instrument called **sukuk** in 2001. Soon after, the new system was adapted to the Turkish financial system. According to the state-owned Ziraat Katılım (participation banking) in Türkiye, sukuk or, as widely known, a "**lease certificate,**"

> refers to assets and bonds issued by an asset leasing company to finance any kind of assets and rights and to ensure that the owners would be beneficiaries of the incomes obtained from such assets and rights in proportion to their rights.
> (Ziraat Katılım-2, August 12, 2022)

Banks engaged in "interest-free" activities are organized under the umbrella of The Participation Banks Association of Türkiye (TKBB), which is a professional public institution.

There are six participation banks in Türkiye, and all are members of the TKBB (see Table 4.2). The aim of TKKB is "to increase the 7.2% market share of participation banking from the banking sector assets as of December 2020 to 15% in 2025" (Gündoğdu, 2021: Abstract, p. vi).

Participation banks are engaged in various "interest-free" (!) transactions ranging from profit–loss sharing, the selling/buying of tangible assets, to the issuance of lease certificates. Lease certificates are used as instruments to finance transactions in various fields ranging from construction to energy and to meet financial needs among nations and the size of the lease certificate market is assumed to reach USD 301 billion in 2014 (see, Görmüş-Albayrak-Yabanlı, 2021, 111–112).

Table 4.2 The List of Participation Banks in Türkiye

Bank	Owner
Emlak Katılım	Türkiye
Vakıf Katılım	Türkiye
Ziraat Katılım	Türkiye
Al Baraka Türk	Bahrein
Kuveyt Türk	Kuwait
Türkiye Finans Katılım	Saudi Arabia

Source: Wikipedia, https://tr.wikipedia.org/wiki/T%C3%B Crkiye%27deki_bankalar_listesi, February 12, 2023.

Issuance of debt assets by the Turkish treasury

In the rest of this chapter, the focus will be only on lease certificates in tangible assets like euros, US dollars, and gold issued by the Ministry of Treasury and Central Bank Türkiye. In a way, it is a "making money from money" process. The rate of rental payments is predetermined by the Central Bank of Türkiye. Lease certificates issued by private companies and all kinds of rental payments accruing from non-tangible assets are excluded.

The steps of a lease certificate issuance in Türkiye are explained below in detail:

1   Within the context of Article 7/A of Law Number 4749 on Regulating Public Finance and Debt Management, the takeover of the public real estate through sale to the Hazine Müsteşarlığı Varlık Kiralama Şirketi[6] is realized. At the same time, the immovables are registered as deeds for **HMVK**.

2   Provided that the beneficiary institutions continue to utilize the assets that are taken over by the **HMVKŞ**, a lease agreement, apart from the deal of takeover through sale stated in Article 1, is signed between the Undersecretariats of Treasury and the **HMVKŞ**. Moreover, a letter of purchase undertaking of these immovables by the Treasury at the end of the lease period is committed. On the other contrary, before the issue, the **HMVKŞ** gave out a declaration to address the preservation of the aforementioned assets in its own name, on its own behalf, and for the account and benefit of certificate holders.

3   In return for the leasing of the assets purchased by the **HMVKŞ** to the Undersecretariat of Treasury, lease certificates are issued that allow investors to merit rental proceeds from the assets on a pro-rata basis.

4   The amount paid by the investors in return for the lease certificates is transferred to the **HMVKŞ**.

5   Proceeds of lease certificates are transferred to Undersecretariats of Treasury from the **HMVKŞ** in return for the asset takeover.

6   In the context of the lease agreement and the purchase undertaking between the Undersecretariat of Treasury and the **HMVKŞ**, rental payments are fulfilled by the Undersecretariat of Treasury to the **HMVKŞ** during the life of the lease contract, and a payment is made in return for the repurchase of immovables by the Undersecretariat of Treasury at the end of the lease agreement.

7 Rental proceeds are allocated on a pro-rata basis, and the principal payment of the lease certificates is allocated to the certificate holders by the HMVKŞ.[7]

The process

The issuer of lease certificates is the Ministry of Treasury and Finance, which establishes an "asset rental company," i.e., **HMVKŞ**, a **Special Purpose Vehicle (SPV)**, with the sole purpose of buying and selling lease certificates. The **HMVKŞ** divides the assets into equal shares before putting them on sale to external investors in return for "rental payment" at a predetermined rate for a given period, say, five years, with installments due every six months or a year. At the end of maturity, the **HMVKŞ** is obliged to buy back the assets at face value, which are then sold back to the original supplier of the assets, in our case, the Ministry of Treasury and Finance. The small investors receive two types of income from the transaction:

1 Periodical rental (coupon) payments at a predetermined rate, say, every six months or a year, and
2 The initial external capital supplied at face value at maturity.

Comparison of returns on conventional bonds and Islamic bonds

According to Investopedia, "Sukuk investors receive profit generated by the underlying asset on a periodic basis, while bond investors receive periodic interest payments." That is because "Sukuk involves asset ownership, while bonds are debt obligations." Is there really a difference in essence between "excess gain," called profit, and "excess gain," called interest? Or is it, in fact, a difference in perception, a play on words?

Let us compare the "permissible gain" accruing from a lease certificate to the "impermissible gain accruing from conventional interest-bearing bonds. The Ministry of Treasury and Finance in Türkiye issued lease certificates in June 2021 with a maturity of five years and a "rental payment" of 5.125%, comparable to interest on bonds (see Table 4.3).

Table 4.3 Foreign Borrowing of the Turkish Treasury in 2021

	Amount (Billion USD)	*Date of Maturity*	*Interest Rate (%)*
January 26	1.75	2026	4.9
January 26	1.75	2031	5.95
June 26	2.5	2026	5.125 (Rental Certificate)
July 08	1.5	2027	4.5
September 20	0.75	2028	5.7
September 20	1.5	2033	6.5
Total	10.0		

Source: www.parahavadis.com/hazinenin-sukuk-ihracinda-birinci-getiri-beklentisi-75-7625/, July 12, 2022.

As we see in Table 4.3, the Turkish Treasury must pay a "**predetermined**" 5.125% rental payment every year until June 2026. In the same month, July 2022, the Turkish Treasury issued a conventional bond with an interest rate of 4.5%. Both rates for periodic payment are predetermined, and the "excess" paid to the so-called Islamic bond or, alternatively, lease certificate is higher. Yet the predetermined rate of "excess" paid to the lease certificate is permissible, while the "excess" income from conventional bonds is un-Islamic and therefore forbidden.

The Ministry of Treasury and Finance of Türkiye only has the privilege to export lease certificates for gold and foreign currencies. Table 4.4 shows the indicative values of various lease certificates with a predetermined "rental payment" compliant with Islamic law and values (!).

In terms of financial instruments gaining a predetermined rate of return, two critical questions arise regarding riba-free Islamic bonds:

1   Is the process of collecting funds through interest-free bonds that guarantee a predetermined rate of return "compliant with Islamic values"?
2   Are the payments at a predetermined rate compliant with Islamic values"?

In short, how Islamic is a rental payment of euros, US dollars, and gold at a predetermined rate?

Table 4.4 Daily Indicative Values of Lease Certificates Determined by the Central Bank of Türkiye as of July 18, 2022[a]

The Values of Gold Lease Certificates for Nominal 1 Piece Issued by the Asset Leasing Company of the Treasury

Maturity Date	Rental Payment
February 21, 2024	1.15
March 20, 2024	1.15
April 12, 2024	1.15

The Values of Euro Lease Certificates Issued by the Asset Leasing Company of the Treasury

Maturity Date	Rental Payment
February 2, 2024	1.40
May 24, 2024	1.50

The Values of USD Lease Certificates Issued by the Asset Leasing Company of the Treasury

Maturity Date	Rental Payment
July 14, 2023	1.75
July 26, 2023	1.50

Source: Central Bank of Türkiye. www.tcmb.gov.tr/wps/wcm/conne ct/060e026b-d4e7-4987-8a20-e7e1bc6e4bbe/dibs1.txt?MOD=AJPE RES&CACHEID=ROOTWORKSPACE-060e026b-d4e7-4987-8a2 0-e7e1bc6e4bbe-o7plj3M.

[a]   For more information, see Appendix.

Concluding remarks

As observed in this chapter, banking transactions on bonds, whether Islamic or non-Islamic, are remarkably similar in that they both gain excess income at predetermined rates of return. In addition, the investment procedure for external capital-owners is almost identical for both traditional and Islamic bonds. Yet the excess gain at predetermined rates of return for conventional bonds is "impermissible," while the excess gain at predetermined rates of return for Islamic bonds is "permissible." How come?

The rationale for the prohibition behind the excess gain called "interest" is that it is said to place the burden of risk entirely on the borrower, who is assumed to be the "weak one" in the transaction. In other words, Islamic law protects the poor or the weak, i.e., the borrower, from the angle of distributive justice; at least this is the claim behind prohibition. But, regarding all kinds of bonds, the protected (!) borrower is the bank, enterprise, or state organ, none of which is actually weak and in need of protection.

The gain from traditional bonds is prohibited by Islamic law because they bear interest at a predetermined rate.

The gain from Islamic bonds or rental payments on lease certificates is permissible because they are "compliant with Islamic law." Yet what is considered permissible is also a gain at a predetermined rate.

The critical question is: Is there indeed any difference, in essence, between conventional bonds and Islamic bonds in terms of excess gain (interest or profit) at a predetermined rate?

Or is the difference perhaps in perception, not in essence?

Usmani says: "the lease transaction is always governed by the rules of Shari'ah prescribed for ijarah" (1998, 110). Who prescribes the rules governing the lease transactions? The experts on Islamic law are neither sacred nor economists by training. How well qualified are they to make a "scientific" economic distinction between returns on conventional interest-bearing bonds and Islamic interest-free bonds for dollars, any currency, or gold at a predetermined rate?

There seem to be no strong rational arguments to justify the excess return at a predetermined rate on lease certificates, i.e., rental payments, as compliant with Islamic law.

An alternative approach to the analysis of "excess" income on Sukuk

So far, the critics have focused on one specific feature: both types of bonds gained an excess at a predetermined rate of return, whether called rental payments or interest. If we define the concept of riba as "unjust" or "unearned" income instead of interest on loans, then we might be able to make a more rational and a more just and fair analysis of the conclusions regarding the permissibility issue.[8]

Acknowledgment

I'm grateful to Orhan Özsöylemez for his contribution to the sukuk process.

Appendix

Daily indicative values of securities and lease certificates determined by the Central Bank of Türkiye on February 10, 2023 (Table 4.A1)

Table 4.A1 Domestic Debt Instruments

Below Are the Values of Coupon Bearing Gold Bonds for Nominal 1 Piece Issued by the Republic of Türkiye Ministry of Treasury and Finance

Maturity		Present Value
Date	Coupon Rate	(per 1 Piece)
February 21, 2024	1.15	1,152.564329
March 20, 2024	1.15	1,150.546848
April 12, 2024	1.15	1,148.889631
June 14, 2024	1.15	1,144.350299
July 5, 2024	1.15	1,142.837188
October 9, 2024	0.75	1,146.001250
January 27, 2025	1.00	1,141.004539
May 21, 2025	1.50	1,147.739918

Below Are the Values of Euro Denominated Government Domestic Debt Instruments Issued by Republic of Türkiye Ministry of Treasury and Finance

Maturity		Present Value
Date	Coupon Rate	(1,000 EUR Equivalent)
February 2, 2024	1.40	20,278.64
May 24, 2024	1.50	20,396.40

Below Are the Values of Euro Denominated Government Domestic Debt Instruments Issued Via Private Placement by Republic of Türkiye Ministry of Treasury and Finance

Maturity	Days	Present Value
Date	to Maturity	(1,000 EUR Equivalent)
April 24, 2024	439	19,195.54
February 25, 2032	3,302	20,267.70
April 24, 2024	439	20,267.70

Below Are the Values of USD Denominated Government Domestic Debt Instruments Issued by Republic of Türkiye Ministry of Treasury and Finance

Maturity		Present Value
Date	Coupon Rate	(1,000 USD Equivalent)
July 14, 2023	1.75	18,895.49
August 9, 2024	2.76	18,844.80
July 26, 2023	1.50	18,869.68
August 25, 2023	1.87	19,170.06

(Continued)

Table 4.A1 (Continued)

Lease Certificates
Below Are the Values of the Ten Selected Consumer Price Indexed Lease
Certificates Issued by the Asset Leasing Company of the Treasury

Maturity Date	Rental Payment	Present Value Including Rental Payment
May 28, 2031	1.59	360.610
May 28, 2031	1.59	360.610
May 28, 2031	1.59	292.454
June 7, 2023	1.59	3.427
December 6, 2023	1.59	3.493
June 5, 2024	1.59	3.560
December 4, 2024	1.59	3.628
June 4, 2025	1.59	3.698
December 3, 2025	1.59	3.770
June 3, 2026	1.59	3.842

Below Are the Values of Gold Lease Certificates for Nominal 1 Piece
Issued by the Asset Leasing Company of the Treasury

Maturity Date	Rental Payment	Present Value (per 1 Piece)
February 21, 2024	1.15	1,152.564329
March 20, 2024	1.15	1,150.546848
April 12, 2024	1.15	1,148.889631
June 14, 2024	1.15	1,144.350299
July 5, 2024	1.15	1,142.837188
October 9, 2024	0.75	1,146.001250
January 27, 2025	1.00	1,141.004539
May 21, 2025	1.50	1,147.739918

Below Are the Values of Euro Lease Certificates Issued by the Asset
Leasing Company of the Treasury

Maturity Date	Rental Payment	Present Value (1000 EUR equivalent)
February 2, 2024	1.40	20,278.64
May 24, 2024	1.50	20,396.40

Below Are the Values of USD Lease Certificates Issued by the Asset
Leasing Company of the Treasury

Maturity Date	Rental Payment	Present Value (1,000 USD equivalent)
July 14, 2023	1.75	18,895.49
July 26, 2023	1.50	18,869.68

Source: https://www.tcmb.gov.tr/wps/wcm/connect/060e026b-d4e7-4987-8a20-e7e1bc6e4 bbe/dibs1.txt?MOD=AJPERES&CACHEID=ROOTWORKSPACE-060e026b-d4e7-4987- 8a20-e7e1bc6e4bbe-o7plj3M, February 10, 2023.

Notes

1 I am grateful to Hakim John Lee who contributed by proofreading the chapter.
2 Original text in Turkish:

> normal bankacılık anlayışına kıyasla çok ciddi farklar söz konusu değildir. Yani fai-
> zli bankacılığın mevcut olduğu bir hesap ile katılım bankasındaki bir hesap arasında
> ciddi farklar göremeyeceksiniz. Ikisinde de hemen hemen aynı şeyleri aynı düzeyde
> yapacaksınız. Bu yüzden faiz kısmına özellikle takılmayan birisi için katılım
> bankacılığının ekstra avantajlara sahip olduğunu söylemek pek mümkün değildir.
> (Ziraat Katılım-1, https://sucte.com/ziraat-katilim-nedir/, 2022-07-09)

3 Asset leasing Special Purpose company owned and controlled by Treasury (Hazine
Müsteşarlığı Varlık Koruma Şirketi, HMVKŞ).
4 "İjarah means 'to give something on rent'. In the Islamic jurisprudence, the term 'ijarah'
is used for two different situations. ... The second type of ijarah relates to the usufructs
of assets and properties, and not to the services of human beings. 'Ijarah' in this sense
means 'to transfer the usufruct of a particular property to another person in exchange for
a rent claimed from him.' In this case, the term 'ijarah' is analogous to the English term
'leasing'." (Usmani, 1998, 109).
5 Types and conditions regarding Lease Certificate issued by Notification on Lease
Certificates:

1 **Lease certificate based on ownership (Ijhara sukuk)**
Lease certificates based on ownership are the lease certificates issued to finance
the assets and rights to be taken over from the source organization by the Asset
Leasing Company so that the same would be leased to the source organization or
third parties or managed on behalf of the asset leasing company.
2 **Lease certificate based on management contract (Sukuk Wakalah)**
Lease certificates based on management contract are lease certificates which are
issued to transfer to the Asset Leasing Company, the revenues which are obtained
as a result of management on behalf of the Asset Leasing Company including the
leasing of the assets and rights of the source organization throughout the fixed
term.
3 **Lease certificate based on purchase and sale (Sukuk al-murabaha)**
Lease certificates based on purchase and sale are lease certificates issued to finance purchase of asset or right in forward sale of any asset or right to the companies with the qualifications stated in the first sub-clause of Article 12 once such
asset or right has been purchased by the Asset Leasing Company.
4 **Lease certificate based on partnership (Mudaraba/Muşaraka sukuk)**
Lease certificates based on partnership are the lease certificates issued by Asset
Leasing Company to be a partner in the joint venture.
5 **Lease certificate based on Agreement for Work (work sukuk)**
Lease certificates based on Agreement for Work are the lease certificates issued
to create a work under an Agreement for Work, to which the Asset Leasing Company is a party acting as the business owner (Ziraat Katilim-2) 2022-08-12.

6 **HMVKŞ**: Asset Leasing Special Purpose Company owned and controlled by
Treasury.
7 Prime Ministry—Undersecretariat of Treasury—**Lease Certificate Investor Guide**:
https://ms.hmb.gov.tr/uploads/sites/2/2018/12/Fixed-Rent-Rate-Lease-Certificate-
Investors-Guide.pdf, 2023-02-14.
8 For details of concepts like "earned vs. unearned" incomes, see Chapter 3 entitled "Is
there a divine definition of riba and its scope?" in this book.

Internet Sources on Islam

Encyclopaedia of Islam. http://referenceworks.brillonline.com/browse/encyclopaedia-of-islam-2/alphaRange/Rh%20-%20Rn/R, 2013-12-01.

Encyclopaedia of Islam, Second Edition. https://referenceworks.brillonline.com/browse/encyclopaedia-of-islam-2/alpha/f?s.start=180, 2022-07-29.

IFSB. Islamic Financial Services Board (IFSB).

Ilmihâl. A Summary of the Principles of Islam – publ. by Diyanet.

Islam. https://islamicline.com/blog/what-is-riba-in-islam.html, 2022-05-08.

Islamic Economics. https://islamiceconomics.net/, 2022-08-07.

Islamic Encyclopeadia. Diyanet. http://www.tdvia.org/index.php, 2014-01-28.

Islamic Financial Services Industry Stability Report 2021. Islamic Financial Services Board (IFSB), 2023-01-30.

Islamic Markets. https://islamicmarkets.com/education/types-of-riba, 2022-05-08.

Islam: Question & Answer. https://islamqa.info/en/answers/129458/what-is-riba, 2022-05-08.

Quran – The Holy Book of Islam. https://quran.com/53, 2022-07-09.

Other Sources

Abozaid, A. 2013. "Role of Fiqh in Islamic Finance", Islam Iktisadı Atölyesi-1, 2–3 Mart-2013, Istanbul.

Ahmad, A.U.F. and Hassan, M.K. 2007. "Riba and Islamic Banking", *Journal of Islamic Economics, Banking and Finance.* Vol.2007, 1–33.

Ahmed, H. (Ed.). 2002. *Theoretical Foundations of Islamic Economics*, Islamic Research & Training Inst., Islamic Dev. Bank, Jeddah.

Akın, C. 1986. *Faizsiz Bankacılık ve Kalkınma*, Kayıhan Yayınları, Ankara.

Ariff, M. 1989. "Islamic Banking in Malaysia", *Journal of Islamic Economics*, Vol.2, No.1, 67. www.iium.edu.my/enmjournal/vol2no1.pdf, 2012-11-15.

Bayındır, A. 2007. "Ticaret ve Faiz" "Trade and Interest", *Süleymaniye Vakfı Yayınları*, Istanbul. www.suleymaniyevakfi.org, 2012-12-26.

———. 2009. "İslam Fıkhı Açısından Borçlanmalarda Enflasyon Farkı". www.suleymaniyevakfi.org/arastirmalar/islam-fikhi-acisindan-borclanmalarda-enflasyon-farki.html, 2013-11-17.

Caliskan, S. 2019. "Banka Faizi Haram mı?" banka-faizi-haram-mc4b1-1.pdf (wordpress.com), 2023-01-08.

Central Bank of Turkiye. https://www.tcmb.gov.tr/wps/wcm/connect/060e026b-d4e7-4987-8a20-e7e1bc6e4bbe/dibs1.txt?MOD=AJPERES&CACHEID=ROOTWORKSPACE-06 0e026b-d4e7-4987-8a20-e7e1bc6e4bbe-o7plj3M, 2022-07-09.

Chapra, M.U. 2001. *What Is Islamic Economics?* Prize Winners' Lecture Serie 9, Islamic Research & Training Inst., Islamic Dev. Bank, Jeddah.

Eskicioğlu, O. 1983. İslam Açısından Enflasyon ve Çözüm Yolları. www.enfal.de/enflasyon.pdf, 2013-04-09.

Euronews. 2022. "Cumhurbaşkanı Erdoğan: Faiz sebeptir, enslasyon neticedir, kusura bakmasınlar". https://tr.euronews.com/2021/11/17/cumhurbaskan-erdogan-faiz-sebeptir-enflasyon-neticedir-kusura-bakmas-nlar, 2022-05-07.

European Central Bank. 2013. Islamic Finance in Europe Occational Paper Serious No. 146, June 2013.

Farooq, M.O. 2012. "Exploitation, Profit and the Riba-Interest Reductionism", *International Journal of Islamic & Middle Eastern Finance & Management.* Vol.5, No.4. Exploitation Profit and the Riba-Interest Reductionism.PDF (mbri.ac.ir).

Görmüş, S., Albayrak, A., and Yabanlı, A. (Eds). 2021. *Yaşayan ve Gelişen Katılım Bankacılığı*, Türkiye Katılım Bankaları Birliği Yayını, Istanbul.

Gözübenli, B. 1992. *"Islam'da Faiz Yasağı ve Paralı Ekonomi"*, in: Heyet (Ed.). *Islam Ekonomisinde*. Finansman Meselel, İlmi Taıtışmalar Dizisi, pp. 77–96, Ensar Neşriyat, Istanbul.

Gündoğdu, A. 2021. *Katılım Bankacılığında Kar Dağıtım Sisteminin Analizi ve Türkiye Uygulaması için Yeni bir Öneri Ph. D. Thesis*, Istanbul S. Zaim Üni, Istanbul.

Gürak, H. 2014. *Islam and Scientific Economics*, PL Academic Publishers, Frankfurt.

Haneef, M.A. and Furqani, H. 2008. "Theory of Profit from Islamic Perspective". http://mpra.ub.uni-muenchen.de/8129/, 2012-10-25.

Hassan, A. 2013. "What Is the Current Situation of Islamic Economics Studies Today and What Is the Future of Them", İslam İktisadı Atölyesi-1, 2–3 Mart-2013, Istanbul.

Hyder, A.S. 2013. "Interest-Free Banking in Sweden: How Much Is It Islamic?", *Paper Presented at Emerging Research Paradigms in Business & Social Research*, 26–28 November, 2013, Dubai.

Iqbal, M., Ali, S.S., and Muljawan, D. (Eds). 2007. *Advances in Islamic Economics and Finance* (Vol.1), Islamic Development Bank, IRTI. www.irtipms.org/PubText/230.pdf, 2013-10-22.

Karaman, H. 2012. "Answer to the Question about Interest". www.hayrettinkaraman.net/sc/00144.htm, 2012-09-19.

Karar (Newspaper). 2022. https://www.karar.com/guncel-haberler/son-dakika-erdogandan-grup-toplantisinda-kritik-aciklamalar-1639765, 2022-05-07.

Kuran, T. 1995. "Islamic Economics and the Islamic Subeconomy". http://econ.duke.edu/uploads/assets/People/Kuran/Islamic%20economics%20and%20Islamic%20 subeconomy.pdf, 2012-11-15.

———. 1997. "The Genesis of Islamic Economics", *Social Research*, Vol.64, No.2. EBSCO Database, 2012-10-31.

Mushtaq. S. and Siddiqui, D.A. 2016. "Effect of Interest Rate on Economic Performance: Evidence from Islamic and Non-Islamic Economies." https://jfin-swufe.springeropen.com/articles/10.1186/s40854-016-0028-7, 2022-10-05.

Neccar, A. 1978. İslam Ekonomisine Giriş, Hilal Yayınları, Istanbul. Çev. R. Nazlı.

Nienhaus, V. 1983. "Profitability of Islamic PLS Banks Cempeting with Interest Banks: Problems and Prospects", *Journal of Research in Islamic Economics,* Vol.1, No.1, 31–39. https://iei.kau.edu.sa/Pages-OVOL-01-01.aspx, 2022-10-05.

Ökte, M.K.S. 2010. "Fundamentals of Islamic Ec. & Finance: Th. & Practice", *Electronic Journal of Social Sciences*, C.9 31. EBSCO Database, 2012-10-31.

Orman, S. 2007. *Gazali'nin İktisat Felsefesi*, İnsan yayınları, Istanbul.

Özsoy, I. 1994. *Faiz ve Problemleri*, Nil Yayınları, Izmir.

Prime Ministry – Undersecretariat of Treasury. "Lease Certificate Investor Guide". https://ms.hmb.gov.tr/uploads/sites/2/2018/12/Fixed-Rent-Rate-Lease-Certificate-Investors-Guide.pdf, 2023-02-14.

Sadr, M.B. 1980. *Islam Ekonomi Doktrini* (Iqtisaduna – Our [Islamic] Economics), Hicret Yayınları, Bursa.

Shahid E.M. 2013. "Frontiers in Islamic Finance: A Critical Perspective". www.bisav.org.tr/yayinlar.aspx?module=makale&yayinid=116&menuID=3_3&yayintipid=3&makaleid=884. 2013-11-09.

Tabakoğlu, A. 2008. *Islam Iktisadına Giriş*, Dergah Yayınları, Istanbul.

Thomas, A. 2017. *Ribâyı Anlamak*, İktisat Yayinlari, Istanbul.

Tok, A. 2009. "İslami Finans Sistemi Çerçevesinde Sukuk (İslami Tahvil) Uygulamaları, Katılım Bankaları ve Türkiue Açısından Değerlendirmeler". https://spk.gov.tr/SiteApps/Yayin/YayinGoster/992, 2022-08-13. SPK, Ankara.

Usmani, M.T. 1998. *An Introduction to Islamic Finance*. https://www.academia.edu/5535927/An_Introduction_to_Islamic_Finance_Taqi_Usmani, 2023-12-13.

Yasmin, S., Hafidhuddin, D., and Najib, M. 2018. "The Impacts of Sharia Bank Customers' Awareness and Attitudes towards Islamic Working Capital Financing Use in Indonesia", *Journal of Islamic Financial Studies*, Vol.4, No.1, 15–27.

Yeni Akit. 2021. Newspaper. www.yeniakit.com.tr/haber/nas-nedir-nas-anlami-ne-1596932.html, 2022-05-28.

Yılmaz, E. 2014. "Yeni Bir Finansal Araç Olarak Sukuk: Çeşitleri, Türkiye Uygulaması ve Vergilendirilmesi", *Muhasebe ve Finansman Dergisi*. Ocak/2014.

Ziraat Katilim-1. 2022. *Katılım katılım nedir?* https://sucte.com/ziraat-katilim-nedir/, 2022-07-09.

Ziraat Katilim-2. 2022. *Lease Certificates* (Sukuk). https://www.ziraatkatilim.com.tr/en/private-banking/investment-and-treasury-products/sukuk, 2022-08-12.

Part 2

President Erdoğan's patented "NAS"—policy and its consequences

5 The NAS is there! President Erdoğan's economic instrument to fight inflation

Hasan Gürak

Introduction

In 2018, Prime Minister Erdoğan was re-elected President of Türkiye endowed with unprecedented economic and political powers. The new system was, as described by many, a "one-man regime," reducing the power of Parliament on all critical issues.

During the election campaign, President Erdoğan said to the electorate: "Vote for me and see how I deal with all the problems." Enough people believed him and voted for him, but huge economic problems that had accumulated in the past years under his rule, among them the high inflation rate, continued to be one of the major problems that had to be dealt with immediately. Every year, ministers appointed by him to be responsible for the economy declared that inflation would be reduced to a one-digit level, the most frequently targeted rate being 5%, but they never succeeded. On the contrary, the harsh economic conditions for working people continued and even worsened. When his son-in-law B. Albayrak, the Minister of the Treasury and Finance from July 10, 2018, to November 08, 2020, said, "Economic conditions in February will be better than in January, in March better than in February, in April better than in March, etc."; this prediction was never realized.

About five years before the presidential election, when Erdoğan was the prime minister, he had promised the people that under his rule, per capita income would rise to USD 25,000 by 2023, the 100th year of the foundation of the Republic of Türkiye. But, since then, per capita income has remained at a much lower level, fluctuating mostly below USD 10,000. In the year 2022, just one year before the 100th year of the foundation of the Turkish Republic, per capita income in USD was far below the targeted goal of USD 25,000. (See some macroeconomic indicators for the years 2020, 2021, and 2022 in Table 5.1.)

Something had to be done urgently to restore the economy and put it on the right path, but how? The critical question was: What was wrong?

For Erdoğan, it was out of the question that his economic policies should fail. He often proudly reminds the Turkish people, "I am an economist," implying that he knows what he is doing. If his policies are not responsible for the economic problems, then there must be "other" factors beyond his control. He had to find a "scapegoat" if his policies were, in principle, appropriate. First, he blamed

DOI: 10.4324/9781032631561-8

Table 5.1 Macroeconomic Indicators (in USD)

	2020	2021	2022
GDP (billion $)	717	807	808
GDP per capita	8,577	9,528	9,485
PPI (year-end)[a]	25.15	79.89	97.72
CPI (year-end)[a]	14.60	36.08	64.27
Inactive unemployment rate (year-end)	28.5	22.6	21.4
Budget balance	−172.7	−192.2	−139.0
Trade balance	−37.9	−29.2	89.7
Current account balance	−36.8	−14.5	−48.8

Source: TUIK, Ministry of Treasury & Finance, Central Bank, BDDK, in: Mahfi Eğilmez, Kendime Yazılar https://www.mahfiegilmez.com/p/gostergeler.html 2023-03-01.

[a] *Author's note:* There is a huge gap between the producer price index and consumer price index (CPI). According to the ENAG, a group of academics, the real CPI was much higher than the official rate declared.

"external powers" like US President Trump and some European leaders, who were allegedly "jealous of the successful policies" of Erdoğan and wanted to prevent the further development of Türkiye by tripping it up. Some people believed that this was the situation without questioning why the United States and Europe were jealous and why they attempted to prevent the economic growth of Türkiye. However, if Türkiye was aware of the hostile attitudes of its so-called Western Friends, why could it not take appropriate measures? After all, many Western leaders, including US President Trump, were "his friends."

Soon after, a new additional threat was successfully presented: "high interest rates," getting and/or paying of which is against Islamic values. After all, "riba" in the form of interest on loans was prohibited in the Holy Quran. If Türkiye has a high inflation problem, the cause must be the riba, the evil thing. Once this problem is overcome, Türkiye will continue to make others "jealous" again.

The Central Bank (CB) of Türkiye raised the lending (policy) rate by 475 base points in November 2020. The next day, in a speech delivered at the 18th Expo Fair, President Erdoğan declared that the main goal was to reduce the inflation rate to single digits. The Turkish economy had to be saved from the cycle of high interest rates and high inflation. In his own words: "Interest makes the rich richer and the poor poorer"[1]. Interest (riba) was the reason sought. Interest is the cause; inflation is the result.

In November 2021, in a speech at Parliament, he declared once again that "Interest is the cause; inflation is the result."[2] To achieve his economic targets, he declared: "As long as I am in office, I will fight interest. NAS[3] is there."

President Erdoğan presented his view as if there were a **NAS** on the *interest–inflation relationship*. Actually, he never made any direct reference to the **NAS** before regarding economic policies. After all, Türkiye has been a secular country since the foundation of the Republic of Türkiye by Atatürk in 1923, and its Constitution, religious values, and laws cannot be used as references. There is always a first time for everything. Who could dare challenge Erdoğan's statement that *NAS is there*?

The related critical questions are as follows:

- Is there really a NAS guiding the Muslims in the fight against inflation?
- Or did Erdoğan just intend to remind them that if Muslims disobey Allah's order on the prohibition of getting/paying interest and bow before evil, they will have to suffer the consequences?

The primary purpose of this section is to shed light on the nature of concepts to find out whether there is indeed a **NAS**, i.e., words in the Holy Quran and/or Hadith, with a specific aim to curb inflation using interest rate as an economic instrument.

The other purpose is to evaluate the outcome of a new economic policy, whether it was a success or a failure, regardless of any reference to **NAS**.

President Erdoğan's Islamic challenge

Speaking at the Group Meeting of the AK Party, which has been in power for about 20 years since 2002 without interruption, President Erdoğan said the following about interest, with an unexpected approach in a secular country:

> As long as I am in office, I will continue my fight against interest until the end. I will continue my fight against inflation. … All we need to know is that **there is a clear NAS in this regard**. (emphasis is mine) … Who cares about what you and I think? *NAS is there*.
>
> (November 17, 2021)[4]

About one month later, President Erdoğan repeated his belief in a speech delivered at the "Academy Awards Ceremony" organized by the Foundation for Dissemination of Science,[5] on December 19, 2021.

> What do they say? We are lowering interest rates. Do not expect anything else from me. *As a Muslim, I will continue to do whatever is required.* (emphasis is mine) *This is the verdict.*[6]

Over a year later, in a TV interview, President Erdoğan repeated his thesis regarding interest rates and inflation:

> Interest and inflation are directly proportional; *Interest is the cause; inflation is the result.* (emphasis is mine) There may be some who do not believe this. **I believe so** (emphasis is mine). As for the field, my field is economics, too.[7]

Since 2002, the year the AK Party came to power, Erdoğan had never made any reference to **NAS** before. There is no doubt, according to Erdoğan, "interest is the cause; inflation is the result." As seen in the citation above, he says, "I believe so." In other words, he expresses his personal belief; he does not quote any holy expression from the Holy Quran or Hadith. This is an important but overlooked detail so far.

Upon Erdoğan's instructions, the CB[8] of Türkiye lowered the lending rate from 18% in September 2021 to 14% in December 2021 (see Table 5.2) while the annual year-end **inflation rate was 36%**. In May 2022, the CB's lending rate was still 14%, while the "official" **inflation rate rose to 73%**. Obviously, something was not in order with the new policy.

In June and July 2022, the CB's lending rate was still 14%, and the living standard of Turkish people was rapidly deteriorating, while both the official and unofficial[9] inflation rates kept rising. And this situation, harming wage-earning people, continued until the end of 2022 (see Table 5.2).

In the following sections, we will first attempt to describe what the term "**NAS**" means and its relation to **RIBA**, e.g., the prohibited excess received or paid.

Riba and NAS

Riba[10]

Muslim or non-Muslim, everybody knows that according to the Islamic faith, getting or paying "riba" is Haram, i.e., forbidden. But what does riba mean? Do we have a definition of riba and its scope?

The Islamic concept of riba means "to increase, to multiply, to heighten, to inflate, to expand". But it also means an "**unjust,**" "**unearned,**" or "**unrequited**" **increase**. Riba is often translated as "interest" and "usury" in relation to loans, as pointed out in the Holy Quran. It is called Quranic riba, which arises as a result of an increase in the amount of debt. There are four verses directly related to the issue of riba, but there is no definition of it or criteria for how to measure it but merely some pronounced examples.

In addition to "Quranic riba" on loans, there is another important concept known as "commodity riba," which arises as a result of the exchange of commodities and is dealt with in the Hadith. To avoid commodity riba, the following exchange conditions reported by the Prophet must be satisfied:

> Gold for Gold, equivalent for equivalent.
> silver for silver, equivalent for equivalent.
> wheat for wheat, equivalent for equivalent.
> barely for barley, equivalent for equivalent.
> salt for salt, equivalent for equivalent.
> dates for dates equivalent for equivalent.

(Ashker-Wilson, 2006)

As we learned from the previous paragraphs, there are two distinct types of riba: (a) **Quranic riba regarding loans**, and (b) **commodity riba regarding exchange conditions**. Our focus in this chapter is "**riba on loans,**" and therefore our reference book is the Holy Quran.

Table 5.2 Central Bank's Lending (Policy) Rates[c] (One-Week Repo Auction Rate) and Price Index

2020 December[a]	2021 March[a]	2021 September[a]	2021 October[a]	2021 November[a]	2021 December[a]	2022 August[a]	2022 September[a]	2022 October[a]	2022 November[a]
17%	19%	18%	16%	15%	14%	13%	12%	10.5%	9.0%

PPI[b] (producer price index)		25.15% 2020 (year-end)			79.89 2021 (year-end)		97.72 2022 (year-end)		
CPI[b] (consumer price index)		14.60 2020 (year-end)			36.08 2021 (year-end)		64.27 2022 (year-end)		

Source: [a]TCMB—1 Hafta Repo, March 1, 2023. [b]In Mahfi Eğilmez, Kendime Yazılar, https://www.mahfiegilmez.com/p/gostergeler.html, March 1, 2023. [c]For detailed data of lending rate in 2022, see Appendix 1.

NAS

NAS is an Islamic concept meaning **the Word of Allah and/or the Prophet**, including his actions. According to the faithful Muslims, including President Erdoğan, the instructions of the **NAS** are in **no way open to debate and/or interpretation**. In other words, if there is a **NAS**, there cannot be any discussion about its validity for Muslims. For instance, the Holy Quran declares that getting or paying interest is forbidden. However, the critical question is:

Is there a "Divine" definition of riba or its scope in the Holy Quran to use in relation to the NAS?[11]

"Interest cause–inflation result" relation in the Holy Quran

The concept riba is used in four surahs and eight verses in the Holy Quran[12] in relation to loans, i.e., *riba Nasi`ah*. The suras, in accordance with the date of Revelation, are as follows:

The Romans

39. That which you give in usury for **increase through the property** of (other) people, will have no increase with Allah: but that which you give for charity, seeking the Countenance of Allah, (will increase): it is these who will get a recompense multiplied.

Women (Nisa)

160. For the iniquity of the Jews We made unlawful for them certain (foods) good and wholesome which had been lawful for them;- in that they hindered many from Allah's Way.

161. That they took usury, though they were forbidden; and that they devoured men's substance wrongfully;- We have prepared for those among them who reject faith a grievous punishment.

The family of Imrân

130. O ye who believe! Devour not usury, doubled, and multiplied, but fear Allah. that ye may (really) prosper.

Baqara

With the revelation of Baqara, we get detailed information on interest:

275. Those who devour usury will not stand except as stand one whom the Satan by his touch Hath driven to madness. That is because they say: "Trade is like usury," but Allah hath permitted trade and forbidden usury. Those who after receiving direction from their Lord, desist, shall be pardoned for the past; their case is for Allah (to judge); but those who repeat (the offense) are companions of the Fire: They will abide therein (forever).

276. Allah will deprive usury of all blessing but will give increase for deeds of charity: For He loveth not any ungrateful and wicked.

278. O ye who believe! Fear Allah and give up what remains of your demand for usury, if ye are indeed believers.

279. If ye do it not, take notice of war from Allah and His Messenger. But if ye repent, ye shall have your capital sums: Deal not unjustly, and ye shall not be dealt with unjustly.

The concept of riba is not infrequently used to refer to "interest" on loans, but it can also be used to refer to "**unjust**" or "**unearned**" income. Regardless of how one uses it, there is no definition of riba or its scope in the Holy Quran. In addition, there is no mention of the concept of "inflation" in the Holy Quran. Accordingly, there is no mention at all of an economic policy in connection with interest and inflation.

In other words, considering the Holy Quran, there are no definitions, explanations, criteria, measures, or even a hint on how to deal with a problem posed as "interest is the cause and inflation is the result."

"Interest cause–inflation result" relationship in the Hadith

Hadith[13] are the collection of sayings and practices of the Prophet Muhammad, revered and received as a major source of religious law and moral guidance, second only to the Holy Quran. When Muslims cannot find the answer they are looking for in the Holy Quran, they refer to Hadiths. Nobody knows exactly how many Hadiths exist. Some say there are thousands of Hadiths. Certainly, not all of them are regarded as sahih,[14] i.e., authentic; most of them are believed to be forgeries.

Al-Bukhari had collected—7,275, Muslim 9,200, Sunan of Abu Dawood around 4,800, al-Tirmidhi around 3,956, Sunan ibn Majah around 4,000, and Muwatta Malik around 1,700 sahih Hadiths (Islamiqate, February 19, 2023). Altogether, there are 30,931 authentic (sahih) Hadith. Their works together are labeled as "**al-kutub al-sittah ("the six books")** and are generally considered the most reliable hadiths for Sunni Muslims" (Encyclopedia Britannica, February 19, 2023).

What is the definition of riba and its scope in the sahih Hadith?

The concept of riba in the Holy Quran referring to "loans" concerns only situations where getting or paying any "additional" or "excess" amount on loans is forbidden. Riba in the Hadith, on the contrary, makes reference, in principle, to an "excess" in trade or, to be more specific, the simultaneous exchange of unequal quantities or qualities of a given commodity known as ***riba al-fadl***,[15] the study of which will be omitted since our focus in this book is on ***riba on loans***, known as ***riba Nasi`ah***.

What does the Hadith say regarding riba on loans?

There are a few Hadith on loans, i.e., ***riba Nasi`ah***, but they, in principle, repeat what the Holy Quran says about it. There is no additional information to find regarding the definition and scope of riba on loans in Hadith.

Given these facts, **where do we go to find a NAS, an Islamic policy, to fight against inflation using interest rates as a tool?**

In Erdoğan's mind, only? If so, would it be wrong to label it as **"Erdoğan-patented" anti-interest policy**?

"Erdoğan-patented" anti-interest policy: success or failure?

Let us summarize what we have at hand:

1. President Erdoğan claimed: ***Interest is the cause; inflation is the result***. And he continued: "As long as I'm in office, I'll fight interest. NAS is there."
2. Yet, as observed in the previous sections, there is no **NAS** to fight inflation. To be more specific:

    1. 2-a. There is no definition of riba or its scope in the Holy Quran. And there is no mention of inflation. Accordingly, there is no policy recommendation on how to cope with inflation.
    2. 2-b. Hadith makes reference to commodity riba, but Erdoğan's claim is about riba on loans. Therefore, Erdoğan's claim regarding interest and inflation cannot be associated with any commodity riba or Hadiths.

If Erdoğan's anti-interest policy cannot be associated with **NAS**, how can we define it?

It can be named an "Erdoğan-patented pro-Islamic anti-inflationary policy."

There is no reason to doubt whether President Erdoğan's intentions "to fight inflation to the end" are sincere or not. Therefore, let us put aside any Islamic connotation and simply evaluate the merits and demerits of Erdoğan's economic policy in the fight against inflation. Can his policy be considered a success? Alternatively, was he, as an "economist,"[16] successful in his fight against inflation?

Let us recall the expectations.

– Inflation would fall.
– Exports would increase, imports would decline, and the balance of payments would improve.
– Foreign currencies would not appreciate.
– Growth would continue, and people's living standards would increase.

(see Babuşçu, 2023)

Did the results meet expectations? Who benefited most from his policies?

We leave the final decision on the results to the readers, who can draw their conclusions after having read the empirical studies in the following chapters written by experts.

Why did NAS suddenly come to the fore in Türkiye?

Why, after being in power for about 20 years (2002–2022), did President Erdoğan suddenly start referring to an Islamic concept like **NAS** in Türkiye, a secular country?

Erdoğan says he has always been against riba as a faithful Muslim. However, until 2021, he had not openly expressed any view for the application of a religion-based economic policy, i.e., **NAS**, to curb inflation and overcome the country's other severe economic problems. However, there is always a first time for everything. What he had in mind could now be applied and tested.

According to some economists, the underlying reason behind President Erdoğan's sudden change in discourse is the severe economic conditions prevailing in Türkiye under his one-man rule. During the 2018 election period, he told the electorate, "Give me your vote and see how to deal with inflation and other major economic problems." The Turkish economy would take off. At least, this was the message.

Erdoğan won the election and was endowed with extreme administrative powers. But he has never managed to reduce the inflation rate to 5%, as projected in the government's three-year plans. However, the high inflation rate was not the only problem. Foreign trade deficits, balance of payment deficits, budget deficits, unemployment, and foreign debt levels were other immense problems waiting to be dealt with. About ten years ago, Erdoğan had promised that per capita income would rise to $25,000 in 2023, but it is far from the projected level; it has been fluctuating around USD 8,000–9,000 for a long time.

Erdoğan, the "economist," has not been performing well since 2018, and he is losing the confidence of the people. He had to do something to save the economy. Many Western-biased economists expected measures in accordance with traditional Western values and norms, such as increasing the interest rate. Accordingly, Türkiye was expected to raise the CB's lending rate partly to protect the value of the Turkish Lira from further depreciation and partly to promote exports to improve the balance of payments.

However, Erdoğan "the economist" had something else in mind, a religiously biased anti-interest policy.

NAS is there, he said. After all, getting and/or paying any kind of Interest is forbidden in the Holy Quran.

According to the Constitution, the Republic of Türkiye is a secular country, but who would dare challenge Erdoğan's new policy?

Concluding remarks

There were two critical questions in relation to Erdoğan's claim: "Interest rate is the cause; inflation is the result. NAS is there."

1 Is there any suggestion in the Holy Quran or Hadith, i.e., any **NAS**, in the fight against inflation by using the CB's lending rate as an economic tool?
2 What are the consequences of the **NAS** policy or rather Erdoğan-patented religion-biased NAS policy implemented in Türkiye in 2022?

As we observed in the previous sections, there is no *NAS* either in the Holy Quran or in Hadith with direct reference to the inflation–interest rate (riba) relationship to guide Muslims **in the fight against inflation**. The Holy Quran has a clear ban forbidding riba but provides no definition of riba or its scope. And there is no statement supporting the cause–result relationship considering riba and inflation.

As to Hadith, they refer, in principle, to commodity riba, not interest on loans, and there is no cause–result relationship considering riba and inflation either.

As to the second question, President Erdoğan's claim that "Interest rate is the cause, inflation is the result" seems to be a hypothesis originating from his brain, influenced by his religious values. There is nothing wrong with presenting a new hypothesis to find a cause–result relationship. In fact, if considered only as Erdoğan's hypothesis, it can be considered a bold attempt. However, it does not seem appropriate to find any relationship between the NAS on riba as suggested in the Holy Quran and the NAS suggested by President Erdoğan in his fight against inflation. Therefore, it seems more appropriate to consider Erdoğan's claim as an "Erdoğan-patented anti-inflationary hypothesis with a religious flavor."

Under the circumstances, how should the results of President Erdoğan's NAS policy be evaluated after one year of experience, between January 2022 and December 2022? Was it a success or a failure?

One year or 12 months is a short period to properly evaluate the results of a "new" approach in the fight against inflation. Nevertheless, this is the only timeframe with data we have access to.

The following chapters, authored by experts in their fields, will evaluate the results of the so-called Erdoğan-patented **NAS** policy based on empirical investigations. The final decision on whether the Erdoğan-patented NAS policy is a success or failure is up to the readers' conclusions.

Appendix A

Table 5.A1

Table 5.A1 Central Bank's Policy Rate (CBPR),[a] Consumer Price Index (CPI)[b] (2003 = 100), Producer Price Index (PPI),[c] Balance of Payments (BoP) in US Dollars[d]

	CBPR (One-Week Repo Auction Rate %)[a]	CPI (Year to Year % Changes)[b]	CPI (Month to Month % Changes)[b]	PPI (Month to Month % Changes)[c]	BoP (Month to Month Changes) in US $
January 2023	9.0	57.68	6.65	4.15	January–December 2022 −12,311
December 2022	9.0	64.27	1.18	−0.24	−2,434
November 2022	9.0	84.39	2.88	0.74	−3,613
October 2022	10.5	85.51	3.54	7.83	−5,059
September 2022	12.0	83.45	3.08	4.78	1,656
August 2022	13.0	80.21	1.46	2.41	−10,786

(Continued)

Table 5.A1 (Continued)

	CBPR (One-Week Repo Auction Rate %)[a]	CPI (Year to Year % Changes)[b]	CPI (Month to Month % Changes)[b]	PPI (Month to Month % Changes)[c]	BoP (Month to Month Changes) in US $
July 2022	14.0	79.60	2.37	5.17	−4,423
June 2022	14.0	78.62	4.95	6.77	1,960
May 2022	14.0	73.50	2.98	8.76	5,939
April 2022	14.0	69.97	7.25	7.67	−3,217
March 2022	14.0	61.14	5.46	9.19	4,506
February 2022	14.0	54.44	4.81	7.22	2,218
January 2022	14.0	48.69	11.10	10.45	942
December 2021	14.0	36.08	13.58	19.08	January– December 2021 −23,330
November 2021	15.0	21.31	3.51	9.99	—
October 2021	16.0	19.89	2.39	5.24	—
September 2021	18.0	19.58	1.25	1.55	—

Source: Turkish Statistical Institute (TÜIK).

[a]   TCMB—1 Hafta Repo, February 25, 2023.
[b]   TCMB—Consumer Prices, Feburary 24, 2023.
[c]   TCMB—Producer Prices, February 25, 2023.
[d]   TCMB—Balance of Payments Statistics, February 25, 2023.

Appendix B

End of NAS- policy?

May 28, 2023: A new finance minister is appointed by President Erdoğan.

After the presidential election, Erdoğan appointed Mehmet ŞİMŞEK as the new Minister of Finance and Treasury, who said that the country has no choice but to return to "rational ground" to ensure predictability in the economy.

What did he mean by "rational ground"? Is the concept of "rational" compatible with the concept of "NAS"?

June 9, 2023: A new Central Bank governor is appointed by President Erdoğan.

President Erdoğan named G. Erkan, a finance executive in the United States, as Central Bank governor.

June 22, 2023: The Central Bank raised its policy rate from 8.5% to **15%**.

July 20, 2023: The Central Bank raised its policy rate from 15% to **17.5%**.

August 24, 2023: The Central Bank of Türkiye raised its policy rate from 17.5% to **25%**.

But what about **NAS**?

Just four months ago, in April 2023, President Erdoğan again emphasized:

As long as this brother is in power, the interest rate cannot rise. Interest rates will continue to fall.[17]

Does **NAS** no longer matter?

Acknowledgment

I am grateful to Kubilay Koş who contributed by proofreading the chapter.

Notes

1 Urging Turkish citizens to keep all savings in the lira and bring their gold savings into the banking system, President Erdoğan stressed in his address to ASKON: "Interest rates make the rich richer and the poor poorer" (a-news, Erdoğan: Interest rates make the rich richer and the poor poorer (anews.com.tr).
2 November 18, 2021, Erdoğan's speech at Parliament. Euronews https://tr.euronews.com/2021/11/17/cumhurbaskan-Erdoğan-faiz-sebeptir-enflasyon-neticedir-kusura-bakmas-nlar, May 7, 2022.
3 Nas is an Islamic concept meaning the Word of Allah and/or the Prophet, including his actions. Since Nas is the textual data of revelation, it forms the basis of law and religious knowledge.
4 Karar (Daily Newspaper), Free translation from Turkish by author, https://www.karar.com/guncel-haberler/son-dakika-Erdoğandan-grup-toplantisinda-kritik-aciklamalar-1639765, 2022-05-07.
5 İlim Yayma Vakfı.
6 "Neymiş efendim faizleri düşürüyormuşuz. Benden başka bir şey beklemeyin. Bir Müslüman olarak naslar neyi gerektiriyorsa onu yapmaya devam edeceğim. Hüküm bu." https://www.tccb.gov.tr/haberler/410/134024/cumhurbaskani-Erdoğan-ilim-yayma-odulleri-toreni-ne-katildi, November 30, 2022.
7 "Faiz ve enflasyon doğru orantılıdır; faiz sebep, enflasyon neticedir. Buna inanmayanlar olabilir. Ben böyle inanıyorum. Alansa, benim alanım da ekonomist." www.tccb.gov.tr/videogaleri/#Video, February 1, 2023.
8 According to law, the Central Bank of Türkiye is an autonomous organization; the fact is different.
9 Unofficial inflation rate is estimated by a group of academics (ENAG) who estimate it twice as much as the official rate of inflation.
10 For an "alternative" interpretation of the concept of Riba, see Chapter 3 in this book entitled: "Is there a 'divine' definition of riba and its scope in the Holy Quran?"
11 The views/comments of the author should in no way be interpreted as criticism of the Holy Quran or Hadith. They are simply logical and rational thoughts open to criticism. If there is criticism anywhere, it is a criticism of human views, such as those of the Ulama or intellectuals.
12 According to the website Alim, the concept riba is referred to in 20 verses. However, the usage does not always refer to loan transactions and is therefore omitted here. www.alim.org/search/?s=riba&page=1&category=quran, February 19, 2023.
13 Our primary reference is Sunni Hadith.
14 "Sahih hadith is the narration whose isnad (chain) compromises the transmission of a trustworthy (adl) narrator whose retention is accurate (dabit) from another upright transmitter who has an accurate retentive ability until the end of the chain and is neither shadh (irregular) or mu'allal (defective)" (Islamiqate, February 19, 2023).
15 "**Riba Al-Fadl** … involves increase in either of the two articles subject to exchange. According to Hadith of the Prophet, six things are susceptible to Riba Al-Fad: gold, silver, wheat, barley, dates, and salt. It is prohibited to charge interest on such transactions where any of the above things are exchanged for articles of the same type. The same holds true with regard to exchanging two articles which bear the same common cause of prohibition. It is, for example, prohibited to exchange a kilo of gold of inferior quality for half a kilo of superior quality. The same is applicable in the case of exchanging a good type of silver, wheat, barley, dates, or salt for a poor type. … It is only

permissible to exchange articles of the above-mentioned things provided that they are equal in weight and the exchange has to be made in a hand-to-hand transaction. However, it is permissible to exchange a kilo of gold for two kilos of silver provided that it is a hand-to-hand transaction. This is because gold and silver are of different types" (**Al-Feqh** February 20, 2023).

16 President Erdoğan often reminds Turkish people that he is an "economist."

17 "Bu kardeşiniz iktidarda olduğu sürece faiz yükselemez. Faiz devamlı düşecektir." https://ekonomi.haber7.com/ekonomi/haber/3319432-cumhurbaskani-erdogandan-faiz-aciklamasi-imf-ile-gorustuler, June 23, 2023.

Internet Sources on Islam

Quran—The Holy Book of Islam. http://www.islamicity.com/mosque/SURAI.HTM, 2013-10-01.

http://unitedamericanmuslim.org/english/2.html, 2013-11-29.

Al-Feqh. https://www.al-feqh.com/en/difference-between-riba-al-fadl-and-riba-al-nasi-ah, 2023-02-20.

Alim. www.alim.org/search/?s=riba&page=1&category=quran, 2023-02-19.

Encyclopaedia of Islam. http://referenceworks.brillonline.com/browse/encyclopaedia-of-islam-2/alphaRange/Rh%20-%20Rn/R, 2013-12-01.

Encyclopaedia of Islam. Second Edition. https://referenceworks.brillonline.com/browse/encyclopaedia-of-islam-2/alpha/f?s.start=180, 2022-07-29.

Ilmihâl. (A summary of the principles of Islam) - Publ. by Diyanet.

Islam. https://islamicline.com/blog/what-is-riba-in-islam.html, 2022-05-08.

Islam, All About Islam. https://islamicline.com/blog/what-is-hadiths-in-islam-solved.html, 2023-02-19.

Islamic Economics. https://islamiceconomics.net/, 2022-08-07.

Islamic Encyclopeadia – Diyanet. http://www.tdvia.org/index.php, 2014-01-28.

Islamic Financial Services Industry Stability Report 2021. Islamic Financial Services Board (IFSB) 2023-01-30.

Islamic Markets. https://islamicmarkets.com/education/types-of-riba, 2022-05-08.

Islam: Question & Answer. https://islamqa.info/en/answers/129458/what-is-riba, 2022-05-08.

Islam–World's Greatest Religion. https://islamgreatreligion.wordpress.com/2012/03/05/interest-riba/, 2022-05-08.

Islamiqate. https://www.islamiqate.com/4788/how-many-hadiths-are-there-the-hadith-collections-sahih-sitta#, 2023-02-19.

Questions on Islam. www.questionsonislam.com/article/what-interest-and-why-it-forbidden, 2013-11-08.

Riba. http://errahman.de/modules.php?name=Encyclopedia&op=content&tid=1158, 2013-11-09.

Other Sources

Abozaid, A. 2013. "Role of Fiqh in Islamic Finance", Islam Iktisadı Atölyesi-1, 2–3 Mart-2013, Istanbul.

Ahmad, A.U.F. and Hassan, M.K. 2007. "Riba and Islamic Banking", *Journal of Islamic Economics, Banking and Finance.* Vol.2007, 1–33.

Ahmed, H. (Ed.). 2002. *Theoretical Foundations of Islamic Economics,* Islamic Research & Training Inst., Islamic Dev. Bank, Jeddah.

Akın, C. 1986. *Faizsiz Bankacılık ve Kalkınma,* Kayıhan Yayınları, Ankara.

Ariff, M. 1989. "Islamic Banking in Malaysia", *Journal of Islamic Economics*, Vol.2, No. 1, 67. www.iium.edu.my/enmjournal/vol2no1.pdf, 2012-11-15.

Ashker, A. and Wilson, R. 2006. "Islamic Economics: A Short History", www.bandung2. co.uk/Books/Files/Economics/Islamic%20Economics%20%28A%20Short%20 History%29.pdf, 2012-11-15.

A-news. https://www.anews.com.tr/world/2021/12/31/erdogan-interest-rates-make-the-rich -richer-and-the-poor-poorer, 2021-31-10.

Babuşçu, Ş. 2023. Cumhuriyet Gazetesi (Daily Newspaper).www.cumhuriyet.com.tr/ ekonomi/ekonomist-senol-babuscu-uyardi-kriz-yilin-ikinci-yarisinda-yeni-bir-yukselise-gececek-2017561?ysclid=ldoe8kor3v675294729, 2023-02-01.

Bayındır, A. 2007. "Ticaret ve Faiz" "Trade and Interest", *Süleymaniye Vakfı Yayınları,* Istanbul. www.suleymaniyevakfi.org, 2012-12-26.

———. 2009. "İslam Fıkhı Açısından Borçlanmalarda Enflasyon Farkı". www.suleymani-yevakfi.org/arastirmalar/islam-fikhi-acisindan-borclanmalarda-enflasyon-farki.html, 2013-11-17.

Chapra, M.U. 2001. *What Is Islamic Economics?* Prize Winners' Lecture Serie 9, Islamic Research & Training Inst., Islamic Dev. Bank, Jeddah.

Eğilmez, M. 2023. Kendime Yazılar. https://www.mahfiegilmez.com/p/gostergeler.html, 2023-03-01.

Ensonhaber. 2021-12-31. https://www.ensonhaber.com/gundem/cumhurbaskani-Erdoğan-f aiz-degerlendirmesini-yineledi?ysclid=ler2z3xei886156087, 2020-03-05.

Ercan, H., Karahanoglu, I., and Walter, G. 2021. "Is Islamic Banking in Turkey Really Interest-Free?" *Society and Economy*, Vol.43, No.4, 391–405.

Eskicioğlu, O. 1983. "İslam Açısından Enflasyon ve Çözüm Yolları". www.enfal.de/ enflasyon.pdf, 2013-04-09.

Euronews. 2022. "Cumhurbaşkanı Erdoğan: Faiz sebeptir, enslasyon neticedir, kusura bakmasınlar". https://tr.euronews.com/2021/11/17/cumhurbaskan-Erdoğan-faiz-sebeptir -enflasyon-neticedir-kusura-bakmas-nlar, 2022-05-07.

European Central Bank. 2013. Islamic Finance in Europe Occational Paper Serious No 146 / June 2013.

Farooq, M.O. 2012. "Exploitation, Profit and the Riba-Interest Reductionism", *International Journal of Islamic & Middle Eastern Finance & Management.* Vol.5, No.4. Exploitation Profit and the Riba-Interest Reductionism.PDF (mbri.ac.ir).

Görmüş, S., Albayrak, A., and Yabanlı, A. (Eds) 2021. *Yaşayan ve Gelişen Katılım Bankacılığı,* Türkiye Katılım Bankaları Birliği Yayını, Istanbul.

Gözübenli, B. 1992. "Islam'da Faiz Yasağı ve Paralı Ekonomi", in: Heyet (Ed.) *Islam Ekonomisinde Finansman Meseleleri,* İlmi Tatıtışmalar Dizisi: 3, pp. 77–96, Ensar Neşriyat, Istanbul.

Gündoğdu, A. 2021. *Katılım Bankacılığında Kar Dağıtım Sisteminin Analizi ve Türkiye Uygulaması için Yeni bir Öneri Doktora Tezi,* Istanbul S. Zaim Üni, Istanbul.

Gürak, H. 2014. *Islam and Scientific Economics*, PL Academic Publishers, Frankfurt.

Haneef, M.A. and Furqani, H. 2008. "Theory of Profit from Islamic Perspective". http:// mpra.ub.uni-muenchen.de/8129/, 2012-10-25.

Hassan, A. 2013. "What Is the Current Situation of Islamic Economics Studies Today and What Is the Future of Them", İslam İktisadı Atölyesi-1, 2–3 Mart-2013, Istanbul.

Iqbal, M., Ali, S.S., and Muljawan, D. (Eds) 2007. *Advances in Islamic Economics and Finance* (Vol.1), Islamic Development Bank, IRTI, Jeddah. www.irtipms.org/PubText/230. pdf, 2013-10-22.

Karaman, H. 2012. "Faiz hakkında soruya yanıt". www.hayrettinkaraman.net/sc/00144.htm, 2012-09-19.

Karar (Newspaper). 2022. https://www.karar.com/guncel-haberler/son-dakika-Erdoğandan-grup-toplantisinda-kritik-aciklamalar-1639765, 2022-05-07.

Kuran, T. 1995. "Islamic Economics and the Islamic Subeconomy". http://econ.duke.edu/uploads/assets/People/Kuran/Islamic%20economics%20and%20Islamic%20subeconomy.pdf, 2012-11-15.

———. 1997. "The Genesis of Islamic Economics", *Social Research*, Vol.64, No.2, EBSCO Database, 2012-10-31.

Mushtaq, S. and Siddiqui, D.A. 2016. "Effect of Interest Rate on Economic Performance: Evidence from Islamic and Non-Islamic Economies." https://jfin-swufe.springeropen.com/articles/10.1186/s40854-016-0028-7, 2022-10-05.

News TR. 2020. "Erdoğan faiz kararı sonrası tezini yineledi: Faiz sebep, enflasyon neticedir". https://www.newstr.net/cumhurbaskani-Erdoğan-faiz-tezini-yineledi-faiz-sebep-e nflasyon-neticedir/, 2023-03-02.

Nienhaus, V. 1983. "Profitability of Islamic PLS Banks Cempeting with Interest Banks: Problems and Prospects". *Journal of Research in Islamic Economics*, Vol.1, No.1, 31–39. https://iei.kau.edu.sa/Pages-OVOL-01-01.aspx, 2022-10-05.

Ökte, M.K.S. 2010. "Fundamentals of Islamic Ec. & Finance: Th. & Practice", *Electronic Journal of Social Sciences*, 2010 C.9 31. EBSCO Database, 2012-10-31.

Özsoy, I. 1994. *Faiz ve Problemleri*, Nil Yayinlari, Izmir.

———. 2012. *Türkiye'de Katılım Bankacılığı*, Türkiye Katılım Bankaları Birliği Yayını, Istanbul.

Sadr, M.B. 1980. *Islam Ekonomi Doktrini (Iqtisaduna - Our [Islamic] Economics)*, Hicret Yayınları, Bursa.

Şeriati, A. 2004. *Islam Ekonomisi*, Dünya Yayınları, Istanbul.

Shahid, E.M. 2013. "Frontiers in Islamic Finance: A Critical Perspective". www.bisav.org.tr/yayinlar.aspx?module=makale&yayinid=116&menuID=3_3&yayintipid=3&makaleid=884, 2013-11-09.

Tabakoğlu, A. 2008. *Islam Iktisadına Giriş*, Dergah Yayınları, Istanbul.

TC Cumhurbaşkanlığı, Strateji ve Bütçe Başk. 2023. https://www.sbb.gov.tr/orta-vadeli-programlar/, 2023-03-09.

Thomas, A. 2017. *Ribâyı Anlamak*, İktisat Yayinlari, Istanbul.

Usmani, M.T. 1998. An Introduction to Islamic Finance. https://www.academia.edu/5535927/An_Introduction_to_Islamic_Finance_Taqi_Usmani, 2023-12-13.

Yasmin, S., Hafidhuddin, D., and Najib, M. 2018. "The Impacts of Sharia Bank Customers' Awareness and Attitudes towards Islamic Working Capital Financing Use in Indonesia", *Journal of Islamic Financial Studies*, Vol.4, No.1, 15–27.

Yeni Akit (Newspaper). 2021. www.yeniakit.com.tr/haber/nas-nedir-nas-anlami-ne-1596932.html, 2022-05-28.

6 The effects of the new economic model on banking sector profitability in Türkiye

Şenol Babuşcu and Adalet Hazar

Introduction

Upon reviewing the economic history of Türkiye over the past 50 years, it becomes apparent that the country has faced persistent challenges in achieving long-term stability, despite implementing numerous economic stability programs. While these programs have occasionally led to short-term improvements, Türkiye has continually grappled with economic problems throughout this period. In the early 2000s, the country appeared to have entered a phase of temporary stability, which lasted until 2015. This stability was facilitated by leveraging the cyclical advantages following the International Monetary Fund (IMF)–supported program. However, since sustainable economic transformation could not be fully achieved, deterioration began to emerge after 2015. The instability further escalated due to the rapid deterioration observed after 2018, coupled with frequent changes in economic policies and fluctuations in the composition of the economic management team. In 2021, amid ongoing fluctuations, interest rates were declared as the primary factor contributing to economic instability. Consequently, the Central Bank of the Republic of Türkiye (CBRT) swiftly initiated a series of reductions in policy rates in response to the rising inflation trend. This unconventional approach, lacking a solid foundation in economic theories, has been attempted to be bolstered through various means. However, the anticipated benefits failed to materialize, exacerbating the economic instability.

Today, the same policy is still being pursued using different practices and tools. However, these tools for producing short-term solutions do not seem to be able to yield lasting benefits.

The vast majority of new tools employed in economic management either directly target banks or individuals and businesses utilizing banking products through the intermediary role of banks. Consequently, it is fair to assert that the application of these tools has the greatest impact on the banking industry. Despite the potential benefits that certain practices may have offered to banks, particularly in 2022, a long-term perspective reveals a framework that harbors and consolidates risks for the future. As a result, the banking sector emerges as an area necessitating heightened oversight in the forthcoming years.

DOI: 10.4324/9781032631561-9

The relationship between interest rates and inflation in the framework of the basic assumption of the new economic model

Interest is defined as the cost incurred by individuals or entities for using capital, either in production or through lending it to others for a specific duration. In other words, it is the cost of the money used by the person in need of funds, and the return gained by the lender for providing the capital. Interest rates, expressed as an annual percentage, are the reward paid by a borrower to a lender for using the money for a period of time (Faure, 2014: 1). In economic theory, interest serves as an incentive to encourage those with surplus funds to save rather than spend and to invest in long-term assets instead of holding cash (Patterson & Lygnerud, 1999: 5). Inflation, on the contrary, is the substantial and consistent increase in the overall price level, indicating a decline in the purchasing power of money (BIS, 2022: 42).

Since changes in interest rates affect macroeconomic equilibrium, the aim of implemented monetary policies in countries is to utilize these effects to maintain economic balance. Central banks, which are responsible for this task, influence economic equilibrium by lowering or raising interest rates based on the prevailing conditions in the country. In fact, the primary aim of central banks is to ensure stability, with a particular emphasis on price stability. This usually entails maintaining a balance between the external and internal values of the national currency. Failure to achieve price stability can result in a decline in the competitiveness of the economy in international markets, reduced efficiency in labor markets, worsened income distribution, and stagnation over time.

The relationship between interest rates and inflation and their reciprocal effects have always been a topic of interest among economists. The interaction between these two interrelated macroeconomic indicators within the economic system holds great significance for the stability of economies. The basis of the studies on this subject revolves around determining which of these indicators influences the other.

The primary work that extensively explores the relationship between interest rates and inflation is the book published by Fisher in 1930. Subsequent studies have been built upon the foundation established in this book. Fisher's study provided evidence that an anticipated change in the price level has an impact on the monetary interest rate (Fisher, 1930: 400). The evidence suggests a clear tendency for interest rates to rise in tandem with price increases. This trend is evident in the majority of cases examined (Fisher, 1930: 411).

Interest rates tend to be higher during periods of high price levels and lower during periods of low-price levels (Fisher, 1930: 438). As a result, the interest rate increases cumulatively during inflationary periods, such that by the end of such a period, when the price level is high, the interest rate is also high (Fisher, 1930: 441).

The long-term relationship between inflation and nominal interest rates is called the Fisher effect. The Fisher hypothesis posits that nominal interest rates are equal to the sum of expected inflation and real interest rates. According to the Fisher equation:

$$i = r^* + \pi$$

i = nominal interest rate
r^* = real interest rate
π = expected inflation rate

Accordingly, expected inflation rates are in a positive relationship with nominal interest rates (Crowder & Hoffman, 1996: 102; Mankiw, 2009: 100–101; Mishkin, 2012: 125).

According to this perspective, a continuous increase in the money supply initially leads to a short-term decrease in nominal interest rates. Subsequently, inflation increases, causing interest rates to rise again. In the long term, both the money supply and interest rates increase at the same rate as inflation.

Following the Fisher equation, a change in the nominal interest rate can occur only if there is a change in either the real interest rate or the inflation rate (Mankiw, 2009: 94). While an increase in inflation rates directly affects nominal interest rates in the long run, monetary imbalances that influence the inflation rate do not affect the real interest rate due to their strong one-to-one relationship (Mankiw, 2009: 100–101).

Consequently, in the long term, the nominal interest rate changes in the same direction as inflation, maintaining a one-to-one relationship. This is because when the inflation rate rises, the real interest earned by the lenders decreases. Lenders, therefore, demand higher nominal interest from borrowers to compensate for the erosion of their position caused by rising inflation. In response to this demand, borrowers pay lenders additional nominal interest, sufficient to offset the increase in inflation. Consequently, with the increase in inflation, the nominal interest rate rises by the same magnitude as the inflation rate, while the real interest rate remains unchanged (Atbaşı, 2019: 71).

Although Fisher's hypothesis is generally accepted in the economics literature, there are challenges in empirically establishing a stable one-to-one relationship between nominal interest rates and inflation rates. According to the Fisher hypothesis, nominal interest rates are the sum of real interest rates and expected inflation. However, it is recognized that real interest rates can change due to various factors, such as policy shifts, although it is assumed that they remain constant (Atbaşı, 2019: 72). Some empirical studies conducted after Fisher's work have found that the estimated inflation has less than a one-unit effect on nominal interest rates and leads to a decrease in real interest rates even in the long term (Fried & Howitt, 1983: 968).

While Fisher's theory acknowledges the potential significance of risk, it falls short in considering the effects of uncertainty on interest rate determination (Ireland, 1996: 22).

Following Fisher's work, John Taylor proposed a new theory in 1993 that outlined the measures central banks should adopt for conducting monetary policy. This approach, known as the Taylor Rule, suggests determining short-term interest rates based on the deviation between actual inflation and targeted inflation, as well as the gap between actual GDP and potential GDP level (Akalın & Tokucu, 2007: 41–42). In other words, the Taylor Rule proposes that central banks set short-term interest rates based on GDP and inflation. According to the Taylor Rule, central banks tend to increase interest rates when there is an expectation that GDP and inflation rates will exceed the target figures, while they tend to lower interest rates in the opposite scenario. The adjustment in short-term interest rates, which central banks employ as a monetary policy tool, is determined by the disparity between actual inflation and the expected level, as well as the deviation of GDP from its potential level.

While Keynes argues that lower interest rates are required for economic recovery, he underscores that the only practical policy for stability is to control inflationary conditions by limiting the expansion rate of the money supply with an increase in interest rate (Hayes, 2008: 199). Keynesian analysis suggests that a decrease in the real money supply disrupts the overall economy, leading to imbalance. This is followed by an increase in the supply of bonds, resulting in low bond prices and high interest rates. Increasing inflation also contributes to higher interest rates (Baktemur, 2021: 1151). The causal relationship between inflation and interest rates implies that with the increase in inflation, the demand for money also increases, leading to higher interest rates (Baktemur, 2021: 1155).

In conditions of very low or negative real interest rates, liquid investment instruments are more in demand. In addition, demand for other capital goods such as foreign currency, precious metals such as jewelry, and land increases as a protection against unexpected increases in the general price level. Increases in the prices of these capital goods can be seen as an indication of potential inflationary pressures spreading to production costs through the cost of utilization. The amount of money is not directly important in this context; the shift in the hierarchy of liquidity preference is driven by the low interest rate on money (Hayes, 2008: 212).

According to the quantity theory, a 1% increase in the growth rate of the money supply results in a 1% increase in the inflation rate. As stated earlier, according to the Fisher equation, a 1% increase in the inflation rate leads to a 1% increase in the nominal interest rate (Mankiw, 2009: 95).

Numerous studies in the literature have raised questions about the impact of inflation changes on interest rates. Some of these studies are mentioned below. According to the study by Mankiw, in the United States between 1955 and 2005, when inflation is high, nominal interest rates are also high, and when inflation is low, nominal interest rates are low (Mankiw, 2009: 96). Figure 6.1 illustrates the relationship between money, price level, and interest rate.

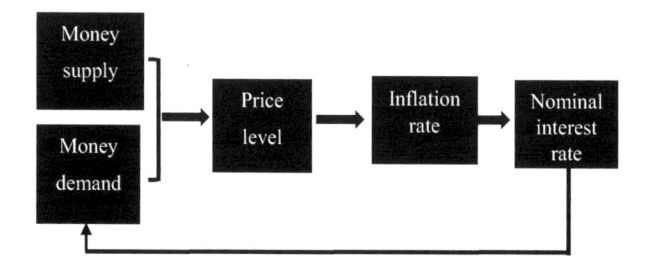

Figure 6.1 The Linkages Among Money, Prices, and Interest Rates.
Source: Mankiw (2009: 99).

As depicted in the figure, the interaction between money supply and money demand determines the price level. Changes in the price level, in turn, determine the inflation rate. The inflation rate has an impact on the nominal interest rate since the nominal interest rate reflects the cost of holding money, which can influence the demand for money (Mankiw, 2009: 99).

Numerous studies on the relationship between interest rates and inflation conducted in different countries or regions in the world, particularly to test the Fisher effect, have reached the conclusion that inflation determines interest rates.

Fama (1975) found that in the US bond market during the period from 1953 to 1971, the market efficiently incorporated all available information about future inflation rates when determining nominal interest rates for durations ranging from one to six months. Nelson and Schwert (1977), in their study on the US bond market to verify Fama's work, concluded that inflation expectations explain most of the changes in short-term interest rates in the postwar period.

In their study, Granville and Mallick (2004) examined the validity of the Fisher effect for England over a long-term period spanning from 1900 to 2000, using the series of inflation and interest rates. They found that the Fisher effect holds true in England. Kasman et al. (2006) conducted a test on the Fisher effect in 33 countries. Using the Engle–Granger cointegration test, they found that the Fisher effect was valid in Korea, Chile, Mexico, Peru, and Malaysia. In addition, through piecewise cointegration tests, they found the Fisher effect to be valid in all countries except Malaysia, the Philippines, Korea, Costa Rica, and the Czech Republic. Westerlund (2005) conducted a study using monthly data from 14 OECD countries for the period 1980–1999. He concluded that the Fisher effect holds true based on his analysis. Beyer et al. (2009) tested the Fisher hypothesis on 15 OECD member countries for the post-1950 period and found evidence supporting the validity of the Fisher effect in the long term. Saymeh and Orabi (2013) conducted a study on Jordan between 2000 and 2010 and found evidence of unidirectional causality from inflation to interest rates. Maghyereh (2006) investigated the relationship between the non-linear trend in interest rates and the inflation rate for Argentina, Brazil, Malaysia, Mexico, South Korea, and Türkiye. The findings showed a statistically significant relationship, indicating a one-to-one relationship between expected inflation rates and nominal interest rates in developing countries.

In the majority of studies on Türkiye, there is evidence supporting the relationship between inflation and interest rates.

Alçam (2003) examined the period from 1987:Q2 to 2002:Q4; Şimşek and Kadilar (2006) studied the period from 1987 to 2004; İncekara et al. (2012) analyzed the period from 1989 to 2011, and Köse et al. (2012) investigated the period from 2002 to 2009. All of these studies found support for the validity of the Fisher effect in Türkiye.

Maxwell (1980) concluded that inflation for the period between 1950 and 1977 was determined by the difference between the rate of change in the nominal money supply and the rate of change in real money demand. Mercan (2013) examined the period from 1991:Q1 to 2013:Q1 and determined that changes in inflation had an impact on interest rates. Dogan et al. (2016) found evidence of unidirectional causality from inflation to interest rates during the period from 2003 to 2015. Tunalı and Erönal (2016) identified a long-term relationship between inflation and interest rates for the period from 2003:Q1 to 2014:Q2, with changes in inflation being the determinant of changes in nominal interest rates. Akıncı and Yılmaz (2016) examined the relationships between different macroeconomic indicators for the period from 1980 to 2012 and found that inflation had an effect on interest rates. Demirgil and Türkay (2017) determined that inflation, along with some macroeconomic variables, had an impact on interest rates during the period from 2007 to 2015.

On the contrary, Civcir and Akçağlayan (2010) and Ersel and Özatay (2008) shared their findings on inflation targeting, which is the basis of the monetary policy in the restructuring program implemented after the November 2000 and February 2001 crises in Türkiye. They found that interest rates were directed as a result of inflation control.

Monetary policy practices in Türkiye after 2000

It has been observed that the policy rates in the monetary policies implemented in the 2000–2021 period in Türkiye were set based on both actual and expected inflation rates, with a particular focus on combating inflation.

In this period, the CBRT initially adopted the overnight interest rate as the official policy rate and later shifted to the weekly repo rate.

Following the banking crisis in 2000–2001, important developments occurred in the country's economy due to the measures taken by the CBRT and the government as part of the "Transition to a Strong Economy Program."

After the initial crisis in November 2000, a three-year "Stand-by Agreement" was signed with the IMF, aimed at reducing the high interest rates. However, contrary to expectations, the increase in the targeted interest rates following the agreement further deteriorated the economic imbalances in an environment of uncertainty. The second crisis in February 2001 witnessed record-high interest rates, leading to the bankruptcy of several banks (Dufour & Orhangazi, 2009). In addition, there was a decrease in the skilled workforce and a significant profit margin contraction even among large holdings (Öniş, 2009).

Following the announcement of the "Transition to a Strong Economy Program" in April 2001, the exchange rate anchor policy was abandoned. The decisions made within the program were formulated with the support of the IMF.

In 2002, the CBRT started to implement "implicit inflation targeting" with a focus on future inflation. Short-term interest rates, among the most frequently used policy instruments, were utilized to control inflation within the framework of policy decisions. The credibility of the CBRT has increased with the successful implementation of implicit inflation targeting and the achievement of desired inflation levels.

In 2002, the CBRT determined the short-term interest rates, which were used as the main monetary policy instrument, only within the framework of the fight against inflation. Overnight borrowing interest rates were reduced from 59% to 44% (CBRT, 2003).

In 2003, short-term interest rates became the main policy instrument for the CBRT. Between April and October, there were six rate cuts, resulting in a decrease in the overnight borrowing rate from 44% in April to 26% in October (CBRT, 2003).

In 2004, interest rates, starting at 26%, were determined considering the risks associated with costs and developments in domestic and foreign demand that could potentially generate inflationary pressures. Throughout the year, four rate cuts were implemented, bringing the interest rate down to 18% by the end of the year (CBRT, 2004).

In 2005, in line with the positive developments, it was decided to remove six zeros from the Turkish lira (TL). Inflation figures fell to 7.72% by the end of the year, and interest rate cuts continued gradually until the end of 2005, resulting in a reduction of short-term interest rates to 13.5% in December (CBRT, 2005).

Following the 2001 crisis, the CBRT aimed at achieving price stability within the framework of implicit inflation targeting between 2002 and 2005. Türkiye switched to explicit inflation targeting in 2006 and started to set the policy rate accordingly. In the second half of 2006, with the fluctuations in the global markets, the risk appetite of international capital decreased, leading to an increase in Türkiye's credit default swap (CDS) premiums and financing costs. As inflation and inflation expectations rose, the TL lost value, and, as a precaution, the CBRT raised policy rates (CBRT, 2006).

Following the collapse of the US mortgage markets in August 2007, which led to a major global crisis in 2008, interest rates decreased both in Türkiye and abroad, in line with the contraction in international activities in the country. Declining growth rates and decreasing inflation resulted in the CBRT lowering interest rates (CBRT, 2008).

In 2009, inflation was suppressed due to the global decline in commodity and energy prices, lowering costs due to tax incentives, and slowing domestic demand. In line with this, the CBRT also decreased interest rates (CBRT, 2009).

Quantitative monetary expansion continued in 2010 due to the effects of the crisis. On the contrary, the slowdown in economic activity in developed countries led international capital to prefer developing countries with relatively high interest rates. Türkiye benefited from increased foreign capital inflows, leading to a loosening of exchange rates and positive impacts on macroeconomic indicators. While keeping inflation under control, the CBRT announced that the weekly repo rate would be accepted as the policy rate. The policy rate decreased in parallel with the decline in inflation (CBRT, 2010).

In 2011, the interest rate corridor was extended downward to mitigate the damage caused by short-term capital inflows and outflows resulting from risk appetite in foreign markets. Efforts were made to control short-term capital movements. During the monetary policy committee meeting in October, the lending interest rate was increased, and the interest rate corridor was widened upward. The lending interest rate was raised to 12.50%, and the interest rate corridor was expanded upward from 400 basis points to 750 basis points (CBRT, 2011).

At the beginning of 2012, there was a gradual improvement in global risk appetite, and the economy began to balance. The tight liquidity policy was maintained in the first half of the year, and later liquidity was increased to keep short-term interest rates close to the lower limit of the interest rate corridor (CBRT, 2012).

In the first half of 2013, the overnight lending rate was reduced to 6.5%, and the one-week repo rate was lowered to 4.5%. However, in the second half of the year, uncertainties started to arise in global markets, leading to a slowdown in capital movements. The monetary policy committee deemed it appropriate to tighten policy for price stability and financial stability, and interest rates were increased (CBRT, 2013).

At the beginning of 2014, the TL experienced a visible depreciation, which had a negative impact on inflation expectations. In response, steps were taken to tighten the monetary policy, and within this framework, the CBRT increased interest rates by up to 10% toward the middle of the year, interest rates were reduced again with the decrease in uncertainties (CBRT, 2014).

Tight monetary policy continued in 2015, similar to the previous year, in order to maintain macroeconomic balances. The weighted average funding rate was gradually increased, and by the end of the year, the policy rate stood at 7.5%. Those measures helped limit the rise in inflation and ensure price stability (CBRT, 2015).

As of March 2016, the monetary policy was simplified, and the CBRT gradually reduced policy rates until September. However, as a result of the increase in global uncertainties in the second half of the year, interest rates were increased again to control the negative expectations concerning the exchange rate and inflation (CBRT, 2016).

In the first half of 2017, the CBRT tightened monetary policy as of January in response to the pressure on inflation caused by the excessive volatility in the exchange rate. Interest rates were raised again to limit upward inflation (CBRT, 2017).

The CBRT continued its tightening stance in the first half of 2018 due to rising inflation, increased risks, and uncertainties. Due to the heightened market risk and excessive volatility in exchange rates, a strong monetary tightening was implemented in September, raising the one-week repo rate to 24% (CBRT, 2018).

The tight monetary policy was maintained in the first half of 2019, and the policy rate was kept constant at 24%. In the second half of the year, the positive effects of the tight monetary policy on the exchange rate and inflation became evident. In line with the positive developments in inflation figures, the policy rate was reduced to 12% in the second half of the year (CBRT, 2019).

In 2020, the Turkish economy started to weaken starting in mid-March due to the impact of the COVID-19 pandemic. While one of the main determinants of consumer inflation was the exchange rate, the increase in commodity prices has added to the inflationary pressures starting from the middle of the year. Cost-side pressures, combined with the expansion of credit-supported demand, pushed inflation up to 14.6% in 2020.

In the first half of 2020, the CBRT continued the interest rate cut process that began in July 2019. As of August, coordinated tightening measures were implemented as part of monetary policy actions. In September, the CBRT decided to increase the policy rate by 200 basis points to support price stability in the face of rising inflation trends. Again, in November and December, the policy rate was increased to 17% to control inflation expectations (CBRT, 2020).

In 2021, inflation in Türkiye continued to rise. Considering the negative developments, the Central Bank took further monetary tightening measures. In March, the policy rate was increased from 17% to 19%. However, in the second half of the year, the CBRT abandoned the monetary policy management method that had been followed since 2000 and introduced different monetary policy practices. Although there was no improvement in inflation expectations, interest rates were cut by 500 points between September and December (CBRT, 2021). These actions marked the beginning of the steps leading to the current situation.

Before moving on to new practices, the monetary policies and interest rates implemented in Türkiye between 2000 and the first half of 2021 were largely influenced by developments and particularly inflation expectations. This approach contributed to a certain period of economic stability in the country.

Since the second half of 2021, Türkiye has entered a very different economic climate, characterized by its divergence from the global community. This disintegration is the basis of the increasing problems in all areas of the economy. Starting from this period, due to policy changes, the CBRT's emphasis on maintaining price stability has effectively eroded in practice, despite its continued existence in written documents.

The new economic model and its effects on the economy

Türkiye started to implement a new economic model in September 2021, known as the "New Economic Model." This model incorporates certain policies that do not comply with conventional economic theories and has been presented to the public as heterodox policies.

The economic challenges which began to surface and intensify in Türkiye particularly after 2015, without viable solutions, have contributed to the exacerbation of these issues. In response to the escalation of problems, temporary measures were taken, and radical solutions were repeatedly postponed. In 2018, the country faced a surge in exchange rates and inflation, resulting from accumulated problems. The disruptions in the economic cycle further increased in Türkiye, along with the global impact of the pandemic in 2020, bringing postponed issues to the forefront once again. As of September 2021, there has been a change in the economic management team and the implementation of the new economic model has commenced. The targets outlined in the presentation of the model are as follows:

- With the lowering of interest rates, a corresponding decrease in inflation can be expected.
- As exports rise and imports decline, a current account surplus will be achieved.
- The growth trajectory will persist, leading to an improvement in the overall welfare of the public.

The foundation of this model, introduced in late 2021, rests on the philosophy that "interest is the cause, and inflation is the outcome." In line with this philosophy, which posits that interest is the root cause of all economic issues, the CBRT initiated a series of interest rate reductions. Starting from September 2021, the policy rate, previously at 19%, has been gradually reduced, reaching 8.5% by February 2023.

The assumption behind the model is that low interest rates will sustain GDP growth and prevent an increase in unemployment.

One of the key principles of the new economic model is that it adopts a negative view of short-term capital flows. This perspective, which associates all historical exchange rate fluctuations with short-term foreign capital movements, has led to certain measures that discourage short-term capital inflows and encourage domestic capital outflows. While most countries opted to raise interest rates in response to global economic developments in 2022, Türkiye aimed to lower interest rates as part of this approach.

Another initial assumption of the model was the use of competitive exchange rates. It was believed that with the devalued TL, exports would be stimulated, and imports would be prevented, thus addressing the current account deficit. In this context, TL devalued significantly at the outset.

It was also revealed that the current account deficit did not close over time but increased. For this reason, in the middle of 2022, this assumption of the model was not mentioned at all and was abandoned. Accordingly, due to persistently high inflation and the efforts of the economy management to prevent further devaluation, the TL regained some value in the later months of the year. However, despite these efforts, the inflation rate continued to rise, reaching historically high levels instead of declining as anticipated.

Below is a detailed explanation of how the utopian philosophy, which initially seemed appealing in theory but proved impractical in practice, affected the country's economy. Upon examining the origins of the model, it becomes evident that it is primarily built upon the following framework:

- To increase production, exports, investment, and employment;
- To exclude short/medium-term portfolio inflows from abroad, often referred to as hot money; and
- To encourage domestic production.

The main expectation of the model, which is based on very ambitious assumptions, is to achieve a permanent surplus in the current account in the long term. Thus, the need for hot money will decrease and there will be no need for a tight monetary policy to control the exchange rate. As a result, interest rates are expected to decrease, providing support to the real economy and promoting growth.

The focal point of the model is the observation that the TL has a higher value than what is considered optimal. Therefore, a moderate depreciation of the currency was deemed necessary. This adjustment was expected to enhance the current account by boosting exports and curbing imports, thereby aligning with the objectives of the model.

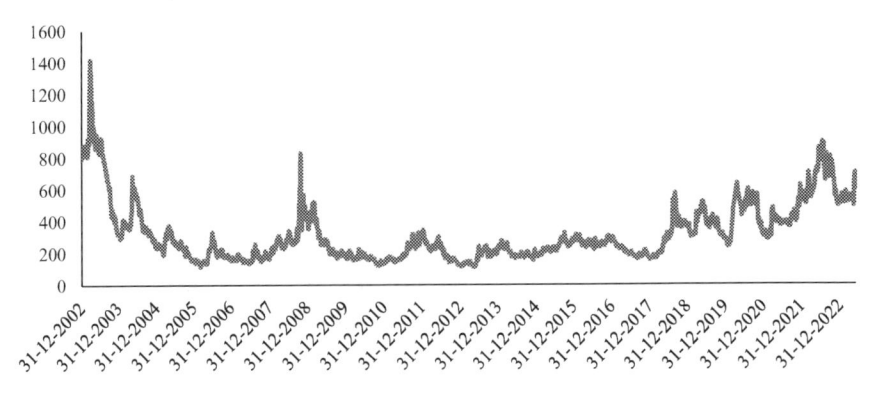

Figure 6.2 CDS Score of Türkiye (December 2002–May 2023).

Source: Author's original representation. The data in the figure was collected from investing.com.

One crucial assumption underlying this model is that all macro variables can be determined by the government. This assumption is confirmed in the model's presentation and subsequent implementation. However, it is worth noting that this approach disregards orthodox monetary policy tools and discourses. As a result, it becomes apparent that the model is not market-friendly.

As a reflection of this, CDS premiums rose as soon as the model was introduced. As can be seen in Figure 6.2, CDS premiums, which have increased especially since September 2021, when the interest rate cuts started, are at the level of 599 points as of the end of May 2023.

In addition to other factors, the timing of implementing the model is not suitable, especially considering the global rise in inflation rates and the tightening measures being taken by central banks. This indicates a timing error in initiating the program.

Another factor contributing to the model's inherent lack of potential for success is the absence of a clear primary objective set at the outset. All economic models, whether orthodox or heterodox, typically have a specific target or anchor. In other words, an economic model should be primarily based on a guiding principle or objective (Flood & Mussa, 1994; Kahn, 1988). However, the new economic model lacks such an anchor. Although there are general targets, there is no fundamental target specified in the model.

In this economic model, the previously stated occurrences have indeed taken place and continue to persist. Since there is no clear set of policies that ensure price stability and despite attempts to implement price controls in almost every sector by the public, it is not possible for such measures to be successful in free market conditions, and as a matter of fact, prices are constantly increasing. As can be seen in Figure 6.3, the inflation rate has started to rise since the CBRT interest rates started to decline, and it has not yet been effectively brought under control.

However, the state's effort to control prices has detrimental effects on the public budget. Moreover, attempts to suppress prices result in increased costs and much higher price increases after a while. Furthermore, policies aimed at mitigating the

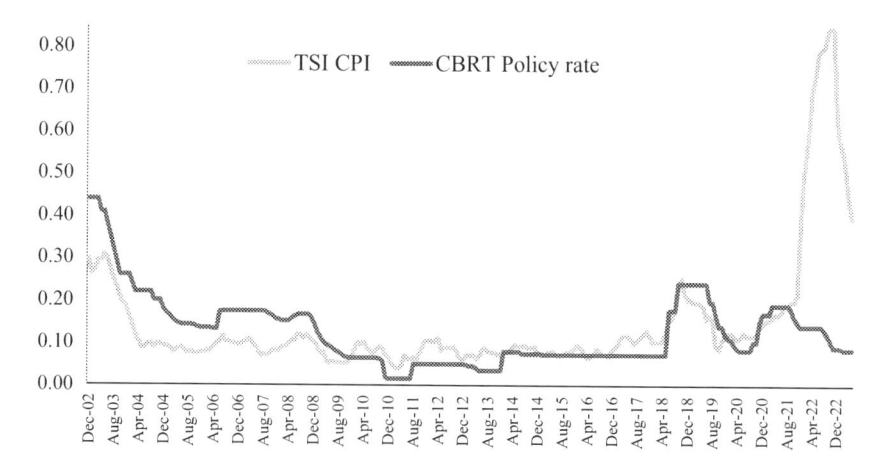

Figure 6.3 Central Bank Policy Rates and Inflation Rates (December 2002–May 2023).

Source: Author's original representation. The data in the figure was collected from the Central Bank Interest Rates and Electronic Data Delivery System (EDDS) of CBRT.

rapid decline in the purchasing power of households (minimum wage hikes, civil servant/retiree hikes, tax reductions) not only increase the burden on the budget but also contribute to inflation through increased demand, labor costs, and monetary expansion. This has resulted in many things being indexed to past inflation.

Inconsistency is another dimension of the issue. Initially, it is stated that the exchange rate level is not taken into account (Kavcıoğlu, 2023), but, later, intense interventions in the market are made to suppress the exchange rate. After a while, it is announced that the only responsible party for the exchange rate imbalances and the implementation of non-raising practices increases uncertainties. This lack of predictability and the environment of insecurity hinder effective measures. Therefore, despite all the measures taken,[1] the demand for foreign currency continues. This situation increases inflation due to the rise in exchange rates and also amplifies the risk of hyperinflation due to the deteriorating inflation expectations. Dollarization plays a significant role in this problem, and the country experiences increased dollarization through currency-protected deposit (CPD)–type products (see Figure 6.4). While CPDs are presented as products designed for converting foreign currency to TL, they actually increase the foreign currency dependency of individuals, since the returns are determined according to exchange rate changes and include TL savings. As a matter of fact, the CBRT acknowledges the effects of reverse currency substitution and continues to implement necessary policy measures to address the issue, as stated in the Summary of the CBRT Monetary Policy Committee meeting dated May 25, 2023 (CBRT, 2023).

One important aspect of the issues at hand is that the country's foreign exchange reserves are depleted to a large extent (see Figure 6.5) to suppress the exchange rate increase and the country's reliance on currency-protected instruments that impose exchange rate risks on the government to discourage the public from turning to

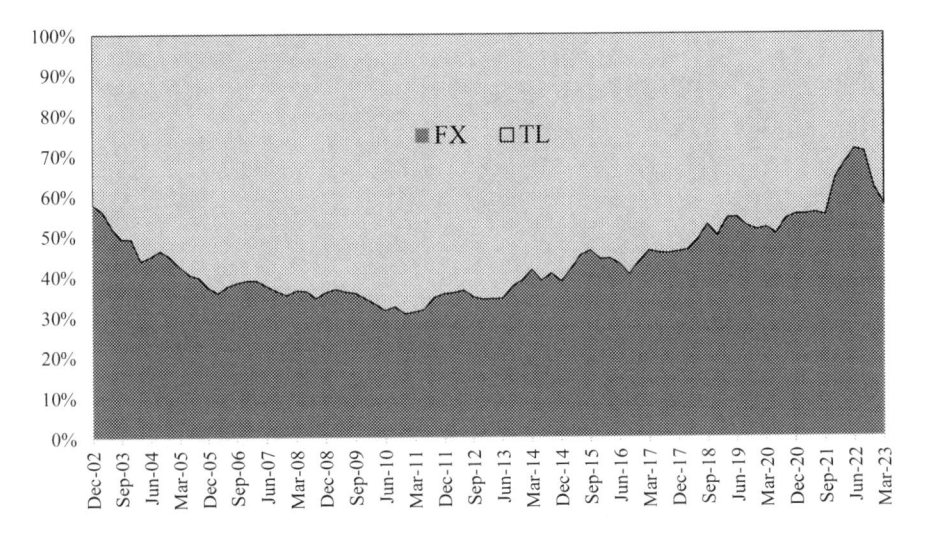

Figure 6.4 TL–FX Distribution of Deposits in the Turkish Banking Sector (December 2002–March 2023).

Source: Author's original representation. The data in the figure was collected from The Statistical Reports of BAT and PBT.

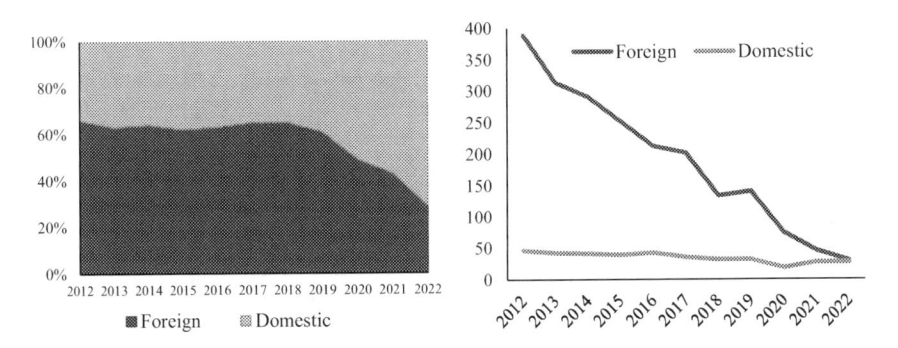

Figure 6.5 Foreign Portfolio Investor Ratio and Retention Periods (Days) (December 2012–December 2022).

Source: Author's original representation. The data in the figure was collected from The Stock Market Trends Reports of TÜYİD between 2013 and 2022.

foreign currency assets. The cost figures associated with these efforts undertaken by the CBRT are not disclosed, but the cost incurred by the Republic of Turkey Ministry of Treasury and Finance is USD 5.6 billion in total for the year 2022 and the first four months of 2023 (RTMTF).

In addition, the CBRT tries to gather foreign currency using unconventional methods to strengthen its foreign exchange reserves. However, the loss of confidence in the management of the economy and institutions, particularly the CBRT, reduces hopes for the implementation of policies that will prevent deterioration in inflation and reinforces the perception of the inflationary spiral. Consequently, the loss of confidence in TL instruments has led to a significant decrease in foreign shares in financial markets at an unprecedented level,[2] and their holding period has declined to less than one month.

As the country's foreign exchange reserves reached critical levels in 2022 and 2023, the Central Bank implemented numerous measures to alter the nature of foreign exchange control. The main measures included the following:

- CPD application,
- A very high provision requirement for foreign currency deposit accounts at the CBRT,
- High taxation in foreign exchange trading,
- The requirement to sell a certain percentage of export revenues to the CBRT,
- Making it mandatory to keep the trading price margin in exchange rates very high,
- Interventions in exchange rates by the Central Bank and public banks,
- Multiple exchange rate system, and
- Permission requirement for foreign exchange transactions above a certain amount.

Figure 6.6 demonstrates that the exchange rate experienced a significant increase following the interest rate cuts. Although it temporarily subsided with the introduction of CPD, it subsequently resumed its upward trajectory.

In reality, a notable portion of the measures implemented following the policy shift in 2022 have been focused on exerting downward pressure on the exchange rate. For this purpose, the CBRT has primarily utilized its reserves. As a result, the CBRT's reserves have significantly decreased, particularly in recent times. As illustrated in Figure 6.7, the latest net central bank reserves have reached negative values, and net reserves excluding swaps have approached minus USD 60 billion.

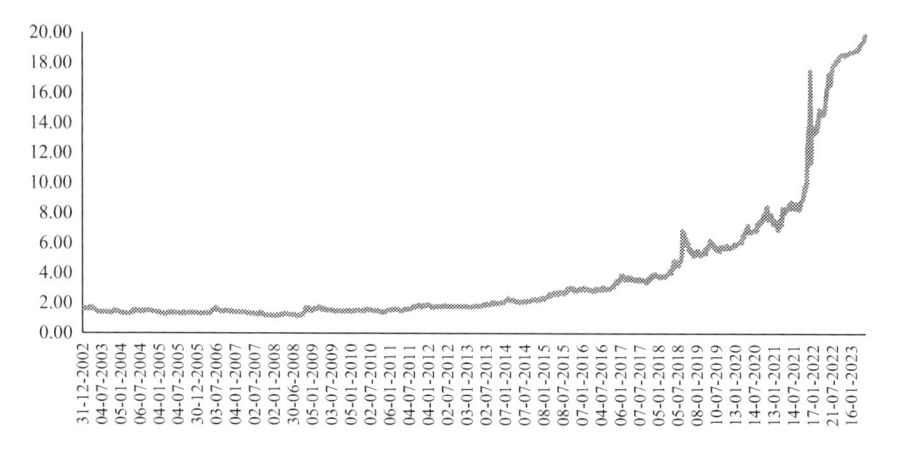

Figure 6.6 TL-USD Exchange Rate Change in Türkiye (December 2002–May 2023).

Source: Author's original representation. The data in the figure was collected from EVDS of CBRT.

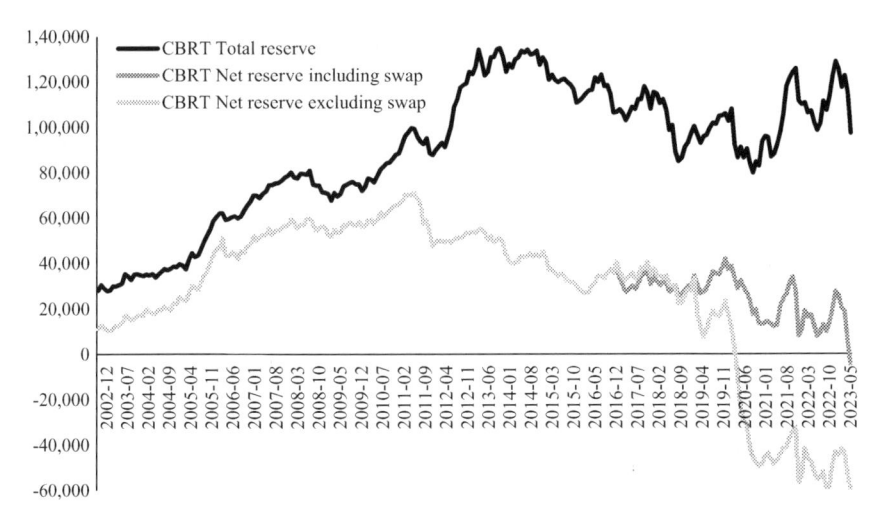

Figure 6.7 Development of Central Bank Reserves by Years (Million USD) (December 2002–May 2023).

Source: Author's original representation. The data in the figure was collected from EVDS of CBRT.

One of the shortcomings of the attempted model is its assumption that exchange rates are the sole determinant of the size of exports and imports. However, it is well-established in the international trade literature that export growth is closely linked to productivity and innovation as much as the exchange rate advantage (Erer & Erer, 2020). Although a depreciation in the exchange rate may provide some marginal benefits in sectoral export volumes, a long-term devaluation of the currency can negatively affect the production structure. In addition, the heavy reliance on imported raw materials and intermediate goods[3] in domestic production undermines the expected foreign trade and current account surplus from the exchange rate advantage. Contrary to the model's ambitious aim of achieving a current account surplus, both the foreign trade deficit and the current account deficit have gradually increased (see Figure 6.8). As new capital inflows could not be ensured, a part of the deficit has been financed through the CBRT reserves. The improvement in the net errors and omissions item in the figure is also remarkable. This account, which records foreign currencies of unknown origin, has maintained a high balance and has played a role in offsetting the current account deficit.

Merely attributing the rise in investments and achievement of growth solely to low interest rates oversimplifies the complex nature of the issue. Factors that will increase investments, which play a crucial role in achieving stable growth, are influenced by various factors besides low interest rates. One significant factor is the increase in predictability, that is, the decrease in uncertainties (Bloom, 2014). Firms tend to become more cautious in their employment decisions and prioritize labor-saving measures in times of increased uncertainty (Altig et al., 2020).

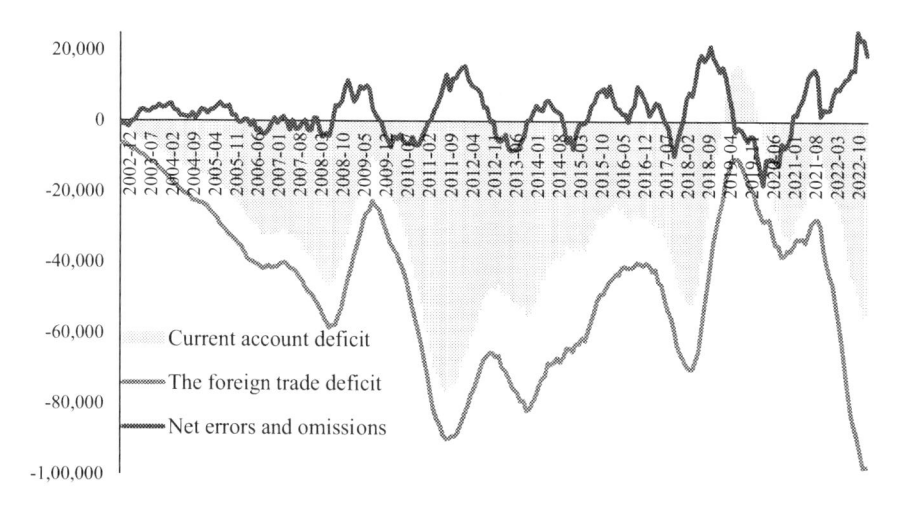

Figure 6.8 Balance of Payments (Million USD) (December 2002–March 2023).

Source: Author's original representation. The data in the figure was collected from EVDS of CBRT.

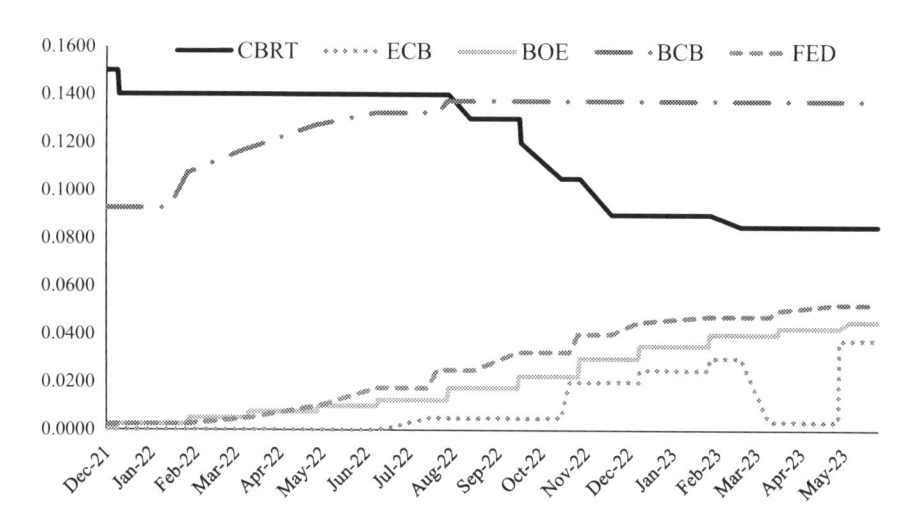

Figure 6.9 Interest Rates of Some Central Banks (December 2021–May 2023).

Source: Author's original representation. The data in the figure was collected from https://tr.investing. com/central-banks/.

Note: CBRT: The Central Bank of The Republic of Türkiye, ECB: The European Central Bank, BOE: Bank of England, BCB: Banco Central do Brazil, FED: Federal Reserve System.

In the present global environment, the persistent decrease in the CBRT's policy rate has exacerbated the adverse effects. As central banks, particularly those in developed countries, respond to inflation risks by increasing policy rates (see Figure 6.9) and tightening monetary policies, the CBRT's reduction in interest rates has made the TL completely vulnerable.

As a result, the country's credit ratings have been substantially downgraded by global rating agencies and the country's risk premiums have escalated to levels comparable to those of the most vulnerable nations. This raises substantial concerns regarding debt sustainability. In recent times, Türkiye's ratings have dropped significantly, and it has ceased to be an investment-grade country (see Table 6.1).

Table 6.1 Credit Ratings of Türkiye as of Year End (2002–May 2023)

Agency	Rating	Outlook	Date	Agency	Rating	Outlook	Date
S&P	B–	Stable	November 7, 2002	Moody's	Baa3	Stable	May 16, 2013
Moody's	B1	Stable	October 21, 2003	S&P	BB+	Negative	February 7, 2014
S&P	B+	Stable	October 16, 2003	Moody's	Baa3	Negative	April 11, 2014
Fitch	B	Positive	September 25, 2003	S&P	BB	Stable	November 4, 2016
Fitch	B+	Positive	August 25, 2004	Fitch	BBB–	Negative	August 19, 2016
Fitch	B+	Stable	February 9, 2004	S&P	BB	Negative	July 20, 2016
S&P	BB–	Stable	August 17, 2004	Moody's	Ba1	Stable	September 23, 2016
Moody's	Ba3	Stable	Dec 14 2005	S&P	BB	Negative	January 27, 2017
Fitch	BB–	Positive	December 6, 2005	Fitch	BB+	Stable	January 27, 2017
Moody's	B1	Positive	February 11, 2005	Moody's	Ba1	Negative	March 17, 2017
S&P	BB–	Stable	June 27, 2006	Fitch	BB	Negative	July 13, 2018
Fitch	BB–	Stable	May 9, 2007	Moody's	Ba3	Negative	August 17, 2018
S&P	BB–	Negative	November 13, 2008	S&P	B+	Stable	August 17, 2018
Fitch	BB+	Stable	December 3, 2009	Fitch	BB–	Stable	November 1, 2019
S&P	BB–	Stable	September 17, 2009	Moody's	B1	Negative	June 14, 2019
Moody's	Ba3	Positive	September 18, 2009	Fitch	BB–	Negative	August 21, 2020
Fitch	BB+	Positive	November 24, 2010	Moody's	B2	Negative	September 11, 2020
Moody's	Ba2	Positive	October 5, 2010	S&P	B+	Negative	December 10, 2021
S&P	BB	Positive	February 19, 2010	Fitch	BB–	Negative	December 2, 2021
Fitch	BB+	Stable	November 23, 2011	Fitch	B	Negative	July 8, 2022
S&P	BB	Stable	May 1, 2012	Moody's	B3	Stable	August 12, 2022

(Continued)

Table 6.1 (Continued)

Agency	Rating	Outlook	Date	Agency	Rating	Outlook	Date
Moody's	Ba1	Positive	June 20, 2012	S&P	B	Stable	September 30, 2022
Fitch	BBB–	Stable	November 5, 2012	S&P	B	Negative	March 31, 2023
S&P	BB+	Stable	March 27, 2013				

Source: Author's original representation. The data in the table were collected from https://tr.tradingeconomics.com/turkey/rating.

Keeping the policy rate low with an irrational (or empirical) approach has increased the short-term and long-term borrowing rates of the Treasury. As explained in the next section, the provision of low-interest loans to specific sectors through public banks and pressure on private banks have increased the risks in the banking sector and losses in public banks' operations. Setting the policy rate at an incorrect level caused the policy rate to become dysfunctional in monetary transmission. This caused interest rates in the banking sector to deviate from the policy rate, leading to increased loan and deposit rates despite attempts to keep them low. This has given rise to multiple interest rate markets.

The new economic model and the Turkish banking sector

In an economy that claims to be closely connected with the global economy, there have been instances where decisions have been made that go against global trends and, at times, even contradict one another. Since it is not possible for these decisions to function autonomously in a market economy, many new decisions have been made since September 2021 to support the model. These decisions are aimed at forcing specific segments to ensure the realization of the assumptions rather than rectifying the flawed aspects of the model. Therefore, while some decisions were intended to regulate the market, the vast majority of them compelled economic actors to behave in a particular manner. The banking sector has been particularly targeted by these decisions, considering its dominant position in the finance sector in Türkiye (82%[4]).

The decisions taken that impact the banking sector can be summarized as follows:

- CPD application,
- Central Bank policy rate changes,
- Inflation-indexed securities,
- Pressures on regulation and implementation regarding deposit and loan sizes and interest rates,
- Applications for foreign exchange transactions, and
- Not applying inflation accounting.

While some of these measures provided periodic advantages to the banks, others forced them to act against their will. As a result, there were significant temporary increases in banks' profits in 2022. The main factors contributing to this increase include the following:

- Providing a cost advantage by transferring some of the deposit costs to the government with the exchange-protected deposit application,
- Decrease in borrowing costs from the CBRT due to the decrease in policy rates,
- Increasing the margin between loan and deposit interest rates,
- On the deposit side, pressure on banks not to raise interest rates on deposits in response to high inflation,
- Increase in the returns of the inflation-indexed public debt securities held by the banks due to rising inflation,
- Especially private banks' being in closed foreign exchange (FX) positions and gaining value due to the depreciation of TL, and
- Improvement in the performance of the banking sector, which had low-profit figures in 2021, making it appear to have a significantly high-profit growth rate in 2022 (base effect).

Table 6.2 illustrates the development of the profitability of the sector over the years. As can be seen in the table, net interest income was the primary factor contributing to the banking sector's profitability in 2022.

Currency-protected deposit application

One of the reasons for the increase in profitability of banks in the last two years is the implementation of CPD. CPD is a banking instrument that individuals can choose in lieu of foreign currency deposits, with the government guaranteeing the difference if the foreign currency exceeds the determined interest rate against the TL at maturity. TL savings holders can also benefit from this product by indexing their money to foreign currency. The amount in the CPD accounts reached 2.5 trillion TL (USD 125.3 billion) by the week of May 26, 2023, since the implementation started in late December 2021. Initially, the interest rate applied by the banks on these accounts was up to three points above the maximum central bank policy rate. The difference in the exchange rate increase beyond this rate was covered by the state. Due to the low policy rate set by the central bank, banks applied low interest rates to these accounts, providing them with a significant cost advantage by shifting a portion of the resource cost to the state. However, at the end of January 2023 for foreign currency conversion accounts, and at the end of March 2023 for accounts with TL conversions, the interest ceiling on these accounts was abolished. With the removal of the interest ceiling, the interest rates applied by the banks to these accounts have considerably increased. Consequently, the advantage of this tool, which played an important role in bank profitability in 2022, diminished.

However, the release of interest rates led to an acceleration in the share of CPD accounts in total deposits. The development of the CPD share in total deposits is

Table 6.2 Banking Sector Income and Expense Development (December 2018–December 2022)

All Banking Sector

Million TL	2018	2019	Chg. %	2020	Chg. %	2021	Chg. %	2022	Chg. %
Interest income	372,930.7	426,241.2	14.3	429,072.3	0.7	646,381.7	50.6	1,416,505	119.1
Interest expenses	222,621.7	258,337	16.0	209,035.4	−19.1	375,436.7	79.6	639,392.5	70.3
Net interest income	150,309	167,904.2	11.7	220,037	31.0	270,945	23.1	777,112.3	186.8
Non-interest income	4,706,180	3,348,132	−28.9	4,438,169	32.6	1,294,0870	191.6	9,470,841	−26.8
Non-interest expenses	4,802,157	3,466,993	−27.8	4,597,221	32.6	13,118,863	185.4	9,816,537	−25.2
Net non-interest income	−95,977	−118,862	23.8	−159,053	33.8	−177,993	11.9	−345,696	94.2
Net profit/losses	54,332.08	49,042.69	−9.7	60,984.42	24.3	92,951.6	52.4	431,416.3	364.1
Exchange rate	5.281	5.94		7.4194		13.329		18.6983	

Million USD	2018	2019	Chg. %	2020	Chg. %	2021	Chg. %	2022	Chg. %
Interest income	70,617	71,758	1.6	57,831	−19.4	48,494	−16.1	75,756	56.2
Interest expenses	42,155	43,491	3.2	28,174	−35.2	28,167	0.0	34,195	21.4
Net interest income	28,462	28,267	−0.7	29,657	4.9	20,327	−31.5	41,561	104.5
Non-interest income	891,153	563,659	−36.7	598,184	6.1	970,881	62.3	506,508	−47.8
Non-interest expenses	909,327	583,669	−35.8	619,622	6.2	984,235	58.8	524,996	−46.7
Net non-interest income	−18,174	−20,010	10.1	−21,437	7.1	−13,354	−37.7	−18,488	38.4
Net profit/losses	10,288	8,256	−19.7	8,220	−0.4	6,974	−15.2	23,072	230.9

Source: Author's original representation. The data in the table was collected from Statistical Reports of BAT.

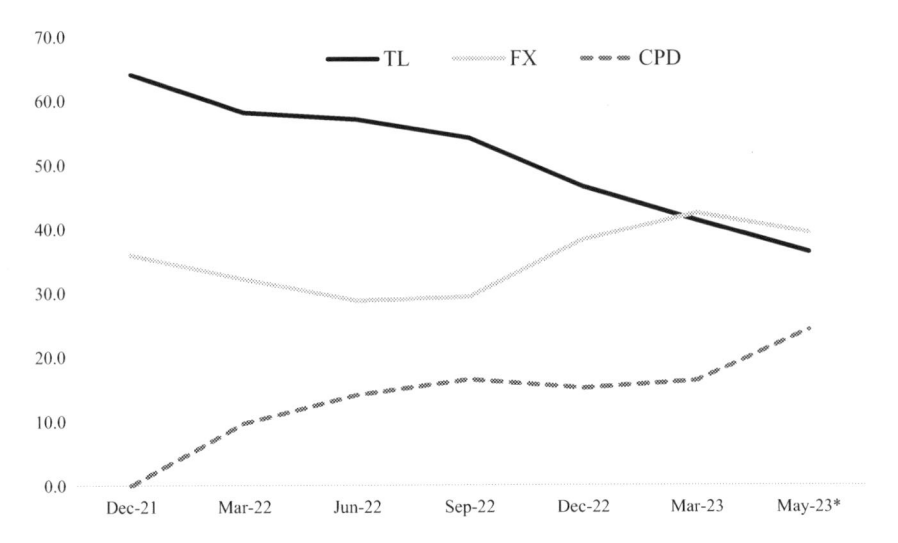

Figure 6.10 Distribution of Total Deposits in TL, FX and CPD (December 2021–May 2023).

Source: Author's original representation. The data in the figure (except CPD) was collected from Statistical Reports of BAT and PBT. All CPD data was collected from the weekly statistical bulletin of the BRSA.

Note: *The data for May was collected from the weekly statistical bulletin of the BRSA.

displayed in Figure 6.10. Since the CPD product has reached a share of more than 20% in total deposits in approximately 1.5 years since its inception, it becomes more challenging to liquidate this product in the future. This product, based on FX-indexed returns, is still encouraged by the economy management, and it appears to present a future issue for both the economy management and the banks.

As depicted in Figure 6.10, while the share of CPDs in total deposits is increasing, the share of both FX deposits and TL deposits is decreasing. However, since the return on CPDs is indexed to the change in exchange rates, they need to be treated like FX. Therefore, if FX deposits and foreign currency-indexed CPD are combined, their share exceeds 60%.

The CBRT's low-interest policy implementation

Another factor contributing to the increased profitability of banks is the policy rate set by the CBRT. As previously mentioned, the new economic model is based on the assumption that high interest rates are the source of various unfavorable outcomes, particularly inflation. In line with this assumption, the CBRT has started to reduce the policy rate as of September 2021, and the policy rate has remained well below the inflation rate since then (see Figure 6.3). Although this situation has had a negative impact on the country's economy, it has been advantageous for banks. In an environment where inflation reached triple digits in 2022, banks obtained funds from the CBRT at a significantly lower interest rate compared to the prevailing inflation rate. Subsequently, they channeled these funds toward the government domestic debt securities with high interest rates or provided loans to individuals at high interest rates, particularly during the first six months of the year. As a result, banks generated significant profits from these transactions in 2022. In 2023, policy rates will still remain far behind the inflation rate. Although the profitability of banks has been impacted by other factors in 2022, this particular factor continues to contribute to their profitability.

The height of the margin between deposit and loan rates and the CBRT's directions for banks' deposit and loan practices

Another factor influencing the profitability of the banking sector is the margin between loan and deposit interest rates. With the introduction of products such as CPD in 2022, banks converted the time deposits they collected at an average interest rate of less than 20% into loans with an average interest rate of 30%. This high margin has played a crucial role in the profitability of banks. However, despite the upward trend in interest rates on time deposits that started at the end of 2022, it is observed that the loan interest rates offered by banks are lagging behind. This can be attributed to the CBRT's regulation requiring banks to purchase low-interest government domestic debt securities in case loan interest rates exceed certain thresholds. Consequently, it is observed that the increase in time deposit costs that began at the end of 2022 has continued into 2023. As a result, the deposit–credit margin of banks reversed with the CBRT regulations (see Figure 6.11). This situation has had a negative impact on the profitability of banks this year.

In the first half of 2022, demand deposits played a significant role in the profitability of banks. Banks do not pay interest on demand deposits. The share of demand

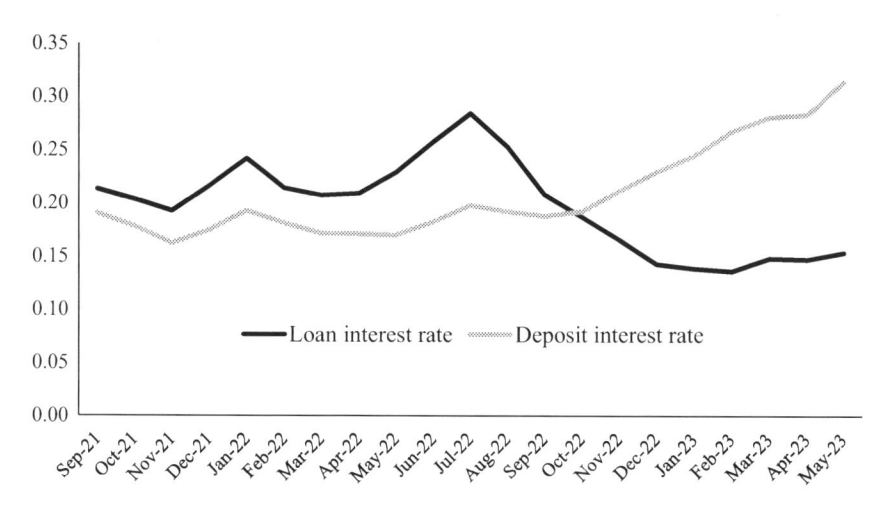

Figure 6.11 Development of Banking Sector Deposit and Loan Interest Rates (September 2021–May 2023).

Source: Author's original representation. The data in the figure was collected from EVDS of CBRT.

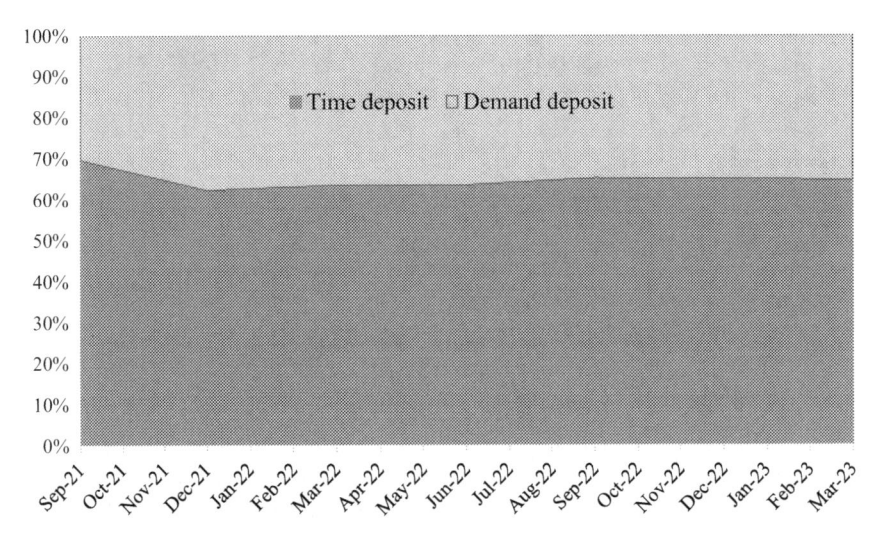

Figure 6.12 Distribution of Demand Deposits and Time Deposits in Banks (September 2021–March 2023).

Source: Author's original representation. The data in the figure was collected from Statistical Reports of BAT and PBT.

deposits in total deposits is around 35%, and this ratio has remained relatively stable in 2022 (see Figure 6.12). In 2023, this rate will remain at approximately the same level. Therefore, the average cost of deposits for banks remains lower. This factor, which has significantly reduced the cost of resources, has also made a substantial contribution to their profitability. It is expected that this factor will continue to contribute to profitability this year as well.

With the effect of this pressure, banks maintained their deposit interest rates at 18% in the first half of the year, allowing them to keep their costs low. However, since the end of 2022 and continuing to the present, there has been a notable rise in deposit rates, as illustrated in Figure 6.11. This rise can be attributed to the challenges faced by banks in retaining deposits amid the prolonged period of low interest rates.

Inflation-indexed securities

One of the primary factors contributing to the significant increase in bank profitability is the presence of inflation-indexed securities in their portfolios. Banks have long-term CPI-indexed securities that they have previously purchased. As illustrated in Figure 6.3, the CPI reached 80% in 2022 with the official figures and closed the year at 64%. Therefore, in this environment, taking into account their low resource costs mentioned earlier, banks made a much higher profit than before the CPI-indexed securities. In 2023, inflation continues to decline due to the base effect. As of May 2023, the inflation rate had decreased to 39.6%. Despite this decline, banks continue to generate profits, although not as much as in the previous year. However, once the base effect diminishes in the second half of the year, there is a possibility that inflation rates may rise again. If this scenario occurs, the income from these inflation-indexed securities may increase further.

Foreign exchange transactions and developments in exchange rates

Foreign exchange profits resulting from developments in exchange rates are another important factor contributing to the increase in bank profits. This factor can be analyzed from two different perspectives. First, in recent times, banks have expanded their margins in foreign exchange purchases and sales, as directed by the government to reduce the demand for foreign currency. The trading margin, which was previously around 0.01%–0.02%, increased to a range of 0.03%–0.05% in 2022. Considering that the demand for foreign currency did not decrease in this period, the higher trading margin contributed to the banks' increased profit. It is seen that this margin has increased to 5% in 2023 with the guidance of the CBRT. Although this directive to restrict the buying and selling of foreign currency by banks in practice limits the purchase of foreign currency, banks still generate significant profits from their transactions due to the margin.

The second aspect of the increase in profits due to exchange rates is related to the foreign exchange positions of the banks. Banks generally held long positions, albeit limited in size, in the first half of the year (see Figure 6.13).

Considering the upward trend of the TL/USD rate in 2022 (see Figure 6.14), banks were able to generate profits from their long positions in foreign exchange. However, as exchange rates have followed a more horizontal trajectory in 2023, their profits in this area have become more limited.

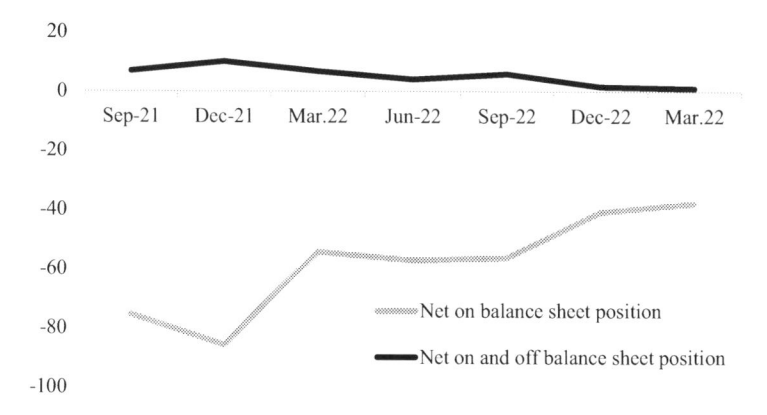

Figure 6.13 FX Positions of Banks (September 2021–March 2023).

Source: Author's original representation. The data in the figure was collected from Statistical Reports of BAT.

Note: Participation banks aren't included.

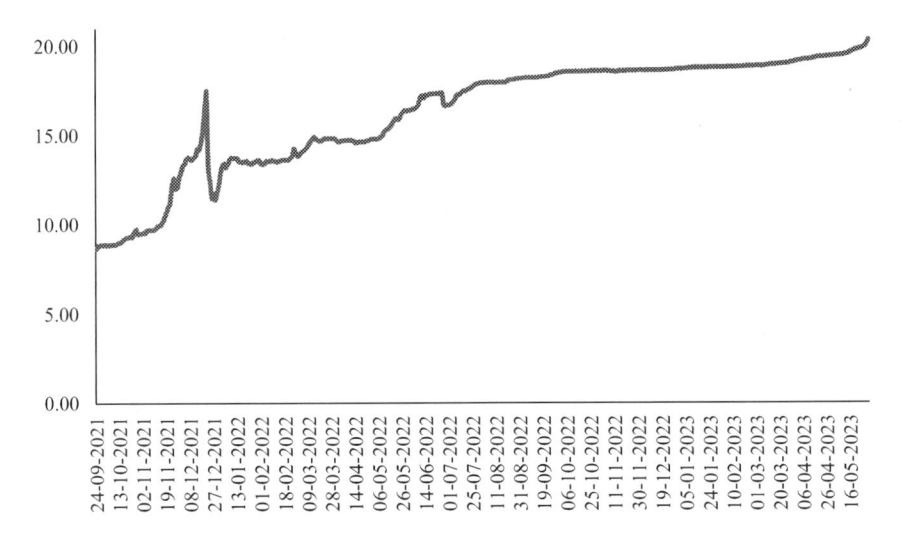

Figure 6.14 Development of Exchange Rates (September 24, 2021–May 31, 2023).

Source: Author's original representation. The data in the figure was collected from EVDS of CBRT.

Effect of high inflation on profits and failure to apply inflation accounting

In 2022, the banking sector's profitability appears to have increased by 230.9% compared to 2021 (Table 6.2). One reason that banks seem to have made exceptionally high profits and experienced a substantial increase in profitability in 2022 is the significantly high inflation rate. Figure 6.15 presents the inflation rate measurements from three different institutions in Türkiye. The Turkish Statistical Institute (TSI) is the government agency responsible for providing official statistical data, while the Istanbul Chamber of Commerce (ICC-İTO) is a professional organization that calculates inflation specifically for Istanbul, Türkiye's largest metropolitan city. The Inflation Research Group (ENAG), on the contrary, is a group of economists that conducts inflation research using various data and provides inflation calculations and explanations for Türkiye. As depicted in the figure, the inflation figures reported by these three institutions are quite different from each other. According to ENAG, the inflation rate in 2022 is 137.5%. If we take into account these high inflation rates when assessing the profitability increases of banks, the rate of increase rate is relatively lower.

One important aspect to consider is the high inflation rate experienced in Türkiye in 2022, which has continued to persist. During periods of significant inflation, it becomes crucial for all businesses, including banks, to incorporate inflation accounting into their balance sheets. This adjustment is essential to ensure greater accuracy and realism in reflecting the impact of inflation on their financial positions. Despite the high inflation in Türkiye, inflation accounting has not been applied in accounting practices. However, the application of inflation accounting would enable a more accurate representation of the real situation of banks. As a result, since

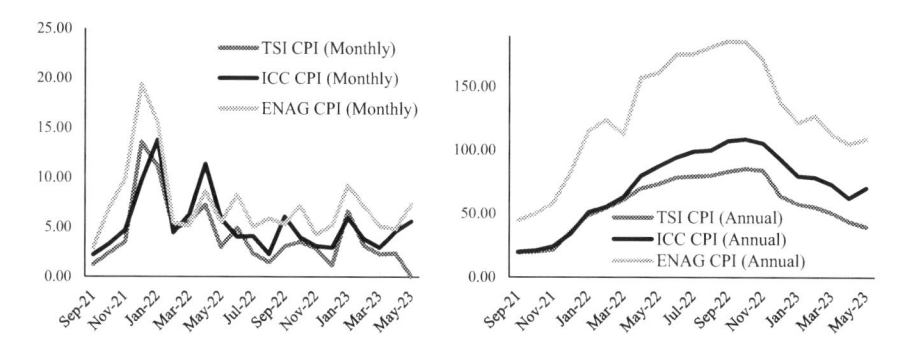

Figure 6.15 Development of Inflation Rates by TSI, ITO (ICC) and ENAG (September 2021–May 2023).

Source: Author's original representation. The data in the figure was collected from TSI, ITO, ENAG.

the announced figures are often provided without adjusting for inflation, they may not fully reflect the truth on paper, and this situation continues to persist.

Base effect

The base effect in 2022 is another factor that contributes to the appearance of high-profit growth for banks. In 2021, the banking sector, especially the public banks, faced challenges in terms of profitability due to various factors, including the pandemic. Consequently, profit figures were lower that year. However, in 2022, with the effect of the factors mentioned earlier, banks increased their profitability. Therefore, when the profit figures for 2022 are compared with the previous year, we observe high-profit growth figures. However, in 2023, this trend is expected to reverse.

Return on equity

The banking sector profitability analysis conducted so far has primarily focused on growth rates and volume. However, taking a broader perspective by considering not only growth rates and quantity but also fundamental profitability ratios and comparing them with various macroeconomic indicators can lead to different outcomes. As in all sectors, profitability ratios are crucial in assessing the performance of the banking sector. The most important ratio among these is the return on equity[5] (ROE).

According to the data from The Bank Association of Türkiye (BAT), as of the end of 2022, the banking sector's ROE stood at 37.66%. Meanwhile, the annual inflation rate is 64.27%. Therefore, although the profits of banks may appear high, the ROE they have generated falls significantly behind the inflation rate. This disparity is clearly illustrated in Figure 6.16. Although the sector's profit figure may initially seem favorable, it remains considerably low when compared to the rate of change in inflation.

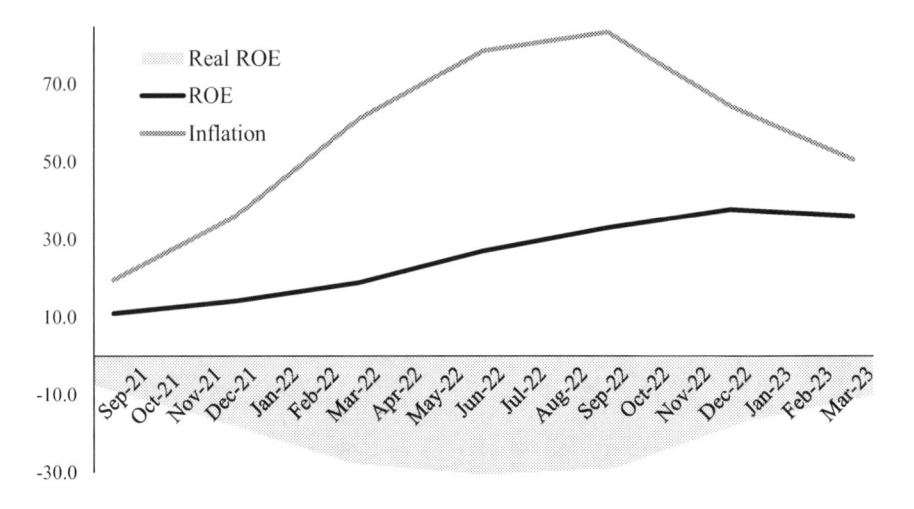

Figure 6.16 ROE of the Banking Sector (September 2021–March 2023).

Source: Author's original representation. The data in the figure was collected from Statistical Reports of BAT and EVDS of CBRT

Note: Participation banks aren't included.

Conclusion

The implementation of the new economic model over the course of 1.5 years has plunged Türkiye into a perilous journey. The decisions made within this framework primarily targeted the banking sector, consequently inflicting the most significant impact on it. When assessing the overall condition of the sector in 2023, there exists a potential for diminished or stagnant profits, despite their initial appearance of being high. Several factors contribute to this possibility, including:

- Loss of cost advantage in CPDs.
- Increasing deposit costs.
- Pressure on banks not to increase loan interest rates.
- Low-interest loan portfolios provided by the sector, especially public banks, in the past.
  - Loss of fixed-income securities in banks' portfolios in the face of possible interest rate increases.
- The decrease in inflation due to the base effect reduces the return on inflation-indexed securities.
- Increase in operational costs due to high inflation rates (high rate of increase in personnel expenses, etc.).

Despite appearing to have ended 2022 on a positive note in terms of profitability, the banking sector's actions and overall developments have actually resulted in the accumulation of future risks for the sector and the economy as a whole.

These risks primarily include interest rate risk, exchange rate risk, liquidity risk due to maturity mismatch, and accumulated credit risk. It can be observed that bank balance sheets have become excessively fragile due to the risks they carry. The extent to which the risks will be realized will depend on the policies implemented in the upcoming period.

Notes

1 The CBRT set the target for the share of TL deposits in total deposits (TL Deposit/Total Deposit≥) as 50% for 2022 and 60% for the first half of 2023.
2 Foreign portfolio investor net inflow/output: USD 5.4 billion inflow in 2012, USD 0.4 billion outflow in 2013, USD 2.3 billion inflow in 2014, USD 2.5 billion outflow in 2015, USD 0.7 billion inflow in 2016, USD 1.8 billion inflows in 2017, USD 2 billion outflows in 2018, USD 0.6 billion outflows in 2019, USD 4.6 billion outflows in 2020, USD 1.6 billion outflows in 2021, 4 in 2022, USD 5 billion output (Stock Market Trends Reports of TUYID between 2013 and 2022).
3 The content of Turkish exports based on foreign raw materials and intermediate goods is above the G20 average (OECD, Trade in Value Added, 1).
4 The data were retrieved from Banks in Türkiye 2021 (data as of 09.2021).
5 Average Return on Shareholders' Equity (ROE) = The Sum of Net Profit (Loss) for the last four individual quarters (year-end Net Profit (Loss) for Decembers)/Average of "Total Shareholders' Equity" for the past four quarters.

References

Akalın, G., & Tokucu, E. (2007). Kurala dayalı-takdire dayalı para politikaları: Taylor kuralı ve Türkiye'de enflasyon hedeflemesi uygulaması. *Marmara Üniversitesi İktisadi ve İdari Bilimler Dergisi*, 22(1), 37–55.

Akıncı, M., & Yılmaz, Ö. (2016). Enflasyon-faiz oranı takası: Fisher hipotezi bağlamında Türkiye ekonomisi için dinamik en küçük kareler yöntemi. *Sosyoekonomi*, 24(27), 33–55. https://doi.org/10.17233/se.81444

Alçam, E. (2003). *Fisher Etkisi ve Türkiye'de Geçerliliğinin sınanması* (Yayımlanmamış yüksek lisans tezi). İstanbul: Marmara Üniversitesi Sosyal Bilimler Enstitüsü.

Altig, D., Baker, D., Barrero, J.M., Bloom, N, Bunn, P., Chen, S., … Thwaites, G. (2020). Economic uncertainty before and during the COVID-19 pandemic. *Journal of Public Economics*, 191(2020), 104274. https://doi.org/10.1016/j.jpubeco.2020.104274

Atbaşı, R. (2019). *Türkiye ekonomisinde kur, faiz ve enflasyon ilişkisi üzerine ampirik bir uygulama* (Yayımlanmamış yüksek lisans tezi). Sakarya: Sakarya Üniversitesi Sosyal Bilimler Enstitüsü.

Baktemur, F.İ. (2021). Enflasyon ile faiz oranları arasındaki doğrusal olmayan nedensellik ilişkisi: Türkiye örneği. *İstanbul Ticaret Üniversitesi Sosyal Bilimler Dergisi*, 20(42), 1147–1158. https://doi.org/10.46928/iticusbe.799437

Banking Regulation and Supervision Agency (BRSA). *Monthly Banking Sector Data* [Dataset]. Retrieved from https://www.bddk.org.tr/BultenAylik/en

Banking Regulation and Supervision Agency (BRSA). *Weekly Banking Sector Data* [Dataset]. Retrieved from https://www.bddk.org.tr/BultenHaftalik/en

Beyer, A., Haug, A., & Dewald, W.G. (2009). *Structural Breaks Cointegration and the Fisher Effect* (European Central Bank Working Paper Series No 1013). Retrieved from https://www.ecb.europa.eu//pub/pdf/scpwps/ecbwp1013.pdf

BIS. (2022). *II. Inflation: A Look Under the Hood* (BIS Annual Economic Report 2022). Retrieved from https://www.bis.org/publ/arpdf/ar2022e2.pdf

Bloom, N. (2014). Fluctuations in uncertainty. *Journal of Economic Perspectives,* 28(2), 153–176. https://doi:10.1257/jep.28.2.153

CBRT. (2003). *General Framework of the Monetary and Exchange Rate Policy in 2003* (CBRT Monetary Policy and Liraization Strategy Text, Number: 2003–2). Retrieved from https://www.tcmb.gov.tr/wps/wcm/connect/eea70927-4238-437d-a94d-0a94dd36fe9c/ANO2003-2.pdf?MOD=AJPERES&CACHEID=ROOTWORKSPACE-eea70927-4238-437d-a94d-0a94dd36fe9c-m4ucbbf

CBRT. (2004). *General Framework of the Monetary and Exchange Rate Policy in 2004* (CBRT Monetary Policy and Liraization Strategy Text, Number: 2004–2). Retrieved from https://www.tcmb.gov.tr/wps/wcm/connect/e7c7ca63-64db-4df7-bfb1-b4ecfe1bea40/ANO2004-2.pdf?MOD=AJPERES&CACHEID=ROOTWORKSPACE-e7c7ca63-64db-4df7-bfb1-b4ecfe1bea40-m4ucb7J

CBRT. (2005). *General Framework of Inflation Targeting Regime and Monetary and Exchange Rate Policy for 2006* (CBRT Monetary Policy and Liraization Strategy Text, Number: 2005–45). Retrieved from https://www.tcmb.gov.tr/wps/wcm/connect/93ebd346-2e3a-4fcd-a24c-25276ea7a01a/ANO2005-45.pdf?MOD=AJPERES&CACHEID=ROOTWORKSPACE-93ebd346-2e3a-4fcd-a24c-25276ea7a01a-m4ucb0p

CBRT. (2006). *Monetary and Exchange Rate Policy for 2007* (CBRT Monetary Policy and Liraization Strategy Text). Retrieved from https://www.tcmb.gov.tr/wps/wcm/connect/309bff4b-862f-4ffb-88e6-e8ffb7621075/2007MonPol.pdf?MOD=AJPERES&CACHEID=ROOTWORKSPACE-309bff4b-862f-4ffb-88e6-e8ffb7621075-m4ucaZ1

CBRT. (2008). *Monetary and Exchange Rate Policy for 2009* (CBRT Monetary Policy and Liraization Strategy Text). Retrieved from https://www.tcmb.gov.tr/wps/wcm/connect/68c4b61d-653a-41fd-a6ec-4a6297fe1c36/Mon_Exc_Pol_2009.pdf?MOD=AJPERES&CACHEID=ROOTWORKSPACE-68c4b61d-653a-41fd-a6ec-4a6297fe1c36-m4ucaP7

CBRT. (2009). *Monetary and Exchange Rate Policy for 2010* (CBRT Monetary Policy and Liraization Strategy Text). Retrieved from https://www.tcmb.gov.tr/wps/wcm/connect/423eca2c-e05d-4030-9a75-c84cad1e51ed/Mon_Exc_Pol_2010.pdf?MOD=AJPERES&CACHEID=ROOTWORKSPACE-423eca2c-e05d-4030-9a75-c84cad1e51ed-m4ucaLK

CBRT. (2010). *Monetary and Exchange Rate Policy for 2011* (CBRT Monetary Policy and Liraization Strategy Text). Retrieved from https://www.tcmb.gov.tr/wps/wcm/connect/07aaa195-d8bd-4698-941c-b5ba1109d337/Mon_Exc_Pol_2011.pdf?MOD=AJPERES&CACHEID=ROOTWORKSPACE-07aaa195-d8bd-4698-941c-b5ba1109d337-m4ucaHX

CBRT. (2011). *Monetary and Exchange Rate Policy for 2012* (CBRT Monetary Policy and Liraization Strategy Text). Retrieved from https://www.tcmb.gov.tr/wps/wcm/connect/5540f91d-2608-4bb4-b5cd-f0c04dd6febe/Mon_Exc_Pol_2012.pdf?MOD=AJPERES&CACHEID=ROOTWORKSPACE-5540f91d-2608-4bb4-b5cd-f0c04dd6febe-m4ucaEu

CBRT. (2012). *Monetary and Exchange Rate Policy for 2013* (CBRT Monetary Policy and Liraization Strategy Text). Retrieved from https://www.tcmb.gov.tr/wps/wcm/connect/8215ba96-4173-42ac-a096-32855032ec35/monetary_2013.pdf?MOD=AJPERES&CACHEID=ROOTWORKSPACE-8215ba96-4173-42ac-a096-32855032ec35-m4ucaAt

CBRT. (2013). *Monetary and Exchange Rate Policy for 2014* (CBRT Monetary Policy and Liraization Strategy Text). Retrieved from https://www.tcmb.gov.tr/wps/wcm/connect/5e52cbaa-5cff-4164-ae01-c4e7e48fe7c3/monetary_2014.pdf?MOD=AJPERES&CACHEID=ROOTWORKSPACE-5e52cbaa-5cff-4164-ae01-c4e7e48fe7c3-m4ucawN

CBRT. (2014). *Monetary and Exchange Rate Policy for 2015* (CBRT Monetary Policy and Liraization Strategy Text). Retrieved from https://www.tcmb.gov.tr/wps/wcm/connect/d6

8e198a-1175-4194-b4f1-9a620a360ec5/2015.pdf?MOD=AJPERES&CACHEID=ROO
TWORKSPACE-d68e198a-1175-4194-b4f1-9a620a360ec5-m4ucasK

CBRT. (2015). *Monetary and Exchange Rate Policy for 2016* (CBRT Monetary Policy and
Liraization Strategy Text). Retrieved from https://www.tcmb.gov.tr/wps/wcm/connect/9b
8077c7-44ac-463d-9b07-09cccd791931/2016.pdf?MOD=AJPERES&CACHEID=ROO
TWORKSPACE-9b8077c7-44ac-463d-9b07-09cccd791931-m4ucao

CBRT. (2016). *Monetary and Exchange Rate Policy for 2017* (CBRT Monetary Policy and
Liraization Strategy Text). Retrieved from https://www.tcmb.gov.tr/wps/wcm/connect/f1
86a672-e81b-423e-a92b-9ec4491a8863/2017MonetaryandExchangeRatePolicy.pdf?MO
D=AJPERES&CACHEID=ROOTWORKSPACE-f186a672-e81b-423e-a92b-9ec4491a
8863-m4ucajm

CBRT. (2017). *Monetary and Exchange Rate Policy for 2018* (CBRT Monetary Policy
and Liraization Strategy Text). Retrieved from https://www.tcmb.gov.tr/wps/wcm/con
nect/92636dde-0107-4ffa-bd25-e6b060621a52/paravekur.politikas_eng.pdf?MOD=AJ
PERES&CACHEID=ROOTWORKSPACE-92636dde-0107-4ffa-bd25-e6b060621a52
-m6U5MTf

CBRT. (2018). *Monetary and Exchange Rate Policy for 2019* (CBRT Monetary Policy and
Liraization Strategy Text). Retrieved from https://www.tcmb.gov.tr/wps/wcm/connect/ac
e5ee96-e2e9-406f-a4ff-1da907304d80/2019MonetaryandExchangeRatePolicy.pdf?MO
D=AJPERES&CACHEID=ROOTWORKSPACE-ace5ee96-e2e9-406f-a4ff-1da907304
d80-mtZhANO

CBRT. (2019). *Monetary and Exchange Rate Policy for 2020* (CBRT Monetary Policy and
Liraization Strategy Text). Retrieved from https://www.tcmb.gov.tr/wps/wcm/connect/0
a520b12-e5de-4948-956a-1a1c4b45b2d0/MonetaryandExchangeRatePolicyfor2020.pdf
?MOD=AJPERES&CACHEID=ROOTWORKSPACE-0a520b12-e5de-4948-956a-1a1c
4b45b2d0-mXk-q8c

CBRT. (2020). *Monetary and Exchange Rate Policy for 2021* (CBRT Monetary Policy and
Liraization Strategy Text). Retrieved from https://www.tcmb.gov.tr/wps/wcm/connect/29
04dff9-d9ae-4a08-a57a-4106aa9ac8a7/PKP2021_ENG.pdf?MOD=AJPERES&CACHE
ID=ROOTWORKSPACE-2904dff9-d9ae-4a08-a57a-4106aa9ac8a7-ns05mRz

CBRT. (2021). *Monetary and Exchange Rate Policy for 2022* (CBRT Monetary Policy
and Liraization Strategy Text). Retrieved from https://www.tcmb.gov.tr/wps/wcm/conn
ect/51be49d9-cbf8-44b3-b8bd-61944857cf5a/Monetary+and+Exchange+Rate+Policy+
for+2022.pdf?MOD=AJPERES&CACHEID=ROOTWORKSPACE-51be49d9-cbf8-44
b3-b8bd-61944857cf5a-nU5oh2S

CBTR. (2023). *Summary of the Monetary Policy Committee Meeting.* Retrieved from https://
www.tcmb.gov.tr/wps/wcm/connect/EN/TCMB+EN/Main+Menu/Announcements/
Press+Releases/2023/ANO2023-21

CBRT. *Central Bank Interest Rates* [Dataset]. Retrieved from https://www.tcmb.gov.tr/
wps/wcm/connect/EN/TCMB+EN/Main+Menu/Core+Functions/Monetary+Policy/
Central+Bank+Interest+Rates/

CBRT. *Electronic Data Delivery System* (EVDS) [Dataset]. Retrieved from https://evds2.
tcmb.gov.tr/index.php?/evds/serieMarket

Civcir, İ., & Akçağlayan, A. (2010). Inflation targeting and the exchange rate: Does it matter in Turkey? *Journal of Policy Modeling*, 32(2010), 339–354. https://doi.org/10.1016/j.
jpolmod.2010.03.002

Crowder, W.J., & Hoffman, D.L. (1996). The long-run relationship between nominal interest
rates and inflation: The Fisher equation revisited. *Journal of Money, Credit, and Banking*,
28(1), 102–118. https://doi.org/10.2307/2077969

Demirgil, B., & Türkay, H. (2017). Türkiye'de faiz oranlarını etkileyen faktörler: Bir ARDL/sınır testi uygulaması. *Gazi Üniversitesi İktisadi ve İdari Bilimler Fakültesi Dergisi*, 19(3), 907–928.

Dogan, B., Eroğlu, Ö., & Değer, O. (2016). Enflasyon ve faiz oranı arasındaki nedensellik ilişkisi: Türkiye örneği. Çankırı Karatekin Üniversitesi İİBF Dergisi, 6(1), 405–425. https://doi.org/10.18074/cnuiibf.258

Dufour, M., & Orhangazi, Ö. (2009). The 2000–2001 Financial crisis in Turkey: A crisis for whom? *Review of Political Economy*, 21(1), 101–122. https://doi.org/10.1080/09538250802517014

Erer, D., & Erer, E. (2020). Industry 4.0 and international trade: The case of Turkey. Akkaya, B. (Ed.), *Agile business leadership methods for industry 4.0* (pp. 69–84). Bingley: Emerald Publishing Limited. https://doi.org/10.1108/978-1-80043-380-920201005

Ersel, H., & Özatay, F. (2008). Fiscal dominance and inflation targeting: Lessons from Turkey. *Emerging Markets Finance and Trade*, 44(6), 38–51. https://doi.org/10.2753/REE1540-496X440603

Fama, E.F. (1975). Short-term interest rates as predictors of inflation. *The American Economic Review*, 65(3), 269–282.

Faure, A.P. (2014). Interest rates 1: What are interest rates? *SSRN Electronic Journal*. http://dx.doi.org/10.2139/ssrn.2542083

Fisher, I. (1930). *The theory of Interest*. New York: Macmillan.

Flood, R., & Mussa, M. (1994). *Issues Concerning Nominal Anchors for Monetary Policy* (NBER Working Paper Series No. 4850). Retrieved from https://www.nber.org/system/files/working_papers/w4850/w4850.pdf.

Fried, J., & Howitt, P. (1983). The effects of inflation on real interest rates. *The American Economic Review*, 73(5), 968–980.

Granville, B., & Mallick, S. (2004). Fisher hypothesis: UK evidence over a century. *Applied Economics Letters*, 11(2), 87–90. https://doi.org/10.1080/1350485042000200169

Hayes, M. (2008). *The Economics of Keynes, A New Guide to the General Theory*. Cheltenham: Edward Elgar Publication.

İncekara, A., Demez, S., & Ustaoğlu, M. (2012). Validity of Fisher effect for Turkish economy: Cointegration analysis. *Social and Behavioral Sciences*, 58, 396–405. https://doi.org/10.1016/j.sbspro.2012.09.1016

Interest rates of some central banks. (n.d.). *Merkez Bankaları* [Dataset]. Retrieved from https://tr.investing.com/central-banks/

Ireland, P.N. (1996). Long-term interest rates and inflation: A Fisherian approach. *Federal Reserve Bank of Richmond Economic Quarterly*, 82(1), 21–35.

İTO. (n.d.). *İTO istatistik verileri* [Dataset]. Retrieved from https://bilgibankasi.ito.org.tr/tr/istatistik-verileri/istanbul-ucretler-gecinme/genel-indeksin-degisim-oranlari/bir-onceki-yil-sonuna-gore-degisim?year=95

Kahn, G.A. (1988). Nominal GNP: An anchor for monetary policy? *Federal Reserve Bank of Kansas City Economic Review*, 73, 18–35

Kasman, S., Kasman, A., & Turgutlu, E. (2006). Fisher hypothesis revisited: A fractional cointegration analysis. *Emerging Markets Finance and Trade*, 42(6), 59–76. https://doi.org/10.2753/REE1540-496X420604

Kavcıoğlu, Ş. (2023). *Governor Şahap Kavcıoğlu's Speech at the Briefing on Inflation Report 2023-II*. Retrieved from: https://www.tcmb.gov.tr/wps/wcm/connect/EN/TCMB+EN/Main+Menu/Announcements/Remarks+by+Governor/2023/SpeechG04_05_2023

Köse, N., Emirmahmutoğlu, F., & Aksoy, S. (2012). The interest rate-inflation relationship under inflation targeting regime: The case of Turkey. *Journal of Asian Economics*, 23(4), 476–485. https://doi.org/10.1016/j.asieco.2012.03.001

Maghyereh, A., & Al-Zoubi, H. (2006). Does Fisher effect apply in developing countries: Evidence from a nonlinear cotrending test applied to Argentina, Brazil, Malaysia, Mexico, South Korea and Turkey. *Applied Econometrics and International Development*, 6(2), 31–46.

Mankiw, N.G. (2009). *Macroeconomics* (7th Edition). New York: Worth Publishers.

Maxwell J.F. (1980). Money, interest, inflation and growth in Turkey. *Journal of Monetary Economics*, 6(4), 535–545. https://doi.org/10.1016/0304-3932(80)90006-9

Mercan, M. (2013). Enflasyon ve nominal faiz oranları arasındaki uzun dönem ilişkinin Fisher hipotezi çerçevesinde test edilmesi: Türkiye örneği. *Atatürk University Journal of Economics & Administrative Sciences*, 27(4), 368–384.

Mishkin, F.S. (2012). *The Economics of Money, Banking, and Financial Markets*. Toronto: Pearson Canada Inc.

Nelson, C.R., & Schwert, W.S. (1977). Short-term interest rates as predictors of inflation: On testing the hypothesis that the real rate of interest is constant. *The American Economic Review*, 67(3), 478–486.

OECD. (n.d). *Trade in Value Added: Turkey*. Retrieved from https://www.oecd.org/sti/ind/CN2021_TUR.pdf

Öniş, Z. (2009). Beyond the 2001 financial crisis: The political economy of the new phase of neo-liberal restructuring in Turkey. *Review of International Political Economy*, 16(3), 409–432. https://doi.org/10.1080/09692290802408642

Participation Banks Association of Turkey (PBT) (2023). *Financial Reports Archive* [Dataset]. Retrieved from https://tkbb.org.tr/veri/financialreports

Patterson, B., & Lygnerud, K. (1999). *The Determination of Interest Rates* (*European Parliament Directorate-General for Research Working Paper, Economic Affairs Series. ECON 116 EN*). Retrieved from https://www.europarl.europa.eu/workingpapers/econ/pdf/116_en.pdf

Republic of Turkey, Ministry of Treasury and Finance (RTMTF). *Central Government Budget Expenditures Ecode4* [Dataset]. Retrieved from https://en.hmb.gov.tr/central-government#

Saymeh, A.A.F., & Orabi, M.M.A. (2013). The effect of interest rate, inflation rate, GDP, on real economic growth rate in Jordan. *Asian Economic and Financial Review*, 3(3), 341–354.

Şimşek, M., & Kadılar, C. (2006). Fisher etkisinin Türkiye verileri ile testi. *Doğuş Üniversitesi Dergisi*, 7(1), 99–111.

The Banks Association of Turkey (BAT) (2021). *Banks in Türkiye 2021* (Publication No: 347 May 2022). Retrieved from https://www.tbb.org.tr/Content/Upload/istatistikiraporlar/ekler/3401/Banks_in_Turkiye_2021.pdf

The Banks Association of Turkey (BAT) (2023). *Statistical Reports*. [Dataset]. Retrieved from https://www.tbb.org.tr/en/banks-and-banking-sector-information/statistics-and-data-query/statistical-reports/20

The Inflation Research Group (ENAG). *ENAGrup Tüketici Fiyat Endeksi* (E-TÜFE) verileri [Dataset]. Retrieved from https://enagrup.org/

Trading Economics. (n.d.). *Turkey—Credit Rating*. Retrieved from https://tradingeconomics.com/turkey/rating

Tunalı, H., & Yıldırım Erönal, Y. (2016). Enflasyon ve faiz oranı ilişkisi: Türkiye'de Fisher etkisinin geçerliliği. *Süleyman Demirel Üniversitesi İktisadi ve İdari Bilimler Fakültesi Dergisi*, 21(4), 1415–1431.

Turkey CDS 5 Years USD. (n.d.). *Turkey CDS 5 Years USD (TRGV5YUSAC=R)* [Dataset]. Retrieved from https://www.investing.com/rates-bonds/turkey-cds-5-year-usd

Turkish Statistical Institute (TSI) (2023). *Data Portal for Statistics* [Dataset]. Retrieved from https://data.tuik.gov.tr/Kategori/GetKategori?p=enflasyon-ve-fiyat-106&dil=1

TUYİD. (2013). *Borsa Trendleri Raporu, Ocak-Aralık 2012*. Retrieved from https://www.tuyid.org/files/yayinlar/Borsa_Trendleri_Raporu_III.pdf

TUYİD. (2014). *BIST Trends Report* (Volume: 7 January-December 2013). Retrieved from https://www.tuyid.org/files/yayinlar/BIST_Trends_Report_VII.pdf

TUYİD. (2015). *BIST Trends Report December* (Volume: 11 January-December 2014). Retrieved from https://www.tuyid.org/files/yayinlar/BIST_Trends_Report_XI.pdf

TUYİD. (2016). *BIST Trends Report* (Volume: 15 January-December 2015). Retrieved from https://www.tuyid.org/files/yayinlar/BIST_Trends_Report_XV.pdf

TUYİD. (2017). *BIST Trends Report* (Volume: 14 January-December 2016). Retrieved from https://www.tuyid.org/files/yayinlar/BIST_Trends_Report_XIX.pdf

TUYİD. (2018a). *BIST Trends Report* (Volume: 23 January-December 2017). Retrieved from https://www.tuyid.org/files/yayinlar/Borsa_Trends_Report_XXIII.pdf

TUYİD. (2018b). *BIST Trends Report* (Volume: 27 January-December 2018). Retrieved from https://www.tuyid.org/files/yayinlar/Borsa_Trends_Report_XXVII_EN.pdf

TUYİD. (2019). *BIST Trends Report* (Volume: 31 January-December 2019). Retrieved from https://www.tuyid.org/files/yayinlar/Borsa_Trends_Report_XXXI_4Q19_EN.pdf

TUYİD. (2020). *BIST Trends Report* (Volume: 35 January-December 2020). Retrieved from https://www.tuyid.org/files/yayinlar/BIST_Trends_Report_XXXV_4Q20_EN.pdf

TUYİD. (2021). *BIST Trends Report* (Volume: 34 January-December 2021). Retrieved from https://www.tuyid.org/files/yayinlar/BTR-Executive-Summary-4Q21.pdf

TUYİD. (2022). Borsa Trendleri Raporu (Sayı: 43 Ocak-Aralık 2022). Retrieved from https://www.tuyid.org/files/yayinlar/BorsaTrendleriRaporu_4C22.pdf

Westerlund, J. (2005). *Panel Cointegration Tests of the Fisher Hypothesis* (Lund University, Department of Economics Working Papers, 2005:10). Retrieved from https://lucris.lub.lu.se/ws/portalfiles/portal/5491579/2061469

7 Empirical evaluation of President Erdoğan's interest rate policy

Haşmet Gökırmak and Fuat Sekmen

Introduction

This study focuses on the impact of the Central Bank of the Republic of Türkiye's (CBRT) decision to reduce the policy interest rate, examining its effects on leading macroeconomic indicators and various markets within the country. Türkiye has grappled with substantial inflationary pressures in recent years, culminating in an annual inflation rate of around 87% in 2022. Several complex and interrelated factors have contributed to this surge in inflation. First, implementing expansionary monetary policies has increased the money supply, contributing directly to inflationary trends. Simultaneously, the Turkish lira's (TL) depreciation against major currencies, such as the US dollars and the euro, has resulted in more costly imports, fueling inflation. External pressures have also played a role, with diplomatic tensions leading to trade disruptions with key partners and subsequent price increases for certain goods. Finally, the global disruption caused by the COVID-19 pandemic has strained supply chains, creating shortages and additional price increases for specific commodities. Together, these elements paint a complex picture of the inflationary landscape in Türkiye, setting the stage for an in-depth exploration of the implications of the CBRT's monetary policy decisions.

CBRT acted upon President Erdogan's claim that interest rates are the cause of inflation and implemented a series of interest rate cuts. A low-interest-rate policy can have positive and negative impacts on the economy of Türkiye, depending on factors such as inflation, foreign exchange rates, and the economy's overall state. Positive effects include a stimulus for economic growth. The lower interest rates are assumed to encourage domestic investment and increase exports. Lower interest rates can incite borrowing and investment for individuals and companies, increase economic activity, and increase economic growth. Low interest rates also reduce the cost of borrowing since they lower the amount to be paid in installments, leaving more money for spending on other goods, services, and investments. It may also create new employment opportunities because of increased economic activity and investments.

Maintaining low interest rates negatively influenced various markets, including goods and services, credit, foreign exchange, and labor. Adopting this low-interest-rate strategy incited inflationary pressures, mainly due to the anticipation

DOI: 10.4324/9781032631561-10

by economic agents of an upward swing in the exchange rate. This expectation implied that the national currency, the TL, would suffer a depreciation when measured against foreign currencies such as the US dollar. The aftermath of this policy decision resulted in significant financial instability. Inflation soared as a direct consequence of the elevated exchange rate, and increased consumption expenditures occurred due to the reduced cost of borrowing. The inflation level reached 87% in the first few months after the sharp plunge in interest rates. Low interest rates also led to about 50% of the depreciation of the TL. Lower interest rates also discouraged foreign investors and increased pressure on currency depreciation. The depreciation of the national currency increased the cost of imported goods, contributing to overall inflation in the country and increasing the current account deficit. Low returns on bank deposits created financial instability by directing deposit owners to invest in foreign currencies, real estate, automobiles, gold, and other commodities. The diversification of investments led to economic instability because of increased real estate leases and the prices of homes and durable products.

After the Justice and Development Party (AKP) assumed power, it implemented a high-interest, low-exchange-rate policy, leading to a significant influx of foreign currency into Türkiye. Consequently, the price of the dollar dipped, and inflation, which was linked to the dollar, followed suit. Nevertheless, the policy perpetuated a growing current account deficit. The AKP maintained that this would not pose a problem as long as it was financed, believing it to be a long-term issue that did not necessitate immediate preventative measures. This period of apparent economic bliss was marked by GDP growth, low interest rates, and inflation declines.

However, the AKP began to change the narrative by promoting the notion that "interest is the cause and inflation is the result." President Erdogan declared that interest rates were the root cause of inflation, supporting his argument with religious reasons. He stated, "Allah has made a decision (nass) on this matter; neither you nor I have the authority to decide." Indeed, the correlation between interest rate and inflation is complex in Türkiye's dual-currency economy. High interest rates can mitigate inflation by reducing the price of foreign currency.

Contrary to this conventional wisdom, the AKP chose to lower interest rates, aiming to depreciate the TL to boost exports rather than curb inflation. As anticipated, the market responded by driving up foreign exchange rates.

Throughout the 1950s and 1960s, the primary opponents of the Keynesians were the *monetarists*. Under the leadership of Milton Friedman, they provided effective opposition to Keynesian policy and theory (Landreth and Colander, 2002, p. 425). Milton Friedman highlighted the monetary system's integral role in his studies. He asserted that "inflation is always and everywhere a monetary phenomenon." This proposition suggests that inflation operates independently of other economic indicators, including growth or shrinkage, unemployment rates, poverty levels, wealth, and income distribution. It does not propose a direct correlation with decreasing interest rates, such as rising or falling inflation. Instead, Friedman claims that inflation is a product of monetary conditions.

In Friedman's perspective, to prevent inflation, policymakers should concentrate on controlling the "quantity, nature, velocity, and interest of money." However, an ambiguity arises here, as Friedman does not explicitly define "money." This becomes particularly relevant in light of the 2008 financial crisis, when the "central bank money" in the United States and EU countries increased while the volume of "bank money created through credit" decreased. The net effect was that overall inflation did not increase because the total quantity of money circulating within the system remained unchanged. Despite prevailing opinions, higher and rising price levels cannot be sustained without monetary expansion, as monetarist economists assert (Cagan, 1979, p. 10).

The causes contributing to the persistent inflation that Türkiye has faced over the past three decades differ substantially from those in Western countries. In these Western nations, which operate within hard-currency economies, excessive demand is typically the catalyst for inflation. Central banks counter this by hiking the borrowing rate, affecting the feasibility calculations for companies considering investing with borrowed funds. This increased borrowing rate, in turn, suppresses household demand for goods and services. By controlling price increases through reducing demand, the economy cools down, and economic growth slows. This way, measures to contain inflation can broadly impact economic dynamics.

In a markedly different approach, President Erdogan, in a speech at his party's group meeting in the Turkish Grand National Assembly before a Central Bank meeting on November 18, 2021, proposed an inverse relationship between interest and inflation. He contended that to quell inflation, it was necessary to lower interest rates. However, when the Central Bank followed through with cutting interest rates, the result was a stark contrast. The official Consumer Price Index (CPI), around 20%, skyrocketed to 85%.

It is important to note that inflation did not rise simply because interest rates were lowered. Instead, the economic agents interpreted the rate cut as an indicator that the price of the dollar would rise, leading to increased demand for the dollar. In this context, it can be concluded that the rising dollar price and the corresponding increase in the exchange rate were the real culprits behind inflation in Türkiye. Unlike in Western economies, Turkish inflation is more closely tied to the dollar price than the interest rate (tr.euronews.com).

Many economists concur that high interest rates can induce numerous detrimental effects, such as unemployment and economic contraction. Notably, the real loan interest rate is more effective in combating inflation than the deposit and bond interest rates. When loan interest rates surge, investment demand diminishes, potentially pushing the economy into a recession. However, this holds only for single-currency economies.

Contrastingly, Türkiye operates a dual-currency economy. In such a scenario, increased interest rates merely attract short-term, speculative capital inflows ("hot money"), resulting in a decrease in foreign currency prices due to the influx from abroad, which in turn leads to a reduction in inflation. However, this often culminates in a current account deficit problem over time.

Social science is the systematic endeavor to categorize real-life events based on hypotheses, theories, and laws formulated through repeated observation and testing, with the level of certainty determining the classification. While social sciences and economics, as a subset, often yield universal results, these results can diverge due to local conditions. For instance, while the exchange rate does not significantly impact inflation in a country like the United States, where the currency is a reserve currency, it can considerably influence inflation in Türkiye, where the currency is not a reserve currency and is subject to the effects of dollarization. Consequently, the causes of inflation can vary across different nations, necessitating a focus on the primary cause in each specific case. In Türkiye, risk escalation is the initial cause of the surge in exchange rates and the ensuing inflation. In such an environment, reducing the interest rate increases the risks. Any risk amplification consequently elevates exchange rates and inflation (https://www.mahfiegilmez.com/2021, October 3, 2021).

Theoretically, several outcomes can be anticipated when a central bank opts to lower the policy interest rate. First, decreasing the policy rate typically leads to a corresponding reduction in both loan and deposit rates. This prompts firms to take on more debt at these more affordable interest rates, amplifying their investment demand. Simultaneously, private consumption escalates as individuals can borrow at lower interest rates. The lower deposit rates also tend to encourage a reduction in savings, with individuals choosing to spend more instead.

Second, lowering the policy rate can instigate increased asset and real estate prices. With reduced interest rates, liquidity increases, boosting demand for assets. This heightened demand causes a rise in prices for financial assets such as stocks, bonds, and real estate. The subsequent appreciation in asset prices can further stimulate investment demand as companies that own these assets find their balance sheets improving. It can also increase consumption demand as individual asset owners increase their wealth.

In summary, a cut in the policy interest rate could drive economic growth by promoting higher levels of investment and consumption. However, it is essential to remember that these outcomes can also depend on other economic conditions and factors.

Expectations do indeed play a critical role in driving inflation. The success of inflation targeting largely hinges on how policy changes influence these expectations. For instance, politically motivated expansionary monetary policies, particularly those enacted in pre-election periods, often lead to deteriorating expectations and an inflation spike surpasses regular periods. The decision to cut the policy interest rate in Türkiye in November 2021 resulted in an unexpected outcome instead of falling, loan rates increased, a deviation linked to the impact of expectations.

In economies like Türkiye, where foreign trade significantly contributes to total income, the exchange rate channel is essential in determining monetary policy's economic impact. Decreases in interest rates often lead to a depreciation in the value of the national currency due to capital outflows. The depreciated exchange rate, in turn, increases the prices of imported consumer goods and raw materials, which hold considerable significance for countries like Türkiye. Therefore, the total demand for domestically produced goods increases.

The interplay between interest rates, exchange rates, and inflation is intricate and multifaceted, shaped by various factors, including economic policies, market expectations, and global economic conditions. It is worth noting, however, that the dynamics may vary significantly across different economies, influenced by factors such as their openness to trade, the stability of their financial systems, and their level of economic development.

Expectations undoubtedly wield significant influence over inflation. The efficacy of inflation targeting relies heavily on the impact policy changes exert on these expectations. An expansionary monetary policy, especially for political motivations such as pre-election periods, can trigger a decline in expectations, resulting in a greater inflation surge than in regular periods. The decision taken in Türkiye to lower the policy interest rate in November 2021 had an unexpected fallout—loan rates increased, not decreased, a deviation associated with expectations.

Delving into the impact of interest on the exchange rate, we find a crucial dynamic in economies like Türkiye, where foreign trade forms a large part of the total income. The exchange rate channel is instrumental in determining the effects of monetary policy on such an economy. Decreasing interest rates often trigger a depreciation in the value of the national currency as capital outflows ensue. This weaker exchange rate subsequently pushes up the prices of imported consumer goods and raw materials—items of significant import for countries like Türkiye. As a result, the total demand for domestically produced goods sees a marked rise.

The interplay between interest rates, exchange rates, and inflation is complex and multifaceted, influenced by various factors, including economic policies, market expectations, and the prevailing global economic climate. It is important to note that these dynamics can significantly differ across economies due to varying factors such as their trade openness, financial systems' robustness, and overall economic development.

There is indeed a theoretical channel through which a reduced interest rate could lead to lower inflation, as advocated by those who favor low interest rates. The argument argues that low interest rates can stimulate production and supply. Inflation could fall if demand does not increase at the same pace.

However, this theory should be considered alongside the many cost factors in price determination. While interest is one of these factors, it often pales in significance compared to other cost elements, such as raw material prices and wages, which could increase due to the lowered policy rate. Therefore, the effect of interest rates on supply tends to be much weaker than their effect on demand.

Additionally, it is worth noting that this theory operates under specific assumptions about how firms and consumers respond to changes in interest rates. Other factors—like economic stability, confidence in monetary policy, and global economic conditions—can also significantly impact the relationship between interest rates and inflation. The complexities of these dynamics mean that lowering interest rates does not always lead to lower inflation, particularly in the short term.

Literature review

In his 1980 study, M.J. Fry presented an analysis of inflation and growth in Türkiye from 1950 to 1977, utilizing a two-equation model. His findings suggested that the discrepancy between the rates of change in the nominal money supply and the real demand for money determined inflation. In the context of Türkiye's economic environment, marked by its disequilibrium institutional interest rate and exchange control systems, the real supply of domestic credit is primarily shaped by the real demand for money. According to Fry, this demand is significantly influenced by the real deposit rate of interest. Fry further proposed that the Central Bank could leverage the nominal money supply and the nominal deposit rate of interest as policy instruments aimed at economic stabilization. When adeptly managed, these tools could contribute to maintaining a balanced economy, ultimately influencing factors such as inflation and economic growth.

In his 2006 research, Bolatoglu (2006) examined the Fisher effect—a concept in economics that describes the relationship between inflation and interest rates—within the context of the Turkish economy from 1990 to 2004. His analysis was based on the assumption of adaptive expectations, a hypothesis suggesting individuals form their future inflation expectations based on their experiences. The empirical results of Bolatoglu's study revealed a long-term relationship between inflation and nominal interest rates in Türkiye during the period under review. In essence, this finding supports the Fisher effect, which posits that changes in expected inflation rates will be directly reflected in nominal interest rates. This link between inflation and interest rates is crucial for policymakers strategizing to manage economic stability and growth.

Gul and Acikalin (2008) explored the validity of the Fisher Hypothesis (FH) for the Turkish economy. The Fisher Hypothesis contends that nominal interest rates adjust on a one-to-one basis in response to expected changes in inflation rates. To test this hypothesis, the authors applied the Johansen cointegration method to the Turkish monthly interest rate and inflation rate data. Their analysis did not reveal a one-to-one relationship between nominal interest rates and inflation, suggesting that the Fisher Hypothesis does not strictly hold for Türkiye from 1990 to 2003. Nevertheless, their results confirmed the presence of a strong Fisher effect, indicating a long-run relationship between nominal interest rates and inflation, albeit not strictly on a one-to-one basis.

Mercan's 2013 study probed the Fisher hypothesis—asserting a positive correlation between nominal interest rates and inflation rate—in the context of the Turkish economy. Mercan used the Autoregressive Distributed Lag (ARDL) bound testing approach to investigate this relationship. This technique provides robust results even in small sample sizes, and he evaluated data from the period spanning from January 1992 to January 2013. The study's conclusions were consistent with the Fisher hypothesis, as Mercan found that the inflation rate significantly and positively impacted the nominal interest rate. This relationship suggests that expectations formed within the Fisher hypothesis framework play a critical role in shaping nominal interest rates in the Turkish economy.

Atgur and Altay (2015) investigated the relationship between inflation and interest rates in Türkiye from 2004 to 2013. Using advanced statistical methodologies—including the Johansen and Lütkepohl-Saikkonen Cointegration Tests and the Dynamic Ordinary Least Squares (DOLS) method—they sought to examine the validity of the Fisher effect in the Turkish context. The study's findings confirmed the presence of the Fisher effect in Türkiye, indicating that nominal interest rates adapted in line with changes in inflation. Moreover, they found a long-run relationship between inflation and nominal interest rates, reinforcing the theoretical underpinnings of the Fisher Effect.

Tunalı and Eronal (2016) examined the validity of the Fisher hypothesis, which postulates a long-term positive relationship between nominal interest rates and inflation rates. Their analysis focused on the effects of inflation on 12-month nominal deposit interest rates and the consumer price index, employing monthly time series data from January 2003 to February 2014. They conducted standard unit root tests and the Zivot Andrews unit root tests for data stability. The Gregory–Hansen cointegration test, which accounts for structural breaks, was applied to determine if there was a long-term correlation between the series. Their findings indicated a nuanced relationship between interest rates and inflation in Türkiye. While the Fisher effect held in the long term, aligning with the hypothesis's central tenet, it was rejected in the short run. In other words, under the inflation targeting strategy, they found that nominal interest rates adjusted to inflation over an extended period. However, this relationship was not observed in the short term.

Alper (2017) explored the causal relationship between interest rates and inflation in the Turkish economy spanning from 1973 to 2016. The research indicated that the Fisher effect was valid in Türkiye, though the relationship was relatively weak during the studied time frame. By employing Fully Modified Ordinary Least Squares (FMOLS) and DOLS tests, Alper discovered that a 1% increase in the inflation rate led to a 0.77% increase in the interest rate. While demonstrating a positive relationship between the variables, this ratio is less than 1, suggesting that the Fisher effect's strength in the Turkish Economy is less robust than the theory's one-to-one correlation premise.

Karahan and Yılgor (2017) conducted a study to contribute fresh insights to ongoing discussions about the causal relationship between interest rates and inflation. Their analysis covered the period from 2002 to 2016 and utilized both cointegration and causality tests to investigate the inflation–interest rate nexus in the Turkish economy. Their findings revealed a unidirectional causality between inflation and interest rates. This essentially suggests that inflation during this period led to corresponding changes in interest rates, but the reverse was not observed. Such a causal relationship could imply that the Central Bank adjusted its interest rate policy in response to changes in inflation. However, changes in interest rates did not necessarily result in corresponding changes in inflation. For policy implications, the authors advised political figures to prioritize price stability to manage interest rates within the Turkish economy effectively.

Altunoz (2020) applied the concept of the Gibson paradox, which postulates a positive correlation between inflation and interest rates, to test the existence and direction of the relationship between these variables in the Turkish economy. This study employed annual data from 1995 to 2019 and utilized the ARDL boundary testing approach for its analysis. The findings revealed that the Gibson paradox applies to the Turkish economy, per the Wicksell–Keynes and Fisher models. This implies that a positive relationship between inflation and interest rates was observed during the period under investigation, supporting the Gibson paradox's proposition. Moreover, the results from the causality analysis concluded that bi-directional causality exists between these two variables. This suggests that changes in interest rates caused changes in inflation, and vice versa, throughout the period studied.

Turna and Ozcan (2021) analyzed the relationship and causality among interest rates, exchange rates, and inflation within the context of the Turkish economy. This study employed quarterly data from 2005Q1 to 2019Q2 and utilized the ARDL model for its analysis. Their short-term analysis revealed that both exchange rates and interest rates have an impact on inflation. Specifically, a 1% increase in the exchange rate led to a 1.11% increase in inflation, and a 1% increase in the interest rate resulted in a 0.29% rise in inflation. They emphasized that changes in the exchange rate had the most substantial impact on inflation in the short term.

Meanwhile, the long-term analysis also indicated that exchange and interest rates significantly affect inflation. A 1% increase in the exchange rate resulted in a 0.80% increase in inflation, while a 1% increase in the interest rate led to a 0.21% increase in inflation. The authors concluded that changes in the exchange rate exerted the most significant influence on inflation in the long run.

Varlık and Gebesoglu (2021) use the ARDL method and the Granger causality test to investigate the validity of the Fisher hypothesis and the Neo-Fisherian approach for Türkiye. These economic theories deal with the relationship between inflation and nominal interest rates.

The Fisher hypothesis, proposed by Irving Fisher, postulates that the real interest rate is independent of monetary measures, particularly the nominal interest rate and inflation rate. This means that changes in expected inflation would be reflected entirely in nominal interest rates. The Neo-Fisherian approach, on the contrary, is a relatively new perspective that suggests raising the nominal interest rate will lead to higher, not lower, inflation in the long run. According to the study results, both inflation uncertainty and the expected inflation rate impact nominal interest rates in Türkiye. This suggests that as uncertainty or expectations about inflation rise, so do nominal interest rates, aligning with the Fisher Hypothesis.

Conversely, it is also found that nominal interest rates affect inflation uncertainty and the expected inflation rate. This latter finding aligns with the Neo-Fisherian approach, as changes in the nominal interest rate can influence inflation expectations and uncertainty. This two-way causality provides significant evidence for the Neo-Fisherian effect and the Fisher Hypothesis in Türkiye. This means the Turkish economy's interaction between inflation and nominal interest rates follows both traditional and newer economic theories. It is a complex relationship where inflation and nominal interest rates are not just cause and effect, but dynamically influence each other. This may imply that monetary policy in Türkiye might need to consider both theories when adjusting to control inflation and stabilize the economy.

Yapraklı (2022) aims to explore the relationship between inflation and interest rates in Türkiye from 2006 to 2021. A set of rigorous econometric techniques is employed in this investigation, including the Ng–Perron unit root test, the Bai–Perron multiple structural breaks test, Johansen's cointegration test, DOLS regression estimation, and a Vector Error Correction (VEC) causality analysis. According to the study's findings, inflation and interest rates in Türkiye move together in the long run. This suggests a long-term equilibrium relationship between these two variables, where any deviation in the short term gets corrected over the long term. Furthermore, the study uncovers a causal relationship between inflation and the interest rate. This means that changes in the inflation rate are likely to lead to changes in the interest rate. This finding supports the Fisher hypothesis, which postulates that changes in expected inflation are fully reflected in the nominal interest rate. This can have important implications for monetary policy, as it suggests that Turkish policymakers must closely monitor and manage inflation to control interest rates, stabilize the economy, and foster sustainable economic growth.

Mercan's 2013 study applied the ARDL bound testing approach to explore the Fisher Hypothesis in the context of the Turkish economy. The study period spans January 1992 (1992:M1) to January 2013 (2013:M1). Mercan conducted ARDL bound tests using this extensive dataset, an econometric technique especially effective in studying long-term equilibrium relationships between variables. The study's results supported the Fisher hypothesis, finding a statistically significant and positive relationship between the inflation rate and the nominal interest rate in Türkiye during the time frame analyzed. This indicates that changes in the inflation rate significantly affect nominal interest rates, in line with expectations as per the Fisher hypothesis.

Turkish economy

Turkish economy is a mixed economy with a growing private sector and centralized economic planning and government regulation. Türkiye has implemented a quasi-command approach, with rigorous government controls over industry, foreign trade, and foreign direct investment. The government has significant involvement in essential sectors such as communication, transport, energy, and banking.

The level of government control has varied over time under different governments. At times, the economy moved toward a more market-oriented economy, and at other times, governments chose to get more control of the market system. During the 1980s, Türkiye implemented many reforms to shift the economy from a command system to a more private-sector and market-based approach. Türkiye has experienced more of the presence of government in all industries and the functioning of the market in recent years, a move toward a command economic system.

The aftermath of a big earthquake in 1999 and ongoing economic stagnation that turned into a financial crisis in 2001 helped the AKP win the elections in late 2002. International Monetary Fund (IMF)–led policies, and a package of financial assistance initiated a year before the national elections, stimulated the economy. AKP stuck to those policies and introduced new reforms to pursue full membership in the European Union. The economic reforms included fiscal discipline and inflation targeting. The most important reform was granting greater independence to the central bank to lower inflation. These policies helped stabilize the economy and attract foreign investment. The inflation went down to 6.4% in 2010. Productivity increased. Annual real economic growth averaged 6.9% between 2002 and

2007 and 5.9% between 2010 and 2017. According to the Turkish Statistical Institute (TUIK), the poverty rate was about 33% and was reduced to 18.5% in 2020, which means that around 15 million people live below the poverty line. Foreign direct investment reached $16 billion in 2015. Turkish manufacturers and construction companies expanded their markets to Africa, the Middle East, and elsewhere. Women's labor force participation rate rose from 25.3% in 2005 to 32.5% in 2021 (Economist, 2023a).

In recent years, Türkiye has faced several challenges, including political instability, a diplomatic crisis with some of its key trading partners, high inflation, and a sharp depreciation of the TL. These factors have contributed to a slowdown in economic growth. The AKP government's goal was to make Türkiye one of the world's ten biggest economies by 2023. The economy has since dropped from 17th to 21st among the world's major economies. The public debt-to-GDP ratio was 41.6% of GDP last year. The rapid depreciation of the TL in recent years has impoverished Turkish citizens. The purchasing power of an average household has diminished substantially. The average income dropped from $12,507 in 2013 to $9,661 in 2021. Over the past two years, skyrocketing prices and falling real wages have pushed millions of Turks into poverty. New economic policies reduce the middle class and increase poverty and income inequality (Figure 7.1).

Economic activity slowed down in recent years. Since 2018, the country has drifted from one currency crisis to another. The low-interest-rate policies caused a flight of foreign capital. Foreign investors cashed in their Turkish bonds and stocks. The TL plunged, and inflation rose to almost 87% in 2022 from 20%. As

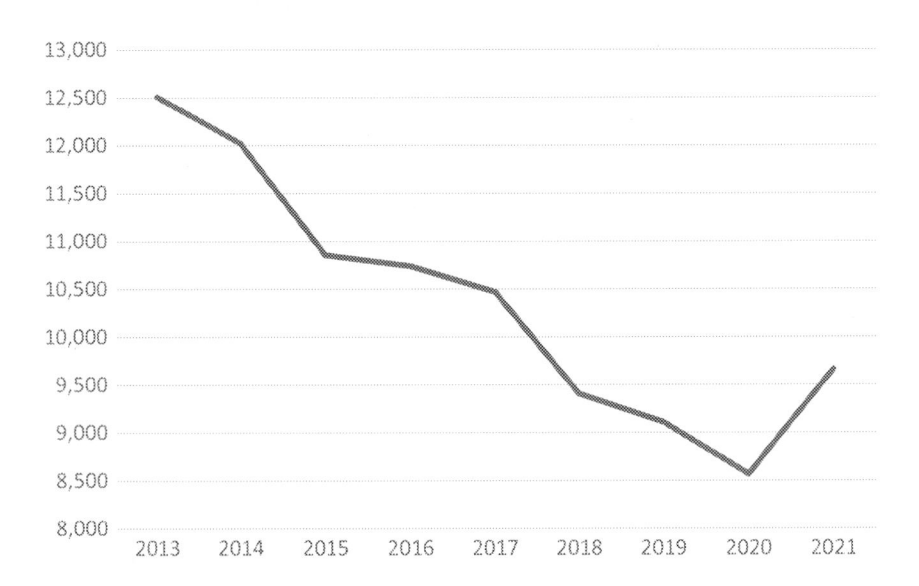

Figure 7.1 GDP per Capita (Current US$).

Source: World Bank, Development Indicators.

economic and political risks increased, foreign investments pulled out of the country, decreased to USD 5.2 billion in 2022 from USD 7.1 billion in 2021, and the TL depreciated rapidly.

The unorthodox economic policies introduced by Mr. Erdogan worsened the economic conditions even further. President Erdogan believes that high interest rates cause inflation. He argues that high interest rates increase production costs since capital, as a factor of production, plays a significant role in the total costs of producing goods and services. This claim, however, is in direct contradiction to mainstream economic principles.

President Erdogan directed CBRT and its monetary policy committee to reduce the policy rate. He aimed to stimulate domestic investment and support export-oriented sectors with low interest rates. He also assumed that the depreciation in the TL would invite more foreign direct investment and increase overall economic growth.

On October 21, 2021, CBRT's interest policy rate was reduced from 19% to 18% in September 2021 and 16% in October 2021. With a 100-basis point decrease in November and December 2021, the policy interest rate was reduced to 14%. The policy rate remained 14% from January 2022 to July 2022; it was reduced to 13% in August 2022. The reduction in the policy interest rate continued in the following months. In November 2022, the policy interest rate was 9%. On February 23, 2023, the policy interest rate was reduced to 8.5%.

As a result, the prevailing negative real interest rates for bank deposits motivated deposit holders to withdraw their TL-dominated savings and convert them to foreign currencies and other higher-return investments. The demand for foreign currency and foreign currency-denominated deposits increased dramatically, putting pressure on the value of the TL. Inflation rose to record levels. The demand for real estate, automobiles, and other durable goods increased. Prices of brand-new and second-hand cars increased dramatically, and real estate prices increased by 120% in 2022.

The government intervened in the foreign exchange market and tried to stabilize the value of the TL. It developed a special exchange rate–protected bank deposit account, which protects depositors against the drop in the value of the TL. The government encouraged people to convert their dollars to TL and deposit them into a bank account Foreign Exchange Protected Deposit Account (EPA) that would pay the interest rate plus any change in the dollar value against the TL. The account holder's balance is adjusted to reflect the original exchange rate. The Treasury pays the exchange rate protection difference to the commercial banks. Some citizens cashed in their investments and deposited their savings into these accounts. The government limited the interest ceiling for EPA deposits converted from Foreign Exchange Deposit Accounts offered by commercial banks to 300 base points above the policy interest rate but later removed the interest ceiling. EPA reached 1.5 trillion liras (USD 80 billion) on February 17, 2023.

The government took many other measures to mitigate the damage to the economy. These measures included pressuring banks to increase personal deposits in TL and providing more TL-dominated loans, forcing banks to purchase Treasury

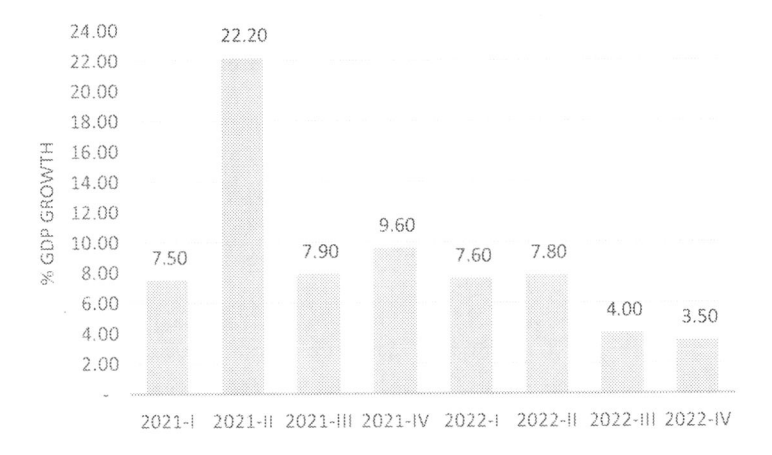

Figure 7.2 GDP Growth Rates by Quarter (2021–2022, %).
Source: CBRT, TUIK.

Bills. The government also requires export companies to keep 40% of their hard-currency earnings at CBRT, making it difficult for companies to pay for vital imports or service debts in dollars and euros.

The government increased controls on the food products chain markets and other retailers not to increase their prices and limited the increase in residential leases to 25%. The government stabilized the value of the TL with these measures.

However, these measures did not satisfy the deposit holders as the commodity prices kept increasing, and they started investing in real estate, other physical goods, and foreign currencies. They were also encouraged to participate in Borsa Istanbul, the Turkish stock market. However, Borsa Istanbul started to decline after being on the rise for a while.

After the earthquake in Eastern Türkiye on February 6, 2023, daily drops at the Borsa Istanbul reached about 8% and it was closed on the February 8. All the transactions were canceled for that day. The Borsa Istanbul resumed on the February 15, 2023.

The low-interest-rate policy, however, stimulates consumption and investments, creating economic stimulus. People with foreign currency-denominated investments are better off with higher exchange rates, and they spend. Wealthy youngsters keep spending despite the high prices. Last year, the Turkish economy grew by 11.4% in 2021 and 5.6%. Figure 7.2 shows the quarterly GDP growth rates for Türkiye.

The impact of low-interest-rate policy on various markets

The most important markets in a functioning economy are the goods and services, credit, foreign exchange, and labor markets. The goods and services market includes stores, the Internet, and other places to purchase and sell provisions, livestock, and other consumable items. The credit market brings together capital owners, households, companies, governments, international and domestic financial institutions, those needing credit for their expenses or investments, and individuals, companies, and governments. The labor market facilitates the interaction between workers and employers in an economy. The foreign exchange market is a global decentralized market where currencies are traded between individuals, banks, corporations, and other financial institutions.

The goods and services market

The Turkish economy depends on imported fuels, raw materials, and intermediate and final products. The currency depreciation increased the cost of goods and services since the Turkish economy relies on imports to manufacture many products, from food products to textiles to export. Türkiye is a net importer of energy. When oil and natural gas prices rise, Türkiye's trade deficit increases. The appreciation of the dollar and other currencies leads to higher prices, increasing the total value of imports and the need for foreign capital. Figure 7.3 shows the consumer and producer price indexes for 2015–2023.

Crude oil prices showed significant increases due to Russia's invasion of Ukraine. Since Türkiye is a net energy importer, increases in oil and natural gas prices, which depend on oil prices, hurt the foreign trade balance (Figure 7.4).

Due to the rising crude oil prices after Russia invaded Ukraine, Türkiye's mineral fuel imports increased by 74% in the first 11 months of 2022, reaching USD 88.3 billion (Figure 7.5).

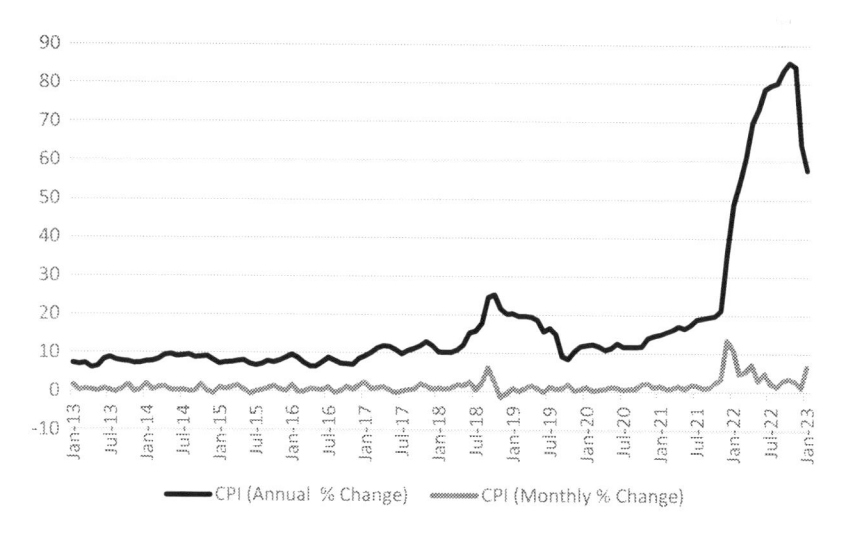

Figure 7.3 The Consumer and Producer Price Indexes (2015–2023, 2003 = 100, % Change).
Source: CBRT, TUIK.

Figure 7.4 Brent Crude Oil Prices (2022, USD/Barrel).
Source: US Energy Information Administration.

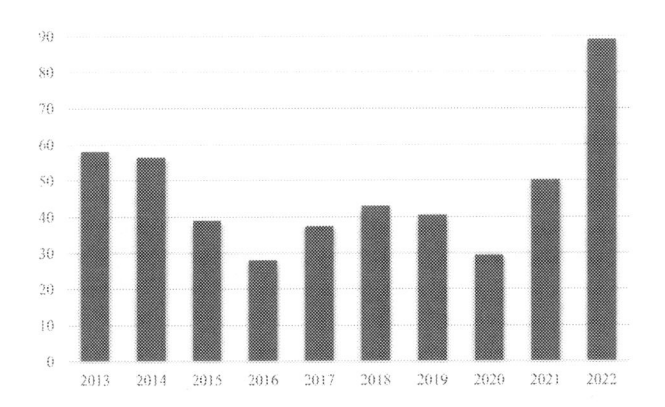

Figure 7.5 Mineral Fuel Imports of Türkiye (2013–November 2022, Thousand USD).
Source: TÜİK.

As the costs of imports increased, the balance of payments deteriorated for Türkiye. The balance of payments is the difference between all the funds flowing into the country and the outflow to the rest of the world at a given period. Due to the Russian occupation of Ukraine on February 24, 2022, the resulting energy crisis (increase in energy prices), and its impact on transportation costs, the deficit in the balance of payments has reached much higher than the values formed in the past 20 years. Türkiye's foreign trade deficit, USD 46 billion in 2021, increased to USD 89.7 billion in 2022. Table 7.1 presents statistics on exports, imports, and foreign trade balance. Türkiye's foreign trade volume increased significantly and reached USD 596.5 billion.

Table 7.1 Exports, Imports, and Foreign Trade Balance (Thousand USD, 2010–2022)

Year	Exports	Imports	Foreign Trade Balance	Foreign Trade Volume	Export–Import Coverage Ratio
2013	161,480,914	260,822,803	−99,341889	422,303,717	60.9
2014	166,504,861	251,142,429	−84,637568	417,647,290	65.3
2015	150,982,114	213,619,211	−62,637097	364,601,325	69.7
2016	149,246,999	202,189,242	−52,942243	351,436,241	72.8
2017	164,494,619	238,715,128	−74,220509	403,209,747	67.9
2018	177,168,756	231,152,483	−53,983,727	408,321,239	75.6
2019	180,832,722	210,345,203	−29,512,481	391,177,925	85.0
2020	169,637,755	219,516,807	−49,879,052	389,154,562	76.3
2021	225,291,385	271,424,473	−46,133,088	496,715,859	82.0
2022	254,200.000	364,400.000	−89,719,000	618,600,000	69.9

Source: TÜİK, World Bank.

The demand for goods and services, however, increased significantly. The low-interest-policy increased the exchange rates and led depositors to take their savings to other investments, such as purchasing other currencies and real estate, automobiles, and other durable goods, increasing the demand and prices of these products. The weak TL also made imported raw materials and intermediate and final products more expensive. Consumers rushed to purchase many goods and services, anticipating further price increases. Many people purchased automobiles, appliances, and imported luxury products, intending to sell them at higher prices to maintain the value of their savings. They were hedging against high inflation.

Another reason for high inflation is advance purchases for households and companies, anticipating further price increases. These advanced purchases of products and supplies put additional pressure on the prices. Due to exchange rate volatility and high inflation, companies prefer to keep their products in stock rather than sell them, creating further pressure on inflation.

The depreciation of a currency is usually assumed to increase exports since that country's products become more competitive in the world market. However, that has yet to happen for Turkish products. One reason might be exports' dependence on imported raw materials and intermediate products. Turkish manufacturers need to increase their prices as these inputs get more expensive. Increased costs partially reduce the impact of the depreciation in the TL. Figure 7.6 shows Türkiye's export and import volumes in US dollars between 2013 and 2022. The level reached by the trade deficit in 2022 is higher than in previous years.

The credit market

While CBRT cut the policy rate by 8.5%, banks' deposit rates continue to increase. According to CBRT data, as of March 10, 2023, the average deposit rate with maturity of up to three months rose to 27.83%, while loan rates remained below this rate. The average interest rates were 26.48% in consumer loans, 24.72% in vehicle loans, 16.40% in housing loans, and 16.17% in commercial loans.

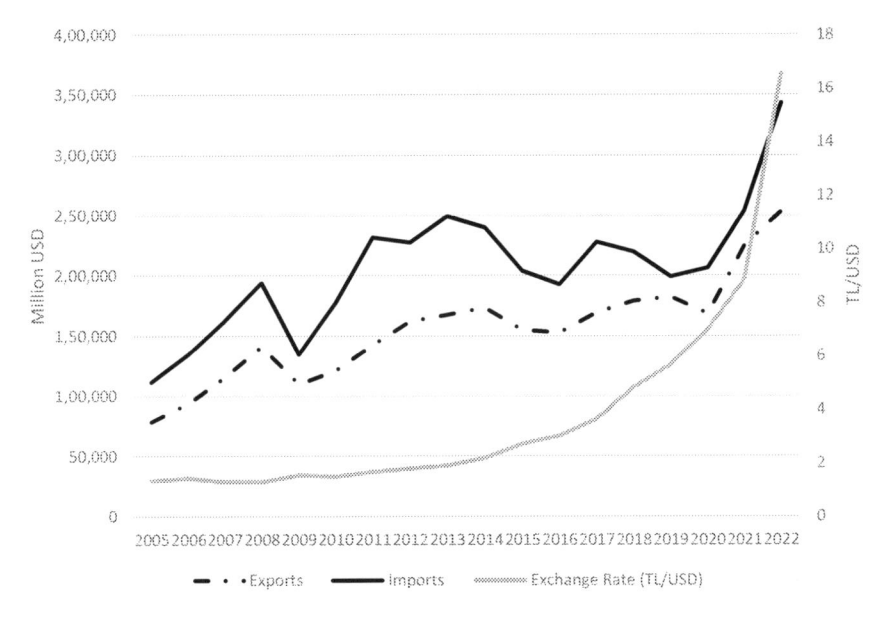

Figure 7.6 Exchange Rates, Export, and Imports (2022, Billion USD, TL/USD).
Source: CBRT.

Although deposit rates have risen, they are still well below the official inflation rate of 55.18%, and there is a loss in real terms. Negative real interest rates lead those with money to the stock market, real estate, gold, and consumption. Interest rates below the inflation encouraged people to borrow money and invest in assets with higher rates of return.

Due to the country's economic developments, there were significant fluctuations in the credit risk premium (credit default swap, CDS) values in 2022. CDS is the risk premium that increases the credit borrowing costs of countries. It is based on complex data and variables such as political stability, default history, and stock market fluctuations. In December 2022, Türkiye's default swap value decreased by 46.94 points compared to January 2022. The percentage change in 2022 was −9.25%. Türkiye's C.D.S. premium in 2022 was the lowest, with 487.15 points on December 15, 2022, and the highest value, with 908.4 points on July 16, 2022 (Figure 7.7).

The foreign exchange market

The Turkish forex market is where foreign currencies are bought and sold in Türkiye. The Turkish forex market is regulated by the Capital Markets Board of Türkiye, which oversees all financial markets in the country.

The TL has depreciated significantly over the past ten years. The lira experienced its most significant drop in value after the interest rate was reduced to

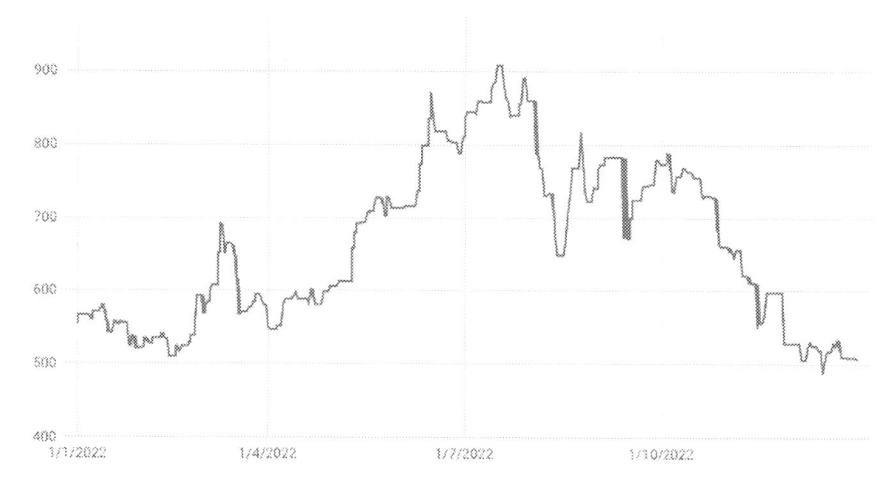

Figure 7.7 Türkiye C.D.S. Change Graph for 2022.

Source: doviz724.com (https://www.doviz724.com/turkiye-2022-yili-cds-grafigi.html).

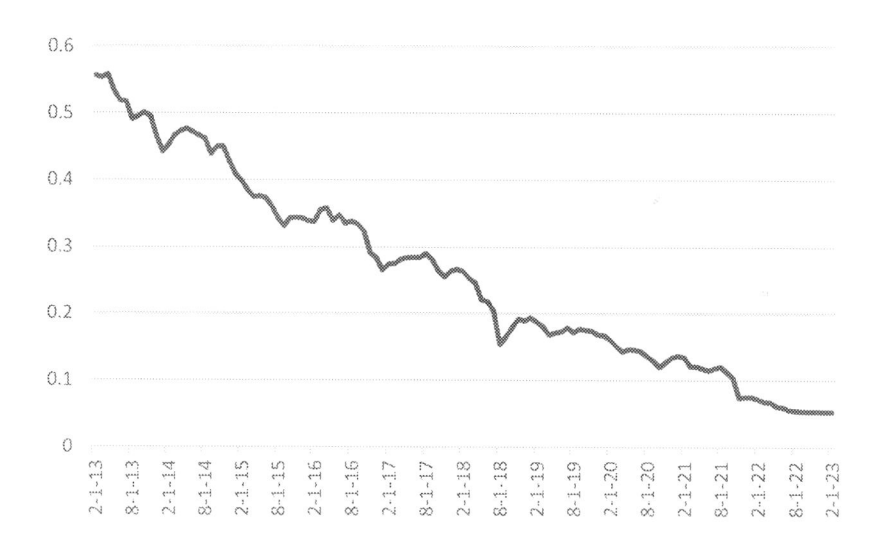

Figure 7.8 Turkish Lira/USD Exchange Rates (2013–2023).

Source: CBRT.

16% on October 21, 2021. The exchange rate for the dollar was TL9.31/USD and reached TL18.70/USD on December 30, 2022. Figure 7.8 shows the steep decline in the value of the TL against the dollar.

The government struggles to limit dollarization and stop the lira from falling further. The government shows heavy involvement in both credit and foreign exchange markets. The government intervenes in the exchange rate market by selling foreign currencies through CBRT, public banks, and public institutions. If the exchange rate increases that day, foreign exchange sales are made in the open markets after markets close. Billions of dollars were spent on this business, and net reserves, excluding swaps, fell to around minus $45 billion (Eğilmez, 2023).

The government is constantly changing the rules regarding the volumes of credit banks should offer, reserve requirements, etc., for the banks. The commercial banks were asked to increase the margin between purchase and sale prices of foreign currencies to discourage people from converting their TLs.

Labor market

The labor or job market refers to the overall demand and supply of labor within a country's economy. Individuals, businesses, and organizations interact to buy and sell labor services. The labor market is closely connected to goods and services and credit markets. The labor market in Türkiye includes both formal and informal employment sectors. The formal employment sector has jobs that offer benefits such as social security. The jobs are not registered or regulated by the government and typically do not provide social security benefits in the informal sector.

Türkiye's labor force participation rate averaged 49% from 2005 until 2022, reaching an all-time high of 54.10% in November 2022. In addition, Türkiye has a large informal sector where small companies avoid minimum wage restrictions, social security payments, and hiring and firing regulations.

In Türkiye, large firms account for 25% of employment and half of the private sectors value added. Some of these large companies are joint ventures with foreign firms. These companies manufacture high-quality, durable goods, car parts, and military hardware for export or generate, transmit, and distribute energy. Small, unregistered firms with low productivity are at the other end of the scale. A third group of medium-sized family firms is in between. Small- and medium-sized enterprises (SMEs) constituted 99.8% of the total enterprises in 2019. SMEs constituted 72.4% of employment, 51.8% of personnel costs, 44.1% of production value, and 44% of added value at factor costs (TUIK, 2019). SMEs have some registered and unregistered workers. The latest two subsequent increases in the minimum wage in recent months forced many SMEs to reduce their employees and hire part-time or unregistered employees whose salaries do not keep up with inflation or minimum-wage laws.

Low interest rates also reduce the cost of borrowing since they lower the amount to be paid in installments, leaving more money for spending on other goods, services, and investments. It may also create new employment opportunities because of increased economic activity and investments.

Another effect of the low-interest policy is an accelerating brain drain. Many young and well-educated Turks leave their homeland because they cannot afford the decent lifestyle they desire. At least 30,000 software developers and 1,400 doctors are said to have left the country in 2021, searching for better opportunities in advanced countries (Economist, 2023b).

Methodology and econometric results

The annual data examined in this study are sourced from the World Bank, the Development Indicators Database, and CBRT. The series investigated within this research include inflation and foreign direct investment, and the sample period spans from January 2000 to June 2023 for Türkiye.

Table 7.2 shows that all variables are nonstationary at the level. After taking the first differences, only the data for inflation become stationary. The other two variables, the exchange and interest rates, become stationary after taking second differences.

According to the traditional Granger (1969) causality test, the series must be stationary to find out the causality relationship between the variables. However, in the Toda–Yamamoto test, stationarity and cointegration are not required to make the causality test. Thus, this study uses a seemingly unrelated regression model with three variables to examine the causal relationship between inflation, exchange rate, and interest rate. If the inflation rate and exchange rate have a common stochastic trend, then it is expected to have a causal relationship between these two variables.

Toda and Yamamoto (1995), to investigate Granger causality (1961), developed a method based on the estimation of an augmented Vector Autoregressive Regression (VAR) model $(k + d_{max})$ where is optimal lag on the VAR model and is the maximum integrated order, two in our model (Table 7.3). VAR model of Toda and Yamamoto causality is set up as follows:

$$\text{inf}_t = \mu_0 + \left(\sum_{i=1}^{k} \alpha_{1t} \text{inf}_{t-i} + \sum_{i=k+1}^{d_{max}} \alpha_{2t} \text{inf}_{t-i} \right) + \left(\sum_{i=1}^{k} \beta_{1t} exc_{t-i} + \sum_{i=k+1}^{d_{max}} \beta_{2t} exc_{t-i} \right) +$$

$$\left(\sum_{i=1}^{k} \delta_{1t} \text{int}_{t-i} + \sum_{i=k+1}^{d_{max}} \delta_{2t} \text{int}_{t-i} \right) + e_{1t}$$

$$exc_t = \phi + \left(\sum_{i=1}^{k} \varphi_{1t} exc_{t-i} + \sum_{i=k+1}^{d_{max}} \varphi_{2t} exc_{t-i} \right) + \left(\sum_{i=1}^{k} \gamma_{1tt-i} + \sum_{i=k+1}^{d_{max}} \gamma_{2t} \text{inf}_{t-i} \right) +$$

$$\left(\sum_{i=1}^{k} \lambda_{1t} \text{int}_{t-i} + \sum_{i=k+1}^{d_{max}} \lambda_{2t} \text{int}_{t-i} \right) + e_{2t}$$

$$\text{int}_t = \mu_0 + \left(\sum_{i=1}^{k} \sigma_{1t} \text{int}_{t-i} + \sum_{i=k+1}^{d_{max}} \sigma_{2t} \text{int}_{t-i} \right) + \left(\sum_{i=1}^{k} \tau_{1t} \text{inf}_{t-i} + \sum_{i=k+1}^{d_{max}} \tau_{2t} \text{inf}_{t-i} \right) +$$

$$\left(\sum_{i=1}^{k} \varsigma_{1t} exc_{t-i} + \sum_{i=k+1}^{d_{max}} \varsigma_{2t} exc_{t-i} \right) + e_{3t}$$

Table 7.2 Unit Root Test Results

	ADF Test						
	Level			*First Difference*			
Variables	*Test Format*	*Test Statistics*	*Critical Value (%5)*	*Test Format*	*Test Statistics*	*Critical Value (% 5)*	*Conclusion*
inf	(c, t)	−3.48	−3.53	(c, t)	−6.395	−3.53	I(1)
exc	(c, t)	−1.423	−3.53	(c, t)	−3.14	−3.53	I(2)
int	(c, t)	−1.237	−3.53	(c, t)	−2.55	−3.53	I(2)

Source: Authors' own calculations using Eviews 10 statistical package.

*Expressions used in the parentheses represent constant terms and trends, respectively. **denotes the critical value of MacKinnon (1996).

Table 7.3 Optimum Lag Selection

Lags (Number of Years)	H.Q. Criterion	AIC Criterion	SIC Criterion
1	10.52	10.33	10.85
2	10.41[a]	10.08[a]	10.99
3	10.74	10.28	11.57
4	11.20	10.60	12.28

Source: Authors' own calculations using Eviews 10 statistical package.

[a] Indicates optimum lag.

Table 7.4 illustrates the bidirectional causality between inflation and the exchange rate within the context of the Turkish economy. When analyzing inflation as the dependent variable, the null hypothesis—that the exchange rate does not cause inflation—can be rejected, given that the p-value is below the 5% threshold. This signifies that the exchange rate indeed influences inflation. This relationship becomes particularly relevant when considering how the reduction in the policy interest rate is perceived by economic agents as an increase in the exchange rate, subsequently leading to heightened inflation.

Conversely, when the exchange rate is treated as the dependent variable, the null hypothesis is likewise rejected, indicating that the exchange rate is affected by inflation, a result that remains consistent and holds significance for the Turkish economy. Fluctuations in inflation in Türkiye correspond with changes in exchange rates rather than interest rates.

Another critical insight, detailed in Table 7.3, pertains to the relationship between fluctuations in the exchange rate and the demand for foreign currency. The consistency of this relationship suggests that economic agents, viewing changes in foreign currency prices as more than mere temporary shifts, may escalate their demand for foreign currency. This, in turn, could prompt further increases in the exchange rate.

Table 7.4 Toda-Yamamoto Causality Test Results

	Lag (k)	Lag (k + d_{max})	Chi²	Prob.	Direction of Causality
Dependent variable: inf	2	2 + 2	17.09735	0.000194	exc→inf
Dependent variable: inf	2	2 + 2	3.688999	0.158104	int ≠ inf
Dependent variable: exc	2	2 + 2	13.20438	0.001357	inf→exc
Dependent variable: exc	2	2 + 2	1.243708	0.536948	int ≠ exc
Dependent variable: exc	2	2 + 2	1212.352	0.00005	exc→exc
Dependent variable: int	2	2 + 2	2.006393	0.366705	inf ≠ int
Dependent variable: int	2	2 + 2	3.126891	0.209413	exc ≠ int

Where inf, exc, and int show inflation, exchange, and interest rates, respectively.

Source: Authors' own calculations using Eviews 10 statistical package.

Lastly, the Turkish economy's mechanism through which interest rates affect inflation is mediated by exchange rates. The absence of a direct causal connection between the interest rate and inflation illuminates this relationship. Furthermore, the consistent interventions by the Turkish Central Bank in interest rates may account for the complex dynamics observed and the difficulty in establishing a clear connection between interest rates and exchange rates.

Conclusion

The year 2022 has been a challenging year for the world and Türkiye. Due to rising energy prices, inflation increased in many countries and economic growth slowed. Türkiye also experienced high inflation and a large current account deficit in 2022. Although the depreciation of the TL in recent years has slightly increased export volumes, the increase in the values of other currencies and commodity prices has increased the cost of importing products and caused a rise in the trade deficit.

CBRT has implemented a low-interest-rate policy to stimulate economic growth since October 2021. However, the low-interest-rate policy dramatically increased inflation and significantly reduced the TL's value.

The ratio of exports to imports decreased significantly compared to the previous year and fell to 69.9%. The deficit in the balance of payments has reached levels much higher than the values observed in the past 20 years. Türkiye's foreign trade deficit increased to USD 110.2 billion in 2022 from USD 46 billion in 2021. Foreign direct investments decreased to USD 5.2 billion in 2022 from USD 7.1 billion in 2021.

The rapid depreciation of the TL was balanced by the measures taken at the end of 2021. However, the high exchange rates caused the prices of raw materials and intermediate products imported from abroad to increase and the production costs to increase. Due to rising oil, raw material, and intermediate product prices, imports increased by 34.0% in 2022, while exports increased by only 12.85%, despite the depreciation of the TL. In 2022, the consumer price index was 72.30% due to increased fuel prices, other export goods, and workers' salaries. Due to adverse developments in the country's economy, credit risk premium values experienced considerable fluctuations in 2022. The credit risk premium and the external debt costs of the country increased.

In conclusion, the complex interplay between inflation and exchange rates in the Turkish economy has been explained in the model findings. The bidirectional causality between inflation and the exchange rate establishes that changes in the exchange rate can cause or be caused by inflation, with *p*-values substantiating these claims. The Turkish economy's unique dynamics reveal that the effect of interest rates on inflation occurs primarily through exchange rates. The Central Bank's constant intervention further complicates the absence of a direct causal relationship between interest rates and inflation. Moreover, the relationship between changes in the exchange rate and the demand for foreign currency, along with how it can trigger further increases in the exchange rate, emphasizes the nuanced nature of these economic phenomena in Türkiye. These insights are consistent and have significant implications for the Turkish economy's policymakers and economic agents.

Türkiye must strive for an appropriate long-term macroeconomic strategy, a conducive political-economic institutional environment, and improve its productive capacity and high value-added export performance to maintain price stability and control current account deficits. The low-interest-rate policy of CBRT cannot be sustained with hyperinflation. Currency swaps and cash from the Gulf countries or Russia may support the lira until the election but not much longer. CBRT should monitor the economy carefully and adjust its policies to maintain stability and promote sustainable economic growth. Without a sound monetary policy, another currency crisis and a further increase in inflation will be unavoidable.

References

Alper, F. O. (2017). Türkiye'deki enflasyon ve nominal faiz oranı ilişkisinin analizi: Bayer-Hanck eşbütünleşme testi. 3nd International Congress on Political, Economic and Social Studies (ICPESS), 09–11 November.

Altunoz, U. (2020). Faiz haddi-enflasyon ilişkisi ve Türkiye'de Gibson çelişkisinin analizi: Keynes-Wicksell ve Fisher örneği. *Journal of Turkish Court of Accounts*, 33 (118), 153–178. http://registericpess.org/index.php/ICPESS/article/view/2163/412

Atgur, M. and Altay, N. O. (2015). Enflasyon ve nominal faiz oranı ilişkisi: Türkiye örneği. *Yönetim ve Ekonomi*, 22 (2), 521–533.

Bolatoglu, N. (2006). Türkiye'de enflasyon ve nominal faiz oranları arasındaki uzun dönemli ilişki: Fisher etkisi. *H.Ü. İktisadi ve İdari Bilimler Fakültesi Dergisi*, 24 (2), 1–15.

Cagan, P. (1979). *Persistent inflation: Historical and policy essays*. Colombia University Press, New York.

CBRT. (2023). Fiat Endeksi (Tüketici Fiyatları) (2003 = 100). Accessed: 16.01.2023. https://www.CBRT.gov.tr/wps/wcm/connect/TR/TCMB+TR/Main+Menu/Istatistikler/Enflasyon+Verileri/Tuketici+Fiyatlari

Eğilmez, M. (2023) Yanlış konomi politikasının sonuçları (mahfiegilmez.com)

The Economist. (2023a). The Turkish economy is in pressing need of reform and repair. 21, January 2023. Accessed: 16.01.2023. https://www.economist.com/special-report/2023/01/16/the-turkish-economy-is-in-pressing-need-of-reform-and-repair

The Economist. (2023b). How has Türkiye's economy kept growing despite raging inflation? Accessed: 17.01.2023. https://www.economist.com/briefing/2022/07/21/how-has-Türkiyes-economy-kept-growing-despite-raging-inflation

Fry, M. J. (1980). Money, interest, inflation, and growth in Türkiye. *Journal of Monetary Economics*, 6 (4), 535–545.

Granger, C. W. (1969). Investigating causal relations by econometric models and cross-spectral methods. *Econometrica: Journal of the Econometric Society*, 37 (3), 424–438.

Gul, E. and Acikalin, S. (2008). An examination of the Fisher hypothesis: The case of Türkiye. *Applied Economics*, 40 (24), 3227–323.

investing.com. (2023). Exchange rates. USD/TRY—Amerikan Doları Türk Lirası. Accessed: 16.01.2023. https://tr.investing.com/currencies/usd-try-historical-data

Karahan, O. and Yılgor, M. (2017). The causal relationship between inflation and interest rate in Türkiye. *Journal of Asian Development Studies*, 6 (2), 15–21.

Landreth, H. and Colander, D. C. (2002). *History of economic thought*. Fourth edition, Houghton Mifflin Company, Boston, USA.

MacKinnon, J. G. (1996). Numerical distribution functions for unit root and cointegration tests. *Journal of Applied Econometrics*, 11, 601–618.

Mercan, M. (2013). Enflasyon ve nominal faiz oranları arasındaki uzun dönem ilişkinin Fisher hipotezi çerçevesinde test edilmesi: Türkiye örneği. *Atatürk Üniversitesi İktisadi ve İdari Bilimler Dergisi*, 27 (4), 368–384.

Toda, H. Y. and Yamamota, T. (1995). Statistical inference in vector autoregressions with possibly integrated process. *Journal of Econometrics*, 66, 225–250.

TUIK. (2019). Accessed: 16.01.2023. https://data.tuik.gov.tr/Bulten/Index?p=Small-and-Medium-Sized-Enterprises-Statistics-2019-37548&dil=2

Tunalı, H. and Eronal, Y. Y. (2016). Relation between inflation and interest rates: Validity of Fisher Effect in Türkiye. *Süleyman Demirel Üniversitesi İktisadi ve İdari Bilimler Fakültesi Dergisi*, 21 (4), 1415–1431.

Turna, Y. and Ozcan, A. (2021). The relationship between foreign exchange rate, interest rate, and inflation in Türkiye: ARDL approach. *Journal of Ekonomi*, 05, 19–23. https://dergipark.org.tr/en/download/article-file/1158260Varlık, N. and Gebesoglu, P. F. (2021). Interest rates: The cause or the result? A chicken and egg problem revisited (The relationship between interest rates and inflation in Türkiye). *International Journal of Contemporary Economics and Administrative Sciences*, XI (1), 076–092.

Yapraklı, S. (2022). The validity of Neo-Fisher effect in the period of explicit inflation targeting: An econometric analysis on Türkiye. *EKOIST Journal of Econometrics and Statistics*, 37, 85–105.

Young, M. (2021). Why is Türkiye's president cutting interest rates, spurring inflation and lowering the value of the Lira? *Diwan. Middle East Insights from Carnegie*. Carnegie Middle East Center. Accessed: 10.01.2022. https://carnegie-mec.org/diwan/85896

8 An analysis of the relationship between Foreign Exchange Rate-Protected Deposit Implementation and exchange rates

Nihat Işık, Efe Can Kılınç, and Suat Serhat Yılmaz

Introduction

The significant depreciation of the Turkish lira (TL) against the dollar, especially since 2018, has brought along the dollarization problem in Türkiye. In response, the economic authorities and the Central Bank of the Republic of Türkiye (CBRT) took some measures under the name of "Dollarization Strategy" and introduced an alternative financial product, the Foreign Exchange Rate-Protected Deposit (FXPD) account. The FXPD implementation is a version of the Convertible Turkish Lira Deposit (CTLD) account implementation introduced in Türkiye in the 1960s to encourage foreign exchange inflows. CTLD accounts were also guaranteed to cover the exchange rate difference from the budget (Yayman, 2022: 1).

While FXPD implementation aims to protect depositors from exchange rate and price changes and to provide high returns in the micro plan, in the macro plan, it aims to prevent exchange rate fluctuations in Türkiye and to restrain the increase in exchange rates. In this context, it is important for policymakers to determine whether the relevant policy has achieved the desired results in the macro plan to understand the success of the implementation. For this purpose, in this section, the impact of the policy on exchange rates is investigated by utilizing time series econometric analysis methods. The analysis uses a weekly data set covering the third week of February 2022 and the second week of April 2023. The US dollar exchange rate, volume of FXPDs, deposit interest rate, and M2 money supply variables are used to measure the impact of the FXPD on exchange rates.

In this chapter, first, the definition, purpose, and functioning of the FXPD, the advantages and disadvantages of this implementation, and the CTLD, which is a similar implementation and has been put into effect in the past, are briefly explained. Then, the definition of exchange rate, its types and exchange rate systems, and the causes of exchange rate fluctuations are discussed. Following these, the effects of the FXPD on the Turkish economy, exchange rate, and inflation are discussed. Finally, the literature on the subject is analyzed under two separate headings: factors affecting the exchange rate and studies on FXPD. Following the related section, the application section is introduced, where the data set used in the study, explanations of the variables, unit root tests for the stationarity of the series, and cointegration

DOI: 10.4324/9781032631561-11

test findings to understand the long-run relationship are presented. Then, the impact of the relevant variables on the exchange rate is analyzed using the Threshold Regression method. This section also includes the theoretical explanations of the Breitung and Candelon's (2006) spectral GC test method and the findings obtained through this method and the related findings are interpreted. A review of the literature reveals that there is no econometric study on the subject. In this respect, the study is considered to contribute to the literature.

Foreign Exchange Rate-Protected Deposit Implementation

In the following sections, the definition, purpose, functioning, advantages, and disadvantages of FXPD and FXPD practices in Türkiye will be discussed, respectively.

Definition, purpose, and functioning of FXPD implementation

FXPDs are a type of deposit that aims to provide high returns in line with changes in exchange rates to protect depositors from the exchange rate and price changes in addition to the interest/profit share in normal deposit accounts. The macroeconomic policy objective of this practice is to prevent exchange rate fluctuations and ensure financial stability in Türkiye. At this point, real and legal persons are encouraged to convert their deposits in foreign currency into TL to prevent fluctuations in exchange rates and ultimately preserve the value of the TL (Çakalı & Baloğlu, 2022: 565).

The functioning of the FXPD implementation was announced by the Republic of Türkiye Ministry of Treasury and Finance on December 21, 2021, with a press release, and the said functioning is as follows (MTF, 2021):

- In the calculation of the return to be provided by the FXPD product, the interest/dividend to be processed on the accounts will be compared with the exchange rates on the date of opening the account and the maturity date, and the depositor will be credited interest by taking into account the higher exchange rate. In addition, there will be no withholding tax on such deposits.
- Foreign exchange buying rates will be announced by the CBRT every day at 11:00 a.m. to calculate the exchange rate changes between the date of opening the account and the maturity date.
- At the end of the term, if the exchange rate change is higher than the interest rate/dividend, the difference will be credited to the client's account in TL.
- FXPD accounts can be opened with maturities of 3, 6, 9, and 12 months. The CBRT interest rate will be taken as the minimum interest rate for these accounts.
- All banks will be able to participate in this system.

Following the announcement of the FXPD implementation on December 21, 2022, the scope of yield guarantees, and tax advantages was gradually expanded in the following months.

A similar practice in the past: convertible TL deposits

In the 1990s, Latin American countries attempted to hedge their national economies against exchange rate fluctuations by using financial instruments that provide treasury-guaranteed currency return options without paying a premium. These instruments have similar features to financial products such as FXPD and Currency Conversion Deposits. These financial instruments offer the option of an exchange rate return guaranteed by the treasury upon payment of a premium. In this way, Latin American countries have aimed to reduce the risks arising from exchange rate fluctuations (Yayman, 2022: 527).

A similar practice of FXPD was tried in Türkiye in 1967 under the name of CTLD. Therefore, the developments regarding this practice are presented below in chronological order, and the purpose and results of the practice are briefly mentioned.

The practice of CTLD was first introduced in Turkish law in 1967 with the Communiqué Serial: VII No. 37 Communiqué on the Decree on the Protection of the Value of Turkish Currency in 1967. Within the scope of this Communiqué, Article 16 of the Communiqué Serial: 1, No. 2 on the Procedural Communiqué on the Protection of the Value of the Turkish Currency was amended, and exchange rate guarantees were introduced for demand deposit accounts for Turkish residents and time deposit accounts for Turkish workers working abroad. In addition, credit utilization through these accounts was encouraged. Subsequently, communiqués dated 08.05.1975, 03.01.1977, and 16.02.1978 amended the scope and interest rates of this practice (Gülerci, 2022: 604).

The main purpose of CTLD is to bring foreign currency abroad into the Turkish economy. These accounts are foreign currency accounts opened in Türkiye by real or legal persons of Turkish or foreign nationality residing abroad. In this way, real or legal Turkish or foreign nationals deposited their foreign currency in a Turkish bank on behalf of a certain person under the exchange rate guarantees given to deposits. At this point, the source of the foreign currency is not asked, and the foreign currency, whether deposited in public or private sector banks, is transferred to the Central Bank. In practice, the holders of these accounts were then entitled to borrow TL against the deposited foreign currency. At the end of the maturity period, those who deposited the foreign currency in the bank have the right to buy it back, and the repayment of the foreign currency and exchange rate differences are guaranteed by the Treasury. These accounts are not affected by devaluation, have high interest rates, and can be converted into foreign currency at any time. In short, this type of account is a type of convertible account in which the state guarantees the deposit of foreign currency and enjoys both a profit guarantee and high interest rates, and in return for the profit, the domestic currency is deposited and used as a loan (Dönek, 1995: 176–177).

Even if the implementation of the CTLD had achieved its objective in the short term, by the end of 1978, the debt burden it created had reached a size corresponding to 52% of Türkiye's total external debt figures, and the related accounts accounted for approximately 2 billion USD of the USD 7.2 billion short-term external debt. Due to the negative effects of the practice, the Bank Credit Agreement signed in 1979 stipulated that authorized banks could not open new CTLDs, and after September 30, 1978, these accounts were converted into foreign exchange deposit accounts in accordance with the instructions of the Ministry of Finance (Mahlebeciler, 2006: 51–52).

Advantages and disadvantages of FXPDs

The introduction of the FXPDs has brought along many debates both in academia and in the press. There are many opinions on the advantages and disadvantages of this practice. In this context, the advantages and disadvantages of this practice will be discussed below.

The first advantage of the FXPD is that it protects economic units from the risks that may arise from exchange rate fluctuations. This practice transfers the exchange rate risk from investors to the treasury and reduces the risk of investors being affected by sudden changes in exchange rates (Kozanoğlu, 2021). Thus, by reducing the fluctuation in the exchange rate, it reduces the pass-through effect of the exchange rate on domestic prices.

The second-most important advantage of this product is that, in addition to providing customers with interest earnings/profit share, it also protects against exchange rate fluctuations. For this purpose, in the operation of the product, the exchange rates at the account opening date and the maturity date are considered, and if the interest/profit share gain is lower than the exchange rate difference return, an additional return is provided to the account holder. In this way, customers both benefit from interest/profit sharing and are not adversely affected by changes in exchange rates (Çakalı & Baloğlu, 2022: 572–573).

The diversification of investments is another advantage of FXPDs. This practice helps investors diversify their portfolios. Thus, investors can hedge against exchange rate fluctuations, spread risks, and diversify their portfolios. Moreover, FXPDs are generally offered by banks. Therefore, investors can be assured that their deposits are safely stored and protected under a specific regulatory framework. Therefore, it is a financial product with a guarantee.

The disadvantages of this practice are the indexation of the national currency to foreign currencies, the tendency to increase the budget deficit, and the CBRT's unnecessary payment of unnecessary difference to those who switch from foreign currency to FXPDs (Eğilmez, 2022b; Özatay, 2022).

Regarding the indexation of the national currency to foreign currencies, it is emphasized that this practice reduces confidence in the national currency. At this point, it is argued that the central bank is in charge of maintaining the credibility of its own currency and therefore, it should trust the money it prints. The indexation of one currency to another creates the impression that the Central Bank does not trust its own currency (Eğilmez, 2022b).

However, the fact that the FXPD system, which was created to prevent the exchange rate spike caused by interest rate cuts, tends to increase the budget deficit is another phenomenon that should be taken into consideration. At this point, the interest burden that should be borne by the normal banking system is transferred to the budget, which carries the risk of increasing the budget deficit (Özatay, 2022).

Another issue raised is that the CBRT may unnecessarily incur losses as a result of paying the difference to those who switched from foreign currency to FXPD accounts. Accordingly, if the CBRT incurs a loss at the end of the year, the Treasury will cover the loss. In this context, just as the CBRT's profits are transferred to the Treasury, its losses will also be covered by the Treasury (Eğilmez, 2022b).

Considering the advantages and disadvantages of the relevant practice together, it can be considered that this practice may be beneficial for investors in the micro plan and in the macro plan in terms of short-term solutions to sudden fluctuations in exchange rates. However, it is clear that in the long run, it will create economic problems both in terms of decreasing confidence in the national currency and the burden it will bring to the treasury. Therefore, this practice should not be continued for a long time and should be seen as temporary. As a matter of fact, the end date of the current implementation is the end of 2023. It is very important that the termination of the FXPD accounts, which have already reached a size of around USD 110 billion, be spread over time and that necessary precautions be taken. Similar to the interest rate hike, although it may help alleviate the exchange rate fever in the short term, in the long term, the root of the problem should be addressed and permanent and healthy solutions to the problem should be produced through measures to be taken at both micro and macro levels. In this context, as an economic policy, special attention should be paid to the foreign trade deficit, the dependence of production on imports of intermediate goods, the external dependence on energy, and the creation of a favorable investment climate for direct investments. Again, expanding the production of high value-added products, which has recently been demonstrated especially in the defense industry, to other sectors, and reducing the need for foreign exchange through measures to increase foreign exchange revenues and reduce foreign exchange expenditures through efforts to reduce foreign dependence on energy will be much healthier than temporary practices such as FXPD.

Exchange rate

As a result of the acceleration of globalization, there has been a significant increase in the trade of goods and services after 1980 and in financial movements after 1990, with the effect of the pro-liberalization policies of countries. As a natural consequence of this situation, the interest in and need for foreign currencies have increased. While the value of the currencies of countries against each other is an important indicator for the competitiveness of countries in one aspect, in another aspect, the difference between currencies has serious effects on many indicators of countries such as growth rate, unemployment rate, inflation rate, interest rate, etc. In the following sections, the definition and types of exchange rates, exchange rate systems, causes and effects of exchange rate fluctuations, FXPDs, stabilization of exchange rates, and the literature on the factors affecting exchange rates will be discussed.

Definition and types of exchange rate

The currencies of foreign countries or highly liquid payment instruments linked to these currencies are called "foreign exchange." These can be in the form of cash or highly liquid assets such as bank transfers, payment orders, foreign exchange policies, certificates of deposit, and traveler's checks. In Türkiye, those in the form of direct cash are called "currency" transactions, while those in the form of assets with high liquidity that can be easily converted into cash are called "foreign exchange" transactions (Seyidoğlu, 2009: 344–345).

The exchange rate is defined as the number of units of domestic currency needed to buy one unit of foreign currency. In other words, it is the ability to exchange one currency in one country for other currencies. The exchange rate, which allows a national currency to be converted into another national currency, is very important in that it facilitates international trade in goods and services and the transfer of funds between countries, while allowing the comparison of prices of different goods (Abdoh et al., 2016: 89).

Exchange rates, which are the quotation of one national currency in terms of another national currency, are quoted in two ways: a unit of national currency that can be exchanged for a unit of foreign currency is known as a direct quotation, while a unit of foreign currency that can be exchanged for a unit of national currency is known as an indirect quotation. Accordingly, for example, the expression of how many TL can be bought with 1 USD in the form of $1 = TL 19.40 is known as direct quotation, while the expression of how many USD can be bought with TL 1 in the form of TL 1 = (1/19.40) is known as indirect quotation. The direct quotation system is also called the European system and is used in Türkiye. In contrast, the indirect quotation system is known as the American system (Yalta, 2020: 186). This distinction is important because a rise in the exchange rate in the direct quotation system implies a depreciation of the national currency, whereas in the indirect quotation system, it implies an appreciation.

In the literature, there are four different types of exchange rates: the nominal exchange rate, the real exchange rate, the effective exchange rate, and the cross rate.

In the current period, the price of foreign currency in terms of the national currency is called the nominal exchange rate. In this context, for example, the exchange rate at foreign exchange bureaus in the market is the nominal exchange rate. The exchange rate obtained by adjusting the nominal exchange rate for inflation is known as the real exchange rate. The real exchange rate between TL and the dollar can be represented as real exchange rate $= (E_{TL/\$} \times P_{US})/P_{TR}$. In this equation, $E_{TL/\$}$ is the nominal exchange rate, P_{US} is the general price level in the United States, and P_{TR} is the general price level in Türkiye. Accordingly, an increase in the real exchange rate implies a depreciation of the TL against the USD. According to the equation, either an increase in the nominal exchange rate or a faster increase in the general price level in the United States than the general price level in Türkiye will lead to an increase in the real exchange rate. On the contrary, the exchange rate of one country is expressed as the average of the changes in the exchange rates of other countries, which is called the effective exchange rate. Finally, the cross rate shows the value of one foreign currency in terms of another foreign currency (Yalta, 2020: 187–188). For example, if USD 1 = TL19.40 and €1 = TL21.30, let's calculate the cross rate between the euro and the dollar. Accordingly, [(Euro/TL) ÷ Dollar/TL)] = 21.30 ÷ 19.40 = 1.097938 is the cross-exchange rates between the euro and the dollar.

Exchange rate systems

"Exchange rate systems," also called "exchange rate regimes," refer to the regime that determines exchange rates and changes in exchange rates. The exchange rate system sets the rules on how, through which power, and at what rates a country's currency will be linked to foreign currencies (Çağdaş, 2018: 3). From the system in which the exchange rate is determined by a central authority to the system in which it is freely determined according to the conditions of supply and demand in the market, many exchange rate systems have been and are being implemented in various economies of the world. Historically, it is observed that exchange rate misalignments have caused or indirectly triggered economic crises. In the literature, it is accepted that the international payment system started with the application of the double metal standard, and when the exchange rate system in the world economy is analyzed in the historical process, a distinction is drawn between the gold monetary standard, the Bretton Woods System and the post-Bretton Woods System period. Countries that have tried to implement national exchange rate systems in accordance with their own conditions and the world conjuncture have tried to renew these policies due to the economic instabilities and crises they have experienced over time. The fact that economic crises have increased worldwide over time and spread from country to country with the spillover effect due to globalization has transformed the crises from being country-specific situations to common problems of the world economy. In this context, organizations such as the International Monetary Fund (IMF) have assumed certain roles and provided loans to developing countries through structural adjustment, in other words, standby agreements and agreements to carry out structural reforms (Su, 2015: 2).

In practice, there are two main exchange rate regimes, fixed and floating, and different exchange rate systems as subregimes of these regimes. In the fixed exchange rate regime, which is the regime in which the external value of the national currency is equalized against foreign currencies by the Central Bank at a certain exchange rate, once the exchange rate is set, it remains the same until it is changed by the Central Bank. The peg regime, which is one way of implementing the fixed exchange rate regime, involves linking the national currency to a specific reserve currency or a basket of several currencies. There are hard currency boards and soft forms. The rigid peg regime does not allow intervention in exchange rate policy. Under this regime, the exchange rate is allowed to vary according to the movement of whichever currency or basket of currencies it is pegged to. The distinctive difference of the currency board regime, which is an advanced stage of this system, is that the printing of national currency is linked to foreign exchange inflows, and the functions of the central bank such as monetary supervision and lender of last resort are not used. The soft peg regime, which is more flexible than the hard peg regime, allows the government to regulate the exchange rate even though the national currency moves in relation to a foreign currency or a basket of currencies (Eğilmez, 2022a).

In a free-floating exchange rate system, exchange rate values are determined by supply and demand in the market. In this system, there is no government intervention in the exchange rate and the central bank is not required to keep exchange rates within the specified limits. In contrast to this feature of the full floating exchange rate system, in the dirty or managed floating exchange rate system, although the exchange rate is determined in the free market, the central bank has the authority to intervene in cases of excessive fluctuations (Abdoh et al., 2016: 89). The managed floating exchange rate regime also has two forms of implementation: continuous intervention and intervention when volatility occurs. Sometimes a band interval is selected for intervention in volatility. In the crawling bands (pegged with horizontal bands) regime, the exchange rate is allowed to fluctuate within a certain band, and the Central Bank intervenes if the exchange rate rises above or below this band. This practice takes the form of fluctuation within the band and interventionist fluctuation outside the band (Eğilmez, 2022a).

An analysis of the exchange rate systems implemented in Türkiye during the historical process reveals that there are differences in terms of periods. In this context, while the fixed exchange rate system was applied in the pre-1980 period, the post-1980 period witnessed a transition from a fixed exchange rate system to a flexible exchange rate system. In the 1980–1989 period, a fixed exchange rate system with frequent devaluations was applied. After full convertibility in 1989, a controlled free exchange rate system was applied in the 1989–1999 period and a fixed exchange rate system with daily increases was applied in the 2000–2001 period. Since the second half of 2001, a free exchange rate system has been applied in which CBRT interventions are limited (Barışık & Demircioğlu, 2006: 72). Although different exchange rate systems have been applied in different periods in the Turkish economy, the impact of the exchange rate on macroeconomic variables such as the balance of trade, inflation, capital movements, growth, money supply, exports, imports, interest rates, and money demand, their interactions with each other and the response to these variables in these regimes are important. For example, if the central bank wants the national currency to appreciate in the floating exchange rate regime, i.e., if it wants the exchange rate to fall, it sells foreign exchange to the market and withdraws money from the market, while in the opposite case, it buys foreign exchange from the market and decreases the value of the national currency by injecting money into the market (Yurdakul, 2016: 5).

Causes and effects of exchange rate fluctuations

Many factors such as inflation rate, real interest rate, current account balance, economic growth, speculation, and political stability can cause changes in exchange rates. For example, the national currency of a country with a lower inflation rate will appreciate. This is because prices of goods and services are cheaper in the country with a lower inflation rate. In this case, the demand for the goods of the country where prices are cheaper, and hence for that country's currency, will increase. By the most basic rule of economics, the price of something whose demand is increasing will increase, everything else being constant. Therefore, the currency of the country with low inflation appreciates. In terms of the real (inflation-adjusted) interest rate, since foreign capital will come to the country with a higher real interest rate, the demand for the national currency will increase and the value of the domestic currency will rise. On the other hand, the value of the national currency of the country with a higher current account deficit will decrease. This is because the foreign exchange income of the country with a current account deficit cannot meet its foreign exchange expenditures. Demand for foreign exchange causes the national currency to depreciate. The national income of the country with a higher growth rate and its demand will increase accordingly. Considering that imports depend on the national income of that country, an increase in the demand for foreign currency will lead to a depreciation of the national currency since some of the increased demand will be for foreign goods and services. Speculation that the value of a country's currency is expected to rise in the future will lead to buying that currency when it is cheap today and selling it when it becomes expensive in the future. An increase in demand for the currency in question would lead to an increase in its value, while a sell-off would lead to a decrease in its value. On the contrary, a country with political stability is more attractive to foreign investors and attracts investment from other countries. An increase in foreign capital inflows leads to an appreciation of the national currency.

Fluctuations in exchange rates are important for countries. This importance is based on the fact that many indicators such as inflation, interest rate balance, economic growth, employment, imports, exports, current account deficit, stock market, money supply, and especially gold prices, which are substitutes for foreign currency in the utilization of savings, energy prices such as oil and natural gas imported by many countries, are affected by exchange rates and exchange rates affect the mentioned indicators. Exchange rate volatility can create serious uncertainty on these indicators and cause economic and financial turbulence. Therefore, determining the causes and effects of exchange rate fluctuations is a much more important issue, especially for capital-strapped developing countries. Determining the factors affecting the exchange rate is also important for the formulation of sound policies for the future. Sudden changes in exchange rates create havoc on the economy and distort economic indicators. In this context, countries try to stabilize exchange rates by intervening in exchange rates from time to time using various methods, primarily monetary policy instruments administered by central banks. Sudden increases in exchange rates lead to an increase in the prices of imported intermediate goods, thereby raising the prices of manufactured goods. This situation reduces the competitiveness of domestic producers in international markets and adversely affects commercial segments doing business in foreign currency (Kartal et al., 2018: 210–211; Yıldız, 2022: 8).[1]

However, the exchange rate channel, one of the monetary transmission mechanisms, affects both aggregate demand and aggregate supply. For example, a monetary expansion that would lead to a decline in domestic real interest rates would result in capital outflows from the country as it would become less profitable for portfolio investors to invest in that country. This process, which will cause the national currency to depreciate, will cause the value of domestically produced goods to become cheaper than foreign goods. These developments in nominal exchange rates will increase net exports and aggregate demand to the extent that these nominal exchange rate changes are reflected in the real exchange rate. An increase in exchange rates would increase the prices of imported goods in terms of national currency and thus lead to a direct increase in inflation. An increase in the prices of imported goods will lead to a decrease in aggregate supply and consequently to an increase in the general level of prices. With the increase in international trade, countries' shift toward flexible exchange rate regimes and globalization, the exchange rate channel plays an important role in the functioning of the monetary transmission mechanism by affecting exports, the level of output gap, and inflation. However, the impact of monetary policy changes on the exchange rate cannot be determined with precise boundaries as it depends on domestic and foreign interest rates and inflation expectations. In general terms, the effect of the exchange rate channel in the transmission mechanism is directly proportional to the degree of openness of countries. Accordingly, the more open a country is, the more effective the exchange rate channel will be (CBRT, 2013: 7).

FXPD implementation and exchange rate stabilization

With the FXPD account, the depositor is offered an opportunity to earn a return depending on the interest rate/profit offered at the time of opening this account, and at the end of the maturity, when the exchange rate return is higher than the interest return, the increase in the exchange rate is paid to the depositor. This practice aims to eliminate exchange rate volatility, reduce the negative effects of exchange rate movements on the markets, prevent the victimization of those who keep their savings in TL, prevent direct intervention in the market (foreign exchange buying and selling), stabilize the TL and limit inflationary pressure due to the high exchange rate pass-through. By the end of December 2021, the FXPD practice started, and while deposits amounting to TL 470 million were accumulated in these accounts in February 2022, this figure reached approximately TL 1 trillion 701 billion 63 million by the end of March 2023. By the second week of May, this figure reached TL 2 trillion 346 billion 755 million.

On December 20, 2021, the USD/TL exchange rate, which peaked at 18.36 in the free market, declined to 13 as of December 21 because of the FXPD decision taken on the same day. It reached TL 14.6 in March and April 2022, TL 15.6 in May, TL 16.9 in June, TL 17 in July and August, and hovered around TL 18 until December. As of April 17, 2023, the official CBRT rate was around TL 19.40. Therefore, the dollar exchange rate has stabilized in parallel with the increase in the number of FXPD accounts. A similar trend was observed in inflation rates. While the inflation rate was 54.4% in February 2022, this rate rose to 78.6% in June, a short period of four months later. The increase in the inflation rate slowed down relatively as of July and reached its highest level of 85.51% in October. Subsequently, a downward trend started, reaching 64.27% in December 2022 and 43.68% in April 2023. A significant deceleration process was observed in exchange rates as of July 2022 and in inflation rates as of December 2022.

Literature review

There are many studies in the literature that examine the factors affecting the exchange rate. However, compared to this field, the literature is quite limited due to the newness of the FXPD implementation. For this reason, this section will first present the literature on the factors affecting the exchange rate and then the studies on the FXPD will be presented under a separate heading.

Literature on factors affecting exchange rate

The studies on the factors affecting the exchange rate are presented below in chronological order.

Bilgin (2004) analyzed the relationship between exchange rate policies implemented in Türkiye and unemployment. According to the results of regression analysis, he finds that there is a close relationship between the exchange rate and the unemployment rate in Türkiye.

Erdem et al. (2005) analyzed the price volatility spillovers in Istanbul Stock Exchange (ISE) indices with monthly data from January 1991 to January 2004 using exchange rate, interest rate, inflation, industrial production, and M1 money supply variables. The Exponential Generalized Autoregressive Conditional Variable Variance Model is used to test univariate volatility spillovers for macroeconomic variables. Accordingly, it is found that there is a strong one-way volatility spillover from inflation and interest rates to all stock price indices. Again, there are spillovers from the M1 money supply to the financial index and from the exchange rate to both ISE 100 and industrial indices. There is no volatility spillover from industrial production to any index.

Brailsford et al. (2006) examined the effects of sharply rising interest rates on Asian exchange rates during the Asian financial crisis using the Granger causality (GC) test. They find that while sharply rising interest rates helped support the exchange rates of South Korea, the Philippines, and Thailand, no significant causal relationship from interest rates to exchange rates was found for Malaysia, as the authorities in Malaysia did not actively adopt a high-interest-rate policy to defend its currency.

Sever and Mızrak (2007) analyzed the relationship between exchange rates, inflation, and interest rates in Türkiye using the Vector Autoregressive Regression (VAR) method for the period from January 1987—to June 2006. According to the findings, the variables are affected by both their own values and shocks occurring in other variables. However, exchange rates are more exogenous than inflation and interest rates and the impact of exchange rate changes on inflation and interest rates is higher. Therefore, exchange rate stability is one of the important factors in stabilizing inflation and interest rates.

Gül et al. (2007) investigated the relationship between nominal exchange rates and interest rates in Türkiye using the Johansen cointegration analysis and the GC test. The findings indicate that there is no cointegration relationship between nominal exchange rates and interest rates, while there is a one-way causality relationship between exchange rates and interest rates from exchange rates to interest rates.

Sujit and Kumar Rajesh (2011) used VAR, impulse–response and variance decomposition, and GC test to analyze the relationship between dollar gold price, stock returns, exchange rate, and dollar oil price using 3,485 daily data for the period from January 2, 1998, to June 5, 2011. The analysis reveals that the exchange rate is highly affected by changes in gold price, stock returns, and oil price.

Şentürk and Akbaş (2012), using monthly data for the period from January 2000—to June 2011 in Türkiye, examined the degree to which the deposit interest rate, USD/TL exchange rate, and international gold (ounce) prices affect the USD-based return of the ISE. The existence of short-run and long-run relationships is tested with ADF, DF-GLS unit root, and Dolado and Lütkepohl GC analyses. The findings indicate that there is a two-way directional causality relationship between the USD/TL exchange rate and the ISE USD-based return and a one-way directional causality relationship between deposit interest rates and the ISE USD-based return, while gold prices have an inverse interaction with the ISE.

Parveen et al. (2012), in their study on some important factors contributing to exchange rate volatility and their relative importance using ordinary least squares method using the annual data for the period 1975–2010, used inflation, growth rate, import, and export variables on exchange rate volatility to control for variability. The findings reveal that the main factor affecting the exchange rate in Pakistan is inflation, while the second, third, and fourth most important variables are economic growth, exports, and the order of change of imports, respectively.

Altıntaş (2013), using quarterly data for the period 1987–2010, found that there is a long-run relationship between exports and their determinants by estimating Türkiye's export function using the Autoregressive Distributed Lag (ARDL) method and causality tests with the help of exports, real income abroad, real exchange rate, real oil prices, and relative export price variables. The GC test findings show that there is a two-way causality between oil price-relative export price and foreign real income exports. This result is interpreted as indicating that exports in Türkiye are more sensitive to external economic developments.

Srinivasan (2014) investigates the relationship between stock prices, gold prices, and exchange rate in India with the help of the ARDL Bounds test and GC test using monthly data for the period from June 1990—to April 2014. The results show that gold and stock prices tend to have a long-run relationship with the exchange rate, whereas there is no stable long-run cointegration relationship between stock and gold price. The findings also indicate that there is no causality from gold prices to stock prices or vice versa in the short run.

Aslan et al. (2014) investigated the relationship between short-term capital flows, economic growth, and the exchange rate in Türkiye. As a result of the analysis, a one-way causality relationship between short-term capital flows and GDP and a two-way causality relationship between short-term capital flows and the real exchange rate were found.

Kaplan and Yapraklı (2014) aim to identify the factors affecting the exchange rate of 12 fragile Emerging Economies (EMEs). For this purpose, the effects of current account deficit/GDP, gross public debt/GDP, private sector domestic credit debt/GDP, foreign exchange reserves/GDP, inflation rate, and external debt/exports variables, which are included in the fragility index announced by the FED for the period 2000–2012, on the exchange rate are analyzed using panel data method with standard error corrected estimators. According to the results of the analysis, the exchange rate is negatively affected by current account deficit/GDP, gross public debt/GDP, private sector domestic credit debt/GDP, and inflation rate variables, while it is positively affected by foreign exchange reserves/GDP and external debt/exports variables. The variable that affects the exchange rate the most is determined as foreign exchange reserve/GDP.

Özdamar (2015) investigates the relationship between domestic producer prices and various macroeconomic variables in Türkiye using monthly data for the period from January 2006—to October 2015 with the ARDL Border test method. The finding that the exchange rate effect on domestic producer prices, in the long run, is low is consistent with the hypothesis that the exchange rate pass-through effect will be lower in a low inflation environment. Other results of the study show that the effect of crude oil prices on producer prices, in the long run, is quite weak, whereas the money supply and the level of industrial production representing domestic income have a strong effect.

Coşkun and Ümit (2016), using monthly data for the period from January 2000—to July 2014, examined the long-run relationship between BIST 100 stock index return and exchange rate, gold price, deposit interest rate, and real house price index using Johansen (1988) and Johansen and Juselius (1990) cointegration test without structural breaks and Maki (2012) cointegration test with multiple structural breaks. Accordingly, while the Johansen test indicates that there is one cointegration relationship between the series, the Maki test finds that there is no long-run relationship between the series.

Hacıevliyagil and Demir (2016) examined the relationship between exchange rate behavior and macroeconomic aggregates in the short and long run between Türkiye and BRICS (T-BRICS) countries based on monthly data for the period from January 2002—to November 2013. As a result of the study, Türkiye is one of the two countries where imports are insignificant variables affecting the exchange rate, while another finding is that Türkiye is one of the countries where inflation rates affect the exchange rate the most with a very high coefficient. These findings reveal that there are some issues that Türkiye should pay attention to be included in the BRICS countries in terms of macro variables affecting the exchange rate.

Abdoh et al. (2016), using the Random Effect Model for selected ASEAN countries, find a significant relationship between exports and exchange rates, but no significant relationship between inflation, interest, and exchange rates.

Mariano et al. (2016) examined the factors affecting the real exchange rate in the Philippines between 1973 and 2014. For this purpose, GDP, volume of money flows, net foreign assets, budget deficit, import restrictions, and oil prices are used. An unrestricted vector autoregressive model was used to investigate the response of the real exchange rate to different macroeconomic variables. The Johansen cointegration test indicates that there is no long-run cointegration relationship between the dependent variable and the independent variables. Variance decomposition shows that GDP and the volume of money flows account for a large share of the real exchange rate movement. In the Philippines, all variables except oil prices have a positive relationship with the real exchange rate.

Lamia and Djelassi (2017), using monthly data for the period January 1993–July 2013, examine the relationship between exchange rate and inflation targeting regimes in six emerging economies that adopted inflation targeting (IT-Inflation Target) regimes with the help of the ARDL model. The study aims to examine how the adoption of inflation targeting affects Exchange Rate Pass Through (ERPT) and volatility. The findings show that for most economies analyzed, the ERPT declines after the adoption of inflation targeting for both the consumer and producer price indexes. Moreover, the results suggest that the inflation targeting regime can reduce exchange rate volatility and inflation volatility in all countries. Thus, the implementation of the inflation targeting regime contributes to price stability by reducing exchange rate pass-through and exchange rate volatility.

Hamza and Elijah (2018) examined the asymmetric relationship between oil prices and exchange rate in Nigeria for the period from January 2008—to December 2017. The analysis using the Nonlinear Autoregressive Distributed Lag (NARDL) model shows that there is a cointegration relationship between oil price increases and decreases and the exchange rate. The study also found that the decrease in oil prices has a negative impact on the exchange rate. Other findings of the study are that the increase in oil price has a negative and insignificant effect on the exchange rate in the long run and that there is an asymmetric relationship between the decrease in the exchange rate and the increase in oil price.

Kartal et al. (2018), with the aim of helping the regulatory and supervisory authorities to keep exchange rates under control by determining the factors affecting the USD and euro exchange rates in Türkiye, using monthly data for the period from January 2006 to June 2017, the most important macroeconomic indicators for the USD exchange rate forecasting model are money supply, budget deficit, foreign investments, unemployment, domestic debt, imports, inflation, and current account deficit, while the most important variables for the euro exchange rate forecasting model are money supply, budget deficit, current account deficit, foreign investments, crude oil imports, and exports.

Singhal et al. (2019) investigate the dynamic relationship between international oil prices, international gold prices, exchange rates, and stock market indexes for the Mexican economy. Using daily data for the period January 2006–April 2018 and the ARDL bounds test cointegration approach, the findings of the study show that international gold prices have a positive effect on the Mexican stock price, while oil prices have a negative effect. At the same time, in the long run, oil prices negatively affect the exchange rate, while gold prices have no significant effect on the exchange rate.

Rahimli and Nazirov (2020) analyze the relationship between oil prices, real effective exchange rate, and real GDP with a VAR model using quarterly data for the period from January 2001—to April 2020. The findings indicate the existence of GC between oil prices and GDP, while a shock to oil prices causes 72% fluctuations in real effective exchange rates. Moreover, although a shock to oil prices has a positive effect on GDP in the short run, the effect is negative in the long run.

A general analysis of the above literature studies reveals that the effects of variables such as unemployment rates, interest rates and inflation rates, industrial production, money supply, gold price, stock returns, international oil prices, foreign exchange reserves, current account deficit/GDP, gross public debt/GDP, budget deficit, private sector domestic debt/GDP, foreign exchange reserves/GDP, real GDP, volume of money flows, net foreign assets, import restrictions, external debt/exports, and current account deficit on exchange rates have been discussed. According to the results of the studies, the finding that there is a close relationship between the exchange rate and the unemployment rate indicates that exchange rate policies are effective in unemployment in Türkiye. Inflation and interest rate variables are found to cause strong volatility spillovers on stock price indices. Moreover, gold prices, stock returns, and oil prices are found to have a significant impact on the exchange rate. To sum up, the general conclusion that can be drawn from the studies is that there are complex and multifaceted relationships between exchange rates and economic variables. However, each study has reached specific results within the framework of its scope and methods.

Literature on FXPD implementation

Since the FXPD account is a relatively new practice, there is a very limited number of studies in the literature. For this reason, no econometric study that considers the effect of FXPD has been found in the literature review. In this context, studies on the FXPD Implementation are presented below.

Köstekçi and Özbay (2023) discussed the FXPD system implemented against the exchange rate shock as a result of the policy changes that emerged with the new economic model in the COVID-19 and the following period in the context of the objectives of taxation. When the results of the study are evaluated in general, they show that the FXPD system has significant advantages for capital holders and the banking sector.

Yurttadur and Taşcı (2023) examined the impact of the FXPD implementation on the financial performance of participation banks. The data set of the study, which covers 12 months of data for 2021 and 9 months of data for 2022, was obtained from the website of the Banking Regulation and Supervision Agency (BRSA). In the analysis section, a hybrid Multi-Criteria Decision-Making

Methods (MCDM) consisting of Criteria Importance Through Intercriteria Correlation (CRITIC) and Weighted Aggregated Sum Product Assessment (WASPAS) methods was used to measure the impact of FXPD implementation on the performance of participation banks. The findings obtained as a result of the analysis indicate that the highest weight in determining the financial performance of participation banks among the criteria considered is the Operating Expense/Total Assets criterion. The results obtained from WASPAS show that participation banks exhibited their worst performance in May 2021 during the analyzed period. According to this analysis, the period in which these banks had the best performance was September 2022.

Yayman (2022) examines whether the tax privileges introduced for the FXPD system are a burden on the state budget. The data sources used in the study are budget statistics published by the Ministry of Treasury and Finance, CBRT's monetary and banking statistics, circulars, communiqués, laws, and statements. The findings reveal that the contingent liability assumed by the public sector through the FXPD reassures residents about the preservation of the financial value of the TL, and the impact of the FXPD on the budget remains low based on the first quarter data of 2022. The study states that since the exchange rate difference in the FXPD is financed by CBRT resources, high inflation risk may be encountered in the coming period, and if the FXPD is implemented until the end of 2022, these tax privileges may put a negative burden on the budget.

Gülerci (2022) aims to make a legal analysis and evaluation of the main arrangements made within the scope of FXPD. In this context, the study analyzed the relations between the Central Bank, the bank, and the account holder, evaluated the legal nature of the exchange rate hedge or the exchange rate or price guarantee, explained the responsibility of the banks at this point, described the meaning of the principal guarantee, and made determinations on the legal nature of the additional payments introduced within the scope of FXPD. As a result of the study, it is concluded that the regulations on participation accounts with exchange rate protected or exchange rate or price guarantees do not comply with the operational logic of participation accounts since they cover a certain payment commitment.

Akgemici (2022), within the framework of the announcement of the Public Oversight Accounting (POA) and Auditing Standards Authority on March 1, 2022 on "Accounting for Currency/Gold Conversion Currency/Price Protected TL Deposit Accounts," provided information and examples on how to classify the FXPD as a financial asset within the scope of TFRS 9 Financial Instruments Standard, how to measure it at the end of the period and how to recognize the income or expenses arising.

Yalçın and Emül (2022) aimed to examine how foreign exchange rate-protected forward accounts are used in enterprises and to offer solutions for the accounting system. The study first discusses the legal infrastructure of these accounts and then examines the accounting and recognition process. The study also includes a monograph for a better understanding of the subject.

Çakalı and Baloğlu (2022) aimed to explain how to account for transactions arising from exchange rate-protected accounts. In this context, they discussed the journal entries to be made by legal customers and banks in detail with examples.

A review of the literature reveals that there is no econometric study that directly examines the effect of FXPD implementation on the exchange rate. However, there is a study that quantitatively examines the impact of FXPD on the financial performance of participation banks. Indeed, Yurttadur and Taşcı (2023) examine the impact of the practice on the financial performance of participation banks. Köstekçi and Özbay (2023) study the FXPD implementation in the context of its objectives, while Yayman (2022) examines whether the tax privileges introduced for the exchange rate-protected accounts system are a burden on the state budget. Gülerci (2022) provides a legal analysis of the general regulations within the scope of the FXPD system. While Akgemici (2022) discusses how to classify FXPD accounts, how to measure them at the end of the period, and how the income or expenses should be recognized, Yalçın and Emül (2022) debate how FXPD accounts are used in enterprises. Finally, Çakalı and Baloğlu (2022) investigate how FXPDs should be accounted for. Therefore, considering the given literature studies, it is seen that there is no econometric study, and, in this respect, the study is expected to contribute to the related literature.

Application

Data, method, and findings

The relationship between FXPDs and the dollar exchange rate in the sample of Türkiye is tested using data from the third week of February 2022 to the second week of April 2023. The variables used in econometric analyses for this purpose are given in Table 8.1. The dollar exchange rate was determined as dependent variable, deposit interest rate, FXPD, and money supply were detected as independent variables. The natural logarithms of the variables are taken to contribute to their stationarity.

In Table 8.2, descriptive statistics of the variables used to test the effect of FXPD implementation on the dollar exchange rate are given. When the skewness

Table 8.1 Data Set

Variable Name	Abbreviation	Definition
Dollar Exchange Rate	LNER	It is the weekly buying rate of the US dollar.
Deposit Interest Rate	LNDIR	It is the interest rate applied to the deposits opened in total TL by Banks.
Foreign Exchange Rate-Protected Deposit (FXPD)	LNFXPD	It is the total amount of TL accumulated in FXPDs.
Money Supply	LNM2	M2 is calculated by adding time deposits to demand deposits with money in circulation.

Source: CBRT, Electronic Data Delivery System. https://evds2.tcmb.gov.tr/ Date of Access: April 24, 2023.

Table 8.2 Descriptive Analysis

Variables	LNER	LNFXPD	LNDIR	LNM2
Mean	2.853211	13.95383	2.828738	22.70065
Median	2.903069	14.11473	2.791778	22.72856
Maximum	2.958549	14.45240	3.033028	22.96531
Minimum	2.607861	13.05885	2.732418	22.39341
Standard Deviation	0.103319	0.344849	0.085754	0.159674
Skewness	−1.014488	−0.964018	0.860556	−0.289920
Kurtosis	2.531793	2.942780	2.560151	1.922559
Jarque-Bera	11.02057	9.456509	8.020730	3.805114
Probability	0.004045	0.008842	0.018127	0.149187
Sum	174.0459	851.1836	172.5530	1384.740
Sum Square Deviation	0.640492	7.135263	0.441220	1.529742
Observations	61	61	61	61

values of the variables are examined in terms of the normal distribution character-istics, it is seen that the LNDIR variable is positively skewed to the right, while the LNER, LNFXPD, and LNM2 variables are negatively skewed to the left. In terms of kurtosis values, since the kurtosis values of the variables are less than 3, it is understood that their distribution is flat compared to the normal distribution. There are 61 observations in the analysis.

Method

In this study, ADF and PP unit root tests, threshold regression, Johansen's (1991, 1995) cointegration test, GC, and Breitung and Candelon's (2006) spectral GC tests were used to test the relationship between FXPD and dollar exchange rate. In this section, as other tests are largely known, especially the mathematical back-ground of the spectral GC test will be given. Since this method is based on the GC test logic, the conventional Granger method will also be explained.

Granger (1969), Toda and Yamamoto (1995), and Dolado and Lütkepohl (1996) time domain causality test graphs show signal differences over time, while fre-quency domain graphs show how the signal lies within each given frequency (ω) band of the frequencies (Hicham et al., 2019: 101). The frequency domain ap-proach allows the investigation of causality dynamics at different frequencies in-stead of relying on a single statistic as in conventional time domain analysis (Bayat et al., 2014: 33).

In the Granger (1969) causality test, it is tested whether the second factor pro-vides useful information in estimating a factor for the future. In this context, the following VAR model is primarily based on the GC analysis (Tuna & Tuna, 2022):

$$Y_t = a_{01} + \sum_{i=1}^{p} a_{1i} Y_{t-i} + \sum_{i=1}^{p} \beta_{1i} X_{t-i} + u_{1i}$$

$$X_t = a_{02} + \sum_{i=1}^{p} a_{2i} Y_{t-i} + \sum_{i=1}^{p} \beta_{2i} X_{t-i} + u_{2i}$$

In the first equation, it is tested that the variable X is not the Granger cause of the variable Y. For this purpose, the residual sum of squares is calculated using the equation $Y_t = a_{01} + \sum_{i=1}^{p} a_{1i} Y_{t-i} + u_{1i}$ of the first model, and then the F statistic is calculated:

$$F = \frac{\left(rss_{\text{restricted}} - rss_{\text{unrestricted}} \right) / m}{rss_{\text{unrestricted}}) / \left(n - k \right)}$$

The calculated F statistic is compared with the F table value, and when the F statistic is greater than the table value, the H_0 hypothesis showing that the Y variable is not the Granger cause of the X variable is rejected (Tuna & Tuna, 2022: 4).

As stated in Geweke (1982), Hosoya (1991), and Breitung and Candelon (2006), the findings obtained from conventional GC tests do not differ according to different frequencies. Breitung and Candelon (2006) developed the Frequency Domain Causality test based on the fact that different causality findings can be obtained for different frequencies (Canbay et al., 2023: 13).

The spectral density function, which is the basis of frequency causation, can be expressed with the following equation (Akdağ et al., 2020: 56; İskenderoğlu & Akdağ, 2017: 629):

$$f_x(\omega) = \frac{1}{2\pi} \left\{ \left| \Psi_{11}\left(e^{-i\omega}\right) \right|^2 \right\} + \left| \Psi_{12}\left(e^{-i\omega}\right) \right|^2$$

However, the problem of using the F test arises during the application of the related tests. This problem has been solved by applying the linear constraints proposed in the study of Breitung and Candelon (2006). Nonlinearity with frequency causality test causality analysis is carried out (Akdağ et al., 2020: 56; İskenderoğlu & Akdağ, 2017: 629). To perform the frequency test, Geweke (1982) and Hosoya (1991) defined a two-dimensional vector of time series $z_t = \left[x_t y_t \right]'$. z_t, has a finite-order VAR:

$$\Theta(L) z_t = \varepsilon_t$$

In this equation, $\Theta(L) = I - \Theta_1 L - \cdots - \Theta_p L^p$ and lag polynomial with $L^k z_t = z_{t-1}$ (Bayat et al., 2014: 34; Şahin, 2018: 401).

Granger (1969) causality at different frequencies is expressed by:

$$M_{y \to x}(\omega) = \log \left[\frac{2\pi f_x(\omega)}{\left| \Psi_{11}\left(e^{-i\omega}\right) \right|^2} \right] = \log \left[1 + \frac{\left| \Psi_{12}\left(e^{-i\omega}\right) \right|^2}{\left| \Psi_{11}\left(e^{-i\omega}\right) \right|^2} \right]$$

Here, if $\left| \Psi_{12}\left(e^{-i\omega} \right) \right|^2 = 0$, there is no GC from variable y to variable x at frequency ω. Breitung and Candelon (2006) developed a new method to test the null hypothesis, which states that there is no causality in their study (Akdağ et al., 2020: 56; İskenderoğlu and Akdağ, 2017: 629).

Breitung and Candelon (2006)'s approach is based on the following linear constraints (Aydin, 2020: 89; Karagöl, 2021: 353)

$$\sum_{k=1}^{p} \theta_{12,k} cos(k\omega) = 0$$

$$\sum_{k=1}^{p} \theta_{12,k} sin(k\omega) = 0$$

To simplify the formula, it is written as $a_j = \theta_{11,j}$ and $\beta_j = \theta_{12,j}$ and VAR equation for x_t is expressed as follow:

$$x_t = a_1 x_{t-1} + \cdots + a_p x_{t-p} + \beta_1 y_{t-1} + \cdots + \beta_p y_{t-p} + \varepsilon_{1t}$$

In Breitung and Candelon's (2006) method, the existence of GC can be tested at any ω frequency value. Accordingly, the hypotheses for each frequency value are as follows:

$$H_0 : R\left(\omega \right)\beta = 0, \beta = \left[\beta_1, \ldots, \beta_p \right] \text{ and } R\left(\omega \right) = \begin{bmatrix} cos\left(\omega \right) & \ldots & cos\left(p\omega \right) \\ sin\left(\omega \right) & \ldots & sin\left(p\omega \right) \end{bmatrix}$$

The significance values of the 0.5, 1.5, and 2.5 frequencies of ω indicate the existence of long-, medium-, and short-term causality, respectively. Here, the $2\pi / \omega$ formula pointed out by Tastan (2015) is used to calculate the duration of the causal relationship (Karagöl, 2021: 353–354).

Findings

In this part, first, whether the variables are stationary or not was investigated using Augmented Dickey–Fuller (ADF) and Phillips–Perron (PP) unit root tests. Considering the unit root test findings in Table 8.3, all variables in the ADF test are not stationary at both intercept and intercept and trending levels. According to the PP test, LNER and LNFXPD variables were found to be stationary at their levels, while LNDIR and LNM2 variables were not stationary. In the case of intercept and trending in the same test, all of the variables are not stationary at their levels. When the ADF and PP unit root tests are evaluated as a whole, it has been determined that all variables are not stationary at their levels, and they become stationary when their first difference is taken.

Table 8.3 Unit Root Tests

Variables/ Tests	ADF		PP	
	Intercept	Intercept and Trend	Intercept	Intercept and Trend
LNER	−2.346645	−1.799700	−3.160828**	−1.691555
LNDIR	0.647500	−1.493139	0.460786	−1.674819
LNFXPD	−2.111512	−2.176863	−4.480560**	−3.424670
LNM2	−1.258004	−2.394555	−1.643304	−2.344728
First differences				
ΔLNER	−4.247972***	−4.787928***	−4.154791***	−4.500240***
ΔLNDIR	−7.533787***	−7.896117***	−7.537735***	−7.888574***
ΔLNFXPD	−4.599611***	−4.550549***	−4.657664***	−4.724636***
ΔLNM2	−9.595347***	−9.609045***	−9.522089***	−9.605981***

*** $p < 0.01$, ** $p < 0.05$.

Table 8.4 Threshold Regression Results

Dependent Variable:	Variable	Coefficient	Robust Standard Error	z	P > |z|
LNER	LNDIR	−0.0832639	0.0560906	−1.48	0.138
	LNM2	0.5634191	0.0810737	6.95	0.000
Region 1	LNFXPD	0.0896749	0.0284058	3.16	0.002
	Cons	−10.94562	1.422275	−7.70	0.000
Region 2	LNFXPD	−0.1304061	0.0516085	−2.53	0.012
	Cons	−7.848961	1.162503	−6.75	0.000

Threshold variable: LNDIR. Threshold value = 2.8178. Number of obs = 61.

Sum of Squared Residuals (SSR) = 0.0127. Bayesian Information Criteria (BIC) = −492.2810.

After testing whether the variables are stationary or not, the effect of FXPD on exchange rates is revealed using threshold regression. Table 8.4 shows the findings obtained from the threshold regression analysis. Among the explanatory variables, the deposit interest rate has a negative but statistically insignificant effect on the dollar exchange rate, while the money supply has a positive and statistically significant effect. The threshold value determined for the logarithm deposit interest rate is 2.8178. When the antilog of this value is taken, it corresponds to 16.74%. "Region 1" shows the region where the deposit interest rate is below 2.8178 (16.74%), while "Region 2" shows the region where the deposit interest rate is above 2.8178 (16.74%). Accordingly, when the deposit interest rate is below 16.74%, the increase in FXPD has a positive effect on the dollar exchange rate, while when the deposit interest rate is above 16.74%, the increase in FXPD has a negative effect. When the interest rate is above 16.74%, it is understood that the expected result of suppressing the dollar exchange rate is obtained from the FXPD.

Since all variables are stationary when the first difference is taken, it can be tested whether there is a long-term relationship between them. In this direction, the possible long-term relationship between the variables was investigated using the Johansen (1991, 1995) cointegration test, and the findings are presented in Table 8.5. The findings show that the coefficients of both Trace and Max-Eigen test statistics are not statistically significant. This situation reveals that there is no long-term relationship between the variables (dollar exchange rate, FXPD, deposit interest rate, and money supply) considered in the study.

Finally, the causality relationship between the variables was investigated using the conventional Granger (1969) causality test and Breitung and Candelon's (2006) spectral causality test. Table 8.6 shows the conventional GC test and Breitung and Candelon's (2006) spectral causality test findings. According to the findings of the conventional GC test, there is a one-way causality relationship from the LNFXPD to the LNDIR, and from the LNER to the LNM2. According to Breitung and Candelon's (2006) spectral causality test findings, there is causality in the medium and long term from the LNER to the LNFXPD, in the short and medium term toward the LNDIR, and in the long term toward the LNM2. In addition, there is a medium and long-term causality relationship between the LNM2 and the LNFXPD.

The results of the Breitung and Candelon's (2006) spectral causality test can also be clearly seen in Figures 8.1 and 8.2. For example, in the first, second, and third rows of the first column in Figure 8.1, causality relationships from FXPD, deposit interest rates, and money supply to the dollar rate are investigated, respectively. Since the test statistics value is smaller than the critical values in all three panels (the blue line is below the green and red lines), it was seen that there is no causality from these variables to the dollar exchange rate. However, it is seen that there are causalities from the dollar rate to FXPD in the first row of the second

Table 8.5 Johansen (1991, 1995) Cointegration Test Results

Unrestricted Cointegration Rank Test (Trace)				
Hypothesized No. of CE(s)	*Eigenvalue*	*Trace Statistic*	*0.05 Critical Value*	*Prob.*
None	0.354856	47.29782	55.24578	0.2074
At most 1	0.189360	21.43918	35.01090	0.6126
At most 2	0.090988	9.053235	18.39771	0.5746
At most 3	0.056395	3.424814	3.841465	0.0642
Unrestricted Cointegration Rank Test (Maximum Eigenvalue)				
Hypothesized No. of CE(s)	*Eigenvalue*	*Max-Eigen Statistic*	*0.05 Critical Value*	*Prob.*
None	0.354856	25.85864	30.81507	0.1792
At most 1	0.189360	12.38595	24.25202	0.7319
At most 2	0.090988	5.628421	17.14769	0.8511
At most 3	0.056395	3.424814	3.841465	0.0642

Note: The lag length is 1, and the fifth model (intercept and trend in CE intercept in VAR is determined as the model).

Table 8.6 Conventional and Breitung–Candelon's (2006) Spectral GC Test Results

Conventional (Time Domain) GC Test			Breitung and Candelon (2006) Frequency Domain Test					
			Long Term		Medium Term		Short Term	
Null Hypothesis:	F-Statistic	p-Value	$\omega = 0.01$	$\omega = 0.05$	$\omega = 1.0$	$\omega = 1.5$	$\omega = 2.0$	$\omega = 2.5$
DLNFXPD => DLNER	0.09352	0.7609	×	×	×	×	×	×
DLNER => DLNFXPD	0.67564	0.4146	√	√	√	√	×	×
DLNDIR => DLNER	1.02153	0.3165	×	×	×	×	×	×
DLNER => DLNDIR	0.01433	0.9052	×	×	×	×	√	×
DLNM2 =>DLNER	3.42391	0.0695	√	√	×	×	×	×
DLNER =>DLNM2	9.20643	0.0037	√	√	√	√	×	×
DLNM2 => DLNFXPD	0.03551	0.8512	×	×	×	×	×	×
DLNFXPD => DLNM2	0.02977	0.8636	×	×	×	×	×	×
DLNDIR => DLNFXPD	1.76939	0.1888	×	×	×	×	×	×
DLNFXPD => DLNDIR	4.25815	0.0437	×	×	×	×	×	×
DLNDIR => DLNM2	0.86206	0.4281	×	×	×	×	×	×
DLNM2 => DLNDIR	0.44603	0.6425	×	×	×	×	×	×

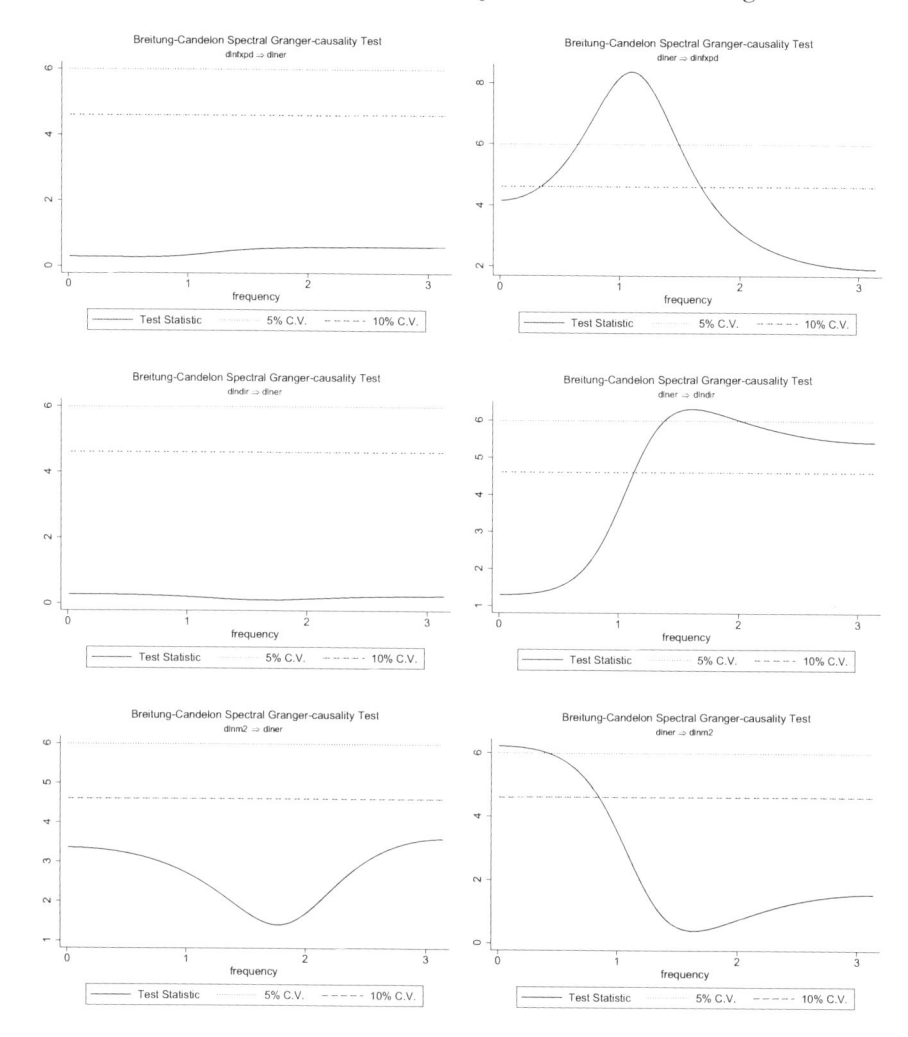

Figure 8.1 Breitung and Candelon's (2006) Spectral GC Test (Graphical Presentation).

column, from the dollar rate to the deposit interest rate in the second row, and from the money supply in the third row (as the blue line stays above the green and red lines in certain periods).

When Figure 8.2 is examined, it can be determined that there is a causality from money supply to FXPD, whereas there is no causality from FXPD to money supply, between FXPD and deposit interest rate, and between money supply and deposit interest rate.

The findings of Breitung and Candelon's (2006) spectral GC test showed that there is no spectral causality from FXPD accounts to dollar exchange rates, but there is medium- and long-term causality from dollar rates to FXPD accounts. This situation reveals that saving holders act regarding FXPD accounts depending on

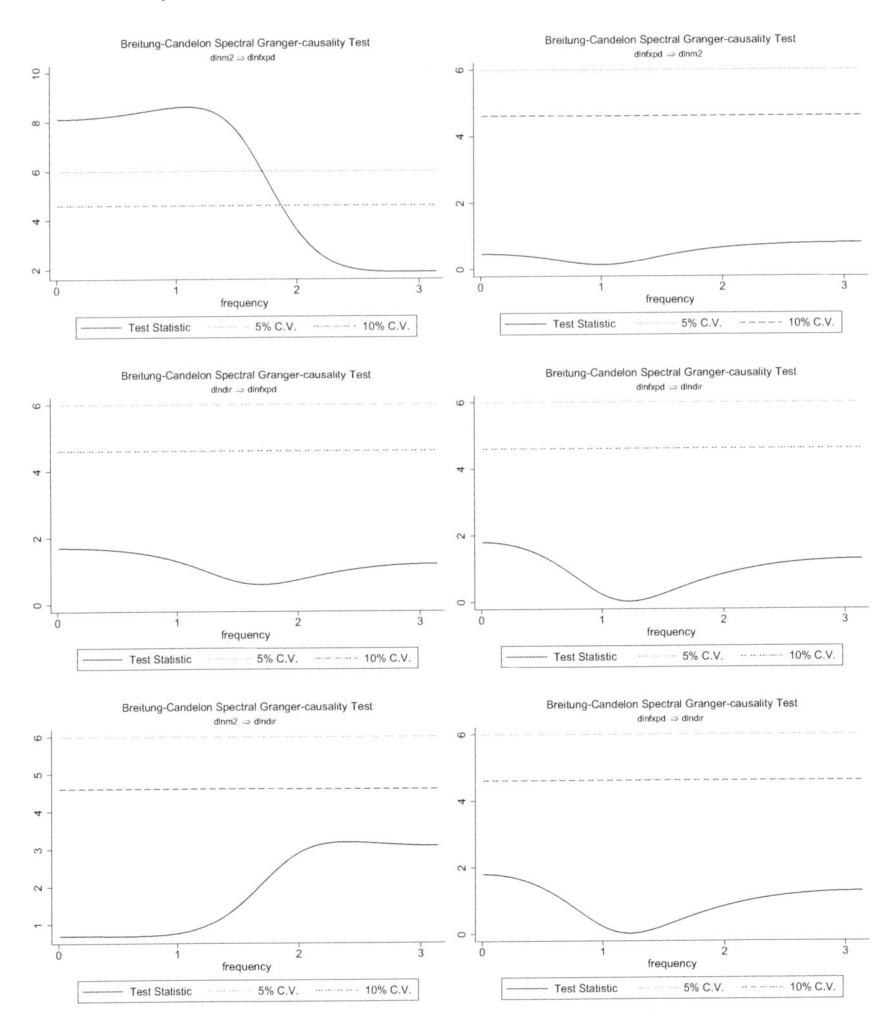

Figure 8.2 Breitung and Candelon's (2006) Spectral GC Test (Graphical Presentation – Continued from Figure 8.1).

the changes in exchange rates in the medium and long term. Considering the maturities of the deposit accounts, it can be considered normal that such a relationship does not exist between the dollar rate and FXPD in the short term.

Conclusion and discussion

The significant depreciation of the TL against the dollar, especially since 2018, has led to the dollarization problem in Türkiye. In response, CBRT and the economic administration introduced a number of measures under the name of the Lirazation Strategy, one of which was the FXPD account.

With the FXPD decision announced on December 21, 2021, The USD/TL exchange rate, which reached its highest point at TL 18.36 in the open market experienced a drop to TL 13. In March, the initial budget expenditures aimed at funding this policy shift were executed, amounting to TL 11.70 billion. This amount corresponds to 5.20% of the total Central Government Budget Expenditures of TL 224.94 billion in the related period. This amount nearly doubled to TL 23.36 billion in June, accounting for 8.95% of total budget expenditures. Subsequently, with the stabilization of the exchange rate, the payments have gradually decreased. In April 2023, the budget allocated approximately TL 650 million in expenditures, representing 0.16% of total budget expenditures. In that month, the exchange rate hovered around TL 19. In total, from March 2022 to April 2023, the budget allocated TL 95.34 billion for FXPD implementation.[2]

In this study, the effects of FXPD on the dollar rate were empirically tested. For this purpose, it was first tested whether the variables were stationary or not, and then the effect of FXPD on the dollar rate was tried to be determined by the threshold value analysis, depending on the threshold value. After the threshold analysis, whether there is a long-term relationship between the variables was investigated using Johansen cointegration, and whether there was a causal relationship using conventional GC and Breitung–Candelon (2006) frequency domain causality tests.

According to the findings obtained from the study, the variables are not stationary at the level of all, but stationary when their first difference is taken. Findings from the threshold analysis have proven that an increase in FXPD causes the dollar exchange rate to be suppressed when the deposit interest rates are above 16.74%, whereas an increase in FXPD causes an increase in the dollar rate when the relevant interest rates are below 16.74%. The decision taken by the CBRT on January 26, 2023, to remove the ceiling on deposit interest rates also supports this result. In addition to keeping the dollar exchange rate within a certain band, when it was perceived that deposit interest rates were not at a level to attract savers to the FXPD system, in other words, when deposit interest rates were not at a level to protect savers' financial rights against inflation, the entry into the FXPD system began to slow down. So much so that starting from the second week of October 2022, the number of entries to the system started to decrease on a weekly basis and this situation continued until the end of the year. In the last two weeks of the year and the first week of 2023, there were outflows from FXPD accounts. In the first week of March, there was an inflow of approximately TL 49 billion, with the effect of the general elections approaching, approximately TL 75.7 billion in the first week of April and TL 113.7 billion in the second week. It is thought that these developments in FXPD accounts create weakness in the emergence of the expected effects of suppression of exchange rates.

However, the Johansen cointegration test showed that there was no long-run relationship between the variables considered to test the relationship between FXPD and the dollar rate, while the traditional GC test showed that there was only one-way causality from exchange rates to money supply and from FXPD to deposit interest rates. The findings of Breitung and Candelon's (2006) spectral GC showed that there is causality in the medium and long term from the dollar exchange rate to the FXPD, in the short and medium term toward the deposit interest rate, and in the long term toward the money supply. In addition, there is a medium- and long-term causality relationship between the money supply and the FXPD.

When the findings obtained from the study are evaluated in general, it is seen that the deposit interest rates should be at a level that will protect the savings of the depositors against the inflation rates to create the desired effect on the exchange rates with the FXPD implementation. It has been shown that the expected effect from the system cannot be created when the input is not provided. When the long-term and causal relationships between FXPD and the dollar rate are considered, it is revealed that there is no long-term relationship for the analysis period, only causality from the dollar rate to FXPD in the medium- and long term. This result revealed that the dollar rate is more determinant in the medium- and long-term inflows to FXPD accounts.

To ensure the stability of the exchange rates in the Turkish economy, primarily to ensure domestic and foreign economic-political stability, to reduce the currency substitution by establishing confidence in the national currency, to take care to keep the added value high in the products subject to export, and to attract more foreign direct investment rather than hot money inflow policy monitoring, is of paramount importance.

Notes

1 For an extensive literature on the factors affecting the exchange rate, see Yıldız (2022) and Kartal et al. (2018).
2 Budget data are obtained from the website of the Republic of Türkiye Ministry of Treasury and Finance. The data are available in 2023 General Government's Financial Statistics section of the related website (URL: https://en.hmb.gov.tr/general-government, Date Accessed: June 20, 2023). Exchange rate data were obtained from the Electronic Data Delivery System of the Central Bank of the Republic of Türkiye (https://evds2.tcmb.gov.tr/index.php?/evds/serieMarket, Date Accessed: June 20, 2023).

References

Abdoh, W. M. Y. M., Yusuf, N. H. M., Zulkifli, S. A. M., Bulot, N. & Ibrahim, N. J. (2016). Macroeconomic Factors That Influence Exchange Rate Fluctuation in ASEAN Countries. *International Academic Research Journal of Social Science*, 2(1), 89–94.

Akdağ, S., İskenderoğlu, Ö. & Alola, A. A. (2020). The Volatility Spillover Effects among Risk Appetite Indexes: Insight from The VIX and the Rise. *Letters in Spatial and Resource Sciences*, 13, 49–65.

Akgemici, A. (2022). Kur Korumalı Mevduat Hesabının TFRS 9 Kapsamında Muhasebeleştirilmesi. *International Social Science Studies Journal*, 8(97), 1347–1352.

Altıntaş, H. (2013). Türkiye'de Petrol Fiyatları, Ihracat ve Reel Döviz Kuru İlişkisi: ARDL Sınır Testi Yaklaşımı ve Dinamik Nedensellik Analizi. *International Journal of Management Economics and Business*, 9(19), 1–30.

Aslan, N., Terzi, N. & Sıampan, E. (2014). Türkiye'de Kısa Vadeli Sermaye Hareketlerinin Ekonomik Büyüme ve Reel Döviz Kuru ile İlişkisi. *The Journal of Financial Research and Studies*, 5(10), ISSN 1309-1123, DOI: 10.14784/JFRS.2014104497.

Aydin, M. (2020). Energy Consumption-Economic Growth Nexus: Causality Approach in Frequency Domain for Türkiye, *Erciyes University Faculty of Economics and Administrative Sciences Journal*, 56, 83–96.

Barışık, S. & Demircioğlu, E. (2006). Türkiye'de Döviz Kuru Rejimi, Konvertibilite, Ihracat-Ithalat İlişkisi (1980–2001). *International Journal of Management Economics and Business*, 2(3), 71–84.

Bayat, T., Senturk, M., & Kayhan, S. (2014). Exchange Rates and Foreign Exchange Reserves in Türkiye: Nonlinear and Frequency Domain Causality Approach. *Theoretical and Applied Economics*, 21(11), 600.

Bilgin, M. H. (2004). Döviz Kuru Işsizlik İlişkisi: Türkiye Üzerine Bir Inceleme. *Kocaeli University Journal of Social Sciences*, 8, 80–94.

Brailsford, T., Penm, J. H. W. & Lai, C. D. (2006). Effectiveness of High Interest Rate Policy on Exchange Rates: A Reexamination of the Asian Financial Crisis. *Journal of Applied Mathematics and Decision Sciences*, 2006(4), 1–9.

Breitung, J. & Candelon, B. (2006). Testing for Short and Long-Run Causality: A Frequency-Domain Approach. *Journal of Econometrics*, 132, 363–378.

Çağdaş, C. (2018). Döviz Kurunun Belirlenmesine Yönelik Teorik Yaklaşımlar. *The Sakarya Journal of Economics*, 7(4), 1–17.

Çakalı, K. R. & Baloğlu, G. (2022). Kur Korumalı Türk Lirası Mevduat Hesaplarının Muhasebeleştirilme Esasları. *Pamukkale University Journal of Business Research*, 9(2), 564–576. DOI: 10.47097/piar.1173156

Canbay, Ş., Coşkun, İ. O. & Kırca, M. (2023). Symmetric and Asymmetric Frequency-Domain Causality between Tourism Demand and Exchange Rates in Türkiye: A Regional Comparison. *International Journal of Emerging Markets*. DOI: https://doi.org/10.1108/IJOEM-06-2022-0899.

CBRT (2013). Parasal Aktarım Mekanizması. https://www.tcmb.gov.tr/wps/wcm/connect/4e99834e-179b-4a08-820c-f2b259032afd/ParasalAktarim.pdf?MOD=AJPERES (Date of Access: 04.04.2023).

CBRT (2023). Electronic Data Delivery System. https://evds2.tcmb.gov.tr/ (Date of Access: 04.24.2023).

Coşkun, Y. & Ümit, Ö. A. (2016). Türkiye'de Hisse Senedi ile Döviz, Mevduat, Altın, Konut Piyasaları Arasındaki Eşbütünleşme Ilişkilerinin Analizi. *Business and Economics Research Journal*, 7(1), 47–69.

Dolado, J. J. & Lütkepohl, H. (1996). Making Wald Tests Work for Co-Integrated VAR Systems. *Econometric Reviews*, 15(4), 369–386.

Dönek, E. (1995). Türkiye'nin Dış Borç Sorunu ve 1980 Sonrası Boyutları. *Ankara University SBF Journal*, 50(01), 173–186.

Eğilmez, M. (2022a). Döviz Kuru Rejimleri ve Türkiye Uygulaması. https://www.mahfiegilmez.com/2022/03/doviz-kuru-rejimleri-ve-turkiye.html (Date Accessed: 02.04.2023).

Eğilmez, M. (2022b). Kur Korumalı Mevduat Üzerine Tartışmalar. https://www.mahfiegilmez.com/2022/08/kur-korumal-mevduat-uzerine-tartsmalar.html (Date Accessed: 02.04.2023).

Erdem, C., Arslan, C. K. & Erdem M. S. (2005). Effect of Macroeconomics Variables on Istanbul Stock Exchange Indexes. *Applied Financial Economics*, 15, 987–994.

Geweke, J. (1982). Measurement of Linear Dependence and Feedback between Multiple Time Series. *Journal of the American Statistical Association*, 77, 304–324.

Granger, C. W. J. (1969). Investigating Causal Relations by Econometric Models and Cross-Spectral Methods. *Econometrica*, 37, 424–438.

Gül, E., Ekinci, A. & Özer, M. (2007). The Causal Relationship between Interest Rates and Exchange Rates in Türkiye: 1984–2006. *Journal of Economic, Management and Finance*, 22(251), 21–31.

Gülerci, A. F. (2022). Kur ve Fiyat Farkı Korumalı Banka Hesapları ile Fiziki Altınların Kaydileştirilmesine İlişkin Düzenlemelerin Hukuki Açidan Değerlendirilmesi. *Necmettin Erbakan University Faculty of Law Review*, 5(2), 603–628.

Hacıevliyagil, N. & Demir, Y. (2016). Döviz Kurunun Temel Makro Ekonomik Değişkenlerle İlişkisi: Türkiye ve BRICS Ülkeleri Karşılaştırması. *Finance, Politics & Economic Reviews*, 53(615), 41–64.

Hamza, N. & Elijah, S. (2018). Testing Asymmetric Effect of Oil Price on Exchange Rate in Nigeria: New Evidence from Nonlinear ARDL Approach. *Gombe Journal of General Studies*, 2(1), 200–210.

Hicham, A., Mostefa, B. & Eddin, S. H. S. (2019). Frequency Domain Causality Relationship Analysis between Poverty, Economic Growth and Financial Development in Algeria. *Review of Economic and Business Studies*, 12(2), 93–111.

Hosoya, Y. (1991). The Decomposition and Measurement of The Interdependence between Second-Order Stationary Process. *Probability Theory and Related Fields*, 88, 429–444.

İskenderoğlu, O. & Akdağ, S. (2017). Investigation of the Validity of Financial Services Confidence Index: The Case of Türkiye. *International Journal of Economic Studies*, 3(4), 625–633.

Johansen, S. (1988). Statistical Analysis of Cointegration Vector. *Journal of Economic Dynamics and Control*, 12(2–3), 231–254.

Johansen, S. (1991). Estimation and Hypothesis Testing of Cointegration Vectors in Gaussian Vector Autoregressive Models. *Econometrica*, 59, 1551–1580.

Johansen, S. (1995). *Likelihood-Based Inference in Cointegrated Vector Autoregressive Models*. OUP, Oxford.

Johansen, S. & Juselius, K. (1990), Maximum Likelihood Estimation and Inference on Cointegration with Application to the Demand for Money. *Oxford Bulletin of Economic and Statistics*, 52, 169–210.

Kaplan, F. & Yapraklı, S. (2014). Ekonomik Kırılganlık Endeksi Göstergelerinin Döviz Kuru Üzerindeki Etkileri: Kırılgan 12 Ülke Üzerine Panel Veri Analizi. *International Journal of Alanya Faculty of Business*, 6(3), 111–121.

Karagöl, V. (2021). Does Global Financial Cycle Cause Business Cycle in Türkiye? A Frequency Domain Analysis. *Maliye Journal*, 180, 345–362.

Kartal, M., Depren, S. K. & Depren, Ö. (2018). Determination of Macroeconomic Indicators Affecting Foreign Exchange Rates in Türkiye: An Examination with MARS Method. *MANAS Journal of Social Studies*, 7(1), 209–229.

Köstekçi, A. & Özbay, F. (2023). Kur Korumalı Mevduat Sistemi ve Vergilemenin Amaçları Üzerine Bir Değerlendirme. *Business Economics and Management Research Journal*, 6(1), 44–56.

Kozanoğlu, H. (2021). 10 Maddede Kur Korumalı TL Vadeli Mevduat: Kâr Özel, Zarar Kamusal, https://www.birgun.net/makale/10-maddede-kur-korumali-tl-vadeli-mevduat-kar-ozel-zarar-kamusal-370729 (Date Accessed: 17.05.2023).

Lamia, B. & Djelassi, M. (2017). The Relationship between Exchange Rate and Inflation Targeting in Emerging Countries. *Asian Economic and Financial Review*, 7 (11), 1028–1038.

Mahlebeciler, Ö. (2006). Türkiye Cumhuriyet Merkez Bankası'nın Rezerv Yönetim Politikaları VE Kredi Mektuplu Döviz Tevdiat Hesaplarının Analizi. Specialization Thesis of the Accounting General Directorate of the Central Bank of the Republic of Turkey, Ankara, October 2006.

Maki, D. (2012). Tests for Cointegration Allowing for An Unknown Number of Breaks. *Economic Modelling*, 29(5), 2011–2015.

Mariano, C. N. Q., Sablan, V. F., Sardon, J. R. C. & Ronald, P. (2016). Investigation of the Factors Affecting Real Exchange Rate in the Philippines. *Review of Integrative Business and Economics Research*, 5(4), 171–202.

Ministry of Treasury and Finance (MTF, 2021). https://www.hmb.gov.tr/duyuru/%20basin-aciklamasi-i-21-12-2021 (Date Accessed: 11.04.2023).

Özatay, F. (2022). %19'u beğenmeyip %48'e razı olmak, https://www.tepav.org.tr/tr/blog/s/7042 (Date Accessed: 17.05.2022).

Özdamar, G. (2015). Türkiye Ekonomisinde Döviz Kuru Geçiş Etkisi: ARDL Sınır Testi Yaklaşımı Bulguları. *Akdeniz University Faculty of Economics and Administrative Sciences*, 32, 66–97.

Parveen, S., Khan, A. Q. & Ismail, M, (2012). Analysis of the Factors Affecting Exchange Rate Variability in Pakistan. *Academic Research International*, 2(3), 670–674.

Rahimli, N. & Nazirov, M. (2020). Impact of Oil Price on Azerbaijan Economy: Relationship between Oil Prices, Real Effective Exchange Rates and Real GDP. *ASERC Journal of Socio-Economics Studies*, 3(1), 37–45.

Şahin, D. (2018). Analysis of Relationship Causality between Exchange Rate and Inflation in Turkey. *Cukurova University Faculty of Economics and Administrative Sciences Journal*, 22(2), 391–408.

Şentürk, M. & Akbaş, Y. (2012). Finansal Aktif Fiyatları ve Borsa Getirisi Ilişkisi: Türkiye Örneği Üzerine Bir Uygulama. *The Journal of Financial Researches and Studies*, 3, 41–53.

Sever, E. & Mızrak, Z. (2007). Döviz Kuru, Enflasyon ve Faiz Oranı Arasındaki Ilişkiler: Türkiye Uygulaması. *The Journal of Social Economic Research*, 13, 265–283.

Seyidoğlu, H. (2009). *Uluslararası Iktisat, Teori, Politika ve Uygulama*, Extended 17th Edition. Güzem Can Publishing, Istanbul.

Singhal, S., Choudhary, S. & Biswal, P. C. (2019). Return and Volatility Linkages among International Crude Oil Price, Gold Price, Exchange Rate and Stock Markets: Evidence from Mexico. *Resources Policy*, 60, 255–261.

Srinivasan, P. (2014). Gold Price, Stock Price and Exchange Rate Nexus: The Case of India. *The Romanian Economic Journal*, XVII(52), 77–94.

Su, Ö. (2015). Türkiye'de Döviz Kurunu Etkileyen Faktörlerin Parasalcı Yaklaşımla Analizi (1980–2010). Unpublished Master's Thesis, Kocaeli University Institute of Social Sciences, Department of Economics, Department of Economic Development and International Economics, Kocaeli.

Sujit, K. & Kumar Rajesh, B. (2011). Study on Dynamic Relationship among Gold Price, Oil Price, Exchange Rate and Stock Market Returns. *International Journal of Applied Business and Economic Research*, 9(2), 145–165.

Tastan, H. (2015). Testing for Spectral Granger Causality. *The Stata Journal*, 15(4), 1157–1166.

CBRT (2013). Parasal Aktarım Mekanizması. https://www.tcmb.gov.tr/wps/wcm/connect/4e99834e-179b-4a08-820c-f2b259032afd/ParasalAktarim.pdf?MOD=AJPERES (Date Accessed: 04.04.2023).

Toda, H. Y. & Yamamoto, T. (1995). Statistical Inference in Vector Autoregressions with Possibly Integrated Processes. *Journal of econometrics*, 66(1–2), 225–250.

Tuna, G. & Tuna, V. E. (2022). Are Effects of COVID-19 Pandemic on Financial Markets Permanent or Temporary? Evidence from Gold, Oil and Stock Markets. *Resources Policy*, 76, 102637.

Yalçın, Z. & Emül, S. (2022). Kur Korumalı TL Vadeli Mevduat Hesaplarını Muhasebeleştirme Sorununa Yönelik Muhasebe Uygulaması ve Çözüm Önerileri. *Munzur University Journal of Social Sciences*, 11(2), 93–116.

Yalta, A. Y. (2020). Para Teorisi ve Politikası Ders Notları, Türkiye Bilimler Akademisi Açık Ders Malzemeleri Projesi, Version 1.1 (April 2020). https://acikders.tuba.gov.tr/pluginfile. php/4391/mod_resource/content/3/ders-notlar%C4%B1-kitap-%28s1%2C1%29.pdf (Date Accessed: 02.04.2023).

Yayman, D. (2022). Kur Korumalı Mevduat Hesabına Tanınan Vergi Ayrıcalıklarının Bütçeye Etkileri. *Journal of Cukurova University Institute of Social Sciences*, 31(2), 526–535.

Yıldız, M. (2022). Dolar ve Euro Kurları Üzerinde Etkili Faktörlerin İki Bağımlı Değişkenli MARS Modeli ile Belirlenmesi. *Journal of Faculty and Administrative Sciences*, 24(1), 6–29.

Yurdakul, F. (2016). Döviz Kuru Modellemesi ve Türkiye Üzerine Bir Uygulama, Inside: Döviz Kurunun Belirleyicileri Kısmi ve Koşullu Granger Nedensellik, SETAR, LSTAR, TVAR Modelleri, Editor: Funda Yurdakul, Ankara, Bookstore, p. 168, ISBN: 978-605-344-469-5.

Yurttadur, M. & Tasci, M. Z. (2023). The Relationship between Currency-Protected Deposits and Bank Performance: Case of Participation Banks. *Journal of Economics Finance and Accounting*, 10(1), 45–54.

9 Women's wage in the Turkish labor market

Handan Kumaş and Atalay Çağlar

Abbreviations

AIC	Akaike Information Criterion
BIC	Bayesian Information Criterion
GOLRM	Generalized Ordinal Logistic Regression Model
HLFSMDS	Household Labor Force Survey Micro Dataset
ILCSMDS	Income and Living Conditions Survey Micro Dataset
ISCO-08	International Standard Classification of Occupations
RC	Reference Category
RCEs	Regular and Casual Employees
TRY	Turkish Lira
TÜRKİYE KAMU-SEN	Confederation of Public Employees' Unions of Türkiye
TURKSTAT	Turkish Statistical Institute
TÜRK-İŞ	Confederation of Turkish Trade Unions

Introduction

The remuneration of female labor constitutes a fundamental subject within both empirical and theoretical investigations. In Türkiye, akin to global trends (ILO, 2022; Neef & Robilliard, 2021), female wages can be influenced by macroeconomic conditions such as inflation (Arslan, 2021), interest rate policies, per capita national income (Aksoy et al., 2019; Arslan, 2021; Tansel, 2002; Tatoğlu, 2022), and minimum wage (Karamızrak, 2019), as well as gender-biased perspectives (Batu Ağırkaya, 2022; Çelik Uğuz & Topbaş, 2016; Cergibozan & Özcan, 2012; Doğan, 2022; Duruoğlu, 2007; Eraslan, 2012; Kılınç, 2020).

According to the Global Gender Gap Index 2022 Rankings by the World Economic Forum (2023), Türkiye ranks 94th among 146 countries in "wage equality for similar work," with a score of 0.612. Furthermore, in Türkiye, the general trend of low female labor force participation and high unemployment rates places a significant emphasis on wage levels for all households. Even the wealthiest households in Türkiye, as evidenced by Duman's (2019) findings from the 2006

DOI: 10.4324/9781032631561-12

to 2017 TURKSTAT Household Budget Survey, derive nearly half of their income from wages. While female labor in Türkiye is influenced by gender-biased perspectives (Ayvaz Kızılgöl, 2012; Çağlayan Akay & Kömüryakan, 2023; Gültekin, 2022; Sayar Özkan & Özkan, 2010; Tansel, 2005), there are studies indicating that women's employment contributes to economic growth (Tütüncü & Zengin, 2020), that economic growth leads to increased female employment (Kılıç & Öztürk, 2014; Özer & Biçerli, 2003; Zeren & Kılınç Savrul, 2018), and that as the female labor force participation rate rises, wage disparities diminish (Aldan, 2021).

In a broader context, directly attributing wage disparities solely to gender-biased perspectives or economic conditions can sometimes fall short of adequately explaining the underlying causes. Wage disparities between women and men, as well as within the female workforce itself, can be influenced by a range of socio-demographic characteristics of individuals, such as education (Bozali & Uğur, 2022; İlkkaracan & Selim, 2007; Kaya & Selim, 2018; Onuk, 2017; Tansel, 2002), occupation (Erdoğan & Yeşilyurt, 2022), marital status (Tunalı & Göksu, 2018), experience (Bozali & Uğur, 2022), sector (Halaçlı & Karaalp Orhan, 2022; Yalçın et al., 2019), and region (Kaya & Selim, 2018; Şentürk & Demir, 2022; Tunalı & Göksu, 2018; Yalçın et al., 2019), along with the characteristics of the occupation itself (Erdem Karahanoğlu & Kumaş, 2022; Kumaş & Çağlar, 2011, 2017). Hence, the fundamental focus of the research lies in examining the determinants of income/wage disparities for women in employment. In this context, the fundamental question of the research was defined as follows: Which individual and job-related factors influence the earnings of women in Türkiye who are categorized as regular and casual employees (RCEs)?"

In the research, wages and women's wages will be examined in the first section, focusing on inflation, varying interest rates, the thresholds of hunger and poverty, and the changes in the minimum wage for the years 2017–2022, and partially for 2023. In the second section, Türkiye's situation regarding annual net earnings and the risk of poverty by gender will be compared with selected country examples. In the third section, using the 2022 Household Labor Force Survey Micro Dataset (HLFSMDS) of the TURKSTAT, through the employment of the Generalized Ordinal Logistic Regression Model (GOLRM), a detailed analysis will be provided on the reasons for wage differences among women working as RCEs, encompassing those who hold salaried, wage-earning, and daily-paid positions, within the context of Türkiye.

The primary source of detailed data concerning the labor market in Türkiye is the HLFSMDS of the TURKSTAT. However, this dataset provides only wage information in a cross-sectional manner and specifically for women working as RCEs. It is important to consider that the findings of this research, which examines the determinants of female wages in Türkiye, encompass a period that includes the effects of COVID-19, the initiation of diverse implementations concerning interest rate policies, and the years following 2018, which also include local and general elections.

Wages in Türkiye: various indicators and country comparisons

The data for the years 2017–2023 in Türkiye demonstrate statistically significant relationships ($\alpha = 0.05$) between minimum wage ($r = 0.821$, $p = 0.023$), poverty and hunger thresholds ($r = 0.821$, $p = 0.023$), consumer loan interest rates including overdraft accounts ($r = 0.786$, $p = 0.036$), and inflation.[1] Within the same period, at $\alpha = 0.10$ significance level, a statistically significant relationship is observed between inflation and the average and median wages ($r = 0.771$, $p = 0.072$). Conversely, there is no statistically significant relationship observed between inflation and policy interest rates ($r = 0.214$, $p = 0.645$). It can be inferred that one of the fundamental causes behind increases in wages is the rise in inflation rates (Table 9.1).

In relation to the years 2017–2023, a discussion regarding the relationship between relative poverty and policy interest rate can be presented: the correlation between the rate of relative poverty for women ($r = 0.90$, $p = 0.037$) and men ($r = 0.975$, $p = 0.005$) working as RCEs and the policy interest rate is statistically significant (Table 9.1). While a statistically significant correlation is observed between the deposit interest rate and the rate of relative poverty for men working as RCEs ($r = 0.975$, $p = 0.005$), a meaningful relationship cannot be established for women working as RCEs ($r = 0.80$, $p = 0.104$) (Table 9.1). According to the data, besides poverty rates, the policy interest rate does not exhibit a relationship with other market interest rates and wage levels, displaying a distinct trend.

During the period of 2017–2022, earnings of employed individuals in Türkiye remained lower than those in the EU-27 and candidate countries, and the poverty risk among the population aged 16 and above is relatively high (Figures 9.1–9.3). The gender wage gap, based on up-to-date data, is lower in Türkiye compared to the OECD average (Figure 9.4).

According to the 2022 HLFSMDS of the TURKSTAT, 6.8% of women and men working as RCEs and declaring their primary income are living in single-person households. In 2022, the net income of a childless individual living alone, representing 50% of the average income in Türkiye based on purchasing power parity, is 77% of the EU-27 average, exhibiting a 43.5% increase compared to the previous year (Figure 9.1). This situation is attributed to the mitigated adverse effects of COVID-19, along with an approximately 3.7-fold increase in inflation and an approximately 72% increase in the minimum wage in 2022 compared to 2021 (Table 9.1).

In Türkiye, wages exhibit a trend closely linked to the minimum wage. According to the 2022 HLFSMDS of the TURKSTAT, 52.7% of all RCEs, 30.5% of RCEs living in single-person households, 31.8% of women, and 28.1% of men earn wages up to the level of TRY 5,500, which is the minimum wage for the second half of 2022. For the same individuals, the nominal average wage is TRY 9,460 for men and TRY 9,092 for women. The ability of female RCEs living in single-person households to escape the minimum wage trap is related to their engagement in skilled professions. Among female RCEs living alone who earn at least twice the minimum wage (TRY 9,754), 83% are in the category of "managers

Table 9.1 Comparison of Wage Levels in Türkiye with Various Indicators

Criteria /year	2017	2018	2019	2020	2021	2022	2023
Inflation Change based on 12-month average CPI (% change from December)[a,b]	11.14	16.33	15.18	12.28	19.60	72.31	46.88[c]
Policy interest rate (%)[b,d]	8.0	13.80	20.27	9.93	17.70	12.80	8.84[c]
Deposit interest rates (%)[b]	10.53	15.70	17.33	9.62	17.00	15.42	17.46[e]
Consumer loan interest rates (including overdraft accounts) (%)[b]	18.33	24.53	23.60	14.83	23.48	26.20	24.18[f]
Credit card default interest rates (%)[b]	2.34	2.48	2.43	1.63	2.29	2.01	1.73[g]
Minimum wage Turkish lira (TRY)	1,404.06	1,603.12	2,020.90	2,324.71	2,825.90	4.876.5[h]	9,954.56[h]
Hunger threshold—TRY TÜRK-İŞ (monthly hunger threshold for a family of four—December)[i]	1,608	1,941.16	2,163	2,590	4,013	8,130	11,658.05 (July)
TÜRK-İŞ (monthly cost of living for a single person—December) TRY[i]	1,989	2,393.25	2,650	3,147	4,927	10,160	15,123 (July)
Hunger threshold—TRY TÜRKİYE KAMU-SEN (monthly hunger threshold for a working individual—December)[j]	2,051.55	2,433.96	2,636.64	2,959.02	3,835.20	6,895.92	7,644.42 (April)
Poverty threshold—TRY TÜRK-İŞ (monthly poverty threshold for a family of four—December)[i]	5,238	6,322.99	7,045	8,436	13,073	26,485	37,974.11 (July)
Poverty threshold—TRY TÜRKİYE KAMU-SEN (monthly poverty threshold for a family of four with a working member—December)[j]	5,468.79	6,500.73	6,897.69	7,862.79	10,372.56	18,746.97	21,316.2 (April)
Poverty threshold—TRY TÜRKİYE KAMU-SEN (monthly poverty threshold for a working individual)[k]	2,663.94	3,127.74	3,408.93	3,832.38	4,891.14	8,659.92	9,691.98 (April)
Criteria/Year	2017	2018	2019	2020	2021	2022	2023

Median wage for RCEs (monthly) TRY[k]	T	2,182.34	2,473.82	2,969.50	3,451.09	4,081.09	6,904.92	N.A.
	F	2,047.95	2,294.54	2,782.96	3,234.17	3,811.18	6,399.58	N.A.
	M	2,238.27	2,552.25	3,054.08	3,548.58	4,203.58	7,151.73	N.A.
Median wage for RCEs (monthly) TRY[k]	T	1,700	2,000	2,350	2,700	3,200	5,500	N.A.
	F	1,500	1,700	2,025.51	2,500	3,000	5,500	N.A.
	M	1,800	2,000	2,500	2,824	3,400	5,510	N.A.
Relative poverty (60% of equivalent household disposable median income) TRY (Annual)[l,m]	T	9,532.29	10,760.11	12,950.35	14,873.17	16,841.14	21,296	N.A.
Gender-based relative poverty rate—for RCEs (%)[m]	F	6.0	7.3	8.0	6.3	6.9	N.A.	N.A.
	M	12.8	13.5	13.9	12.8	13.6	N.A.	N.A.
Gender-based poverty rate—for RCEs (%)[m]	F	15.7	18.3	20.2	17	18	N.A.	N.A.
	M	84.3	81.7	79.8	83	82	N.A.	N.A.
USDTRY (exchange rates-banknotes selling)[n]	M	3.66	4.83	5.69	7.03	8.91	16.62	19.77[o]

[a] Central Bank of the Republic of Türkiye (2023a).

[b] The monthly or weekly rates were converted to annual figures by calculating the geometric mean.

[c] It encompasses the first six months' data (Central Bank of the Republic of Türkiye, 2023a).

[d] Starting from June 1, 2018, the policy interest rate is the "one-week repo auction rate" (Central Bank of the Republic of Türkiye, 2023b).

[e] It is the geometric mean of the first five months' rates (Central Bank of the Republic of Türkiye, 2023c).

[f] It is the geometric mean of the first six months' rates (Central Bank of the Republic of Türkiye, 2023d).

[g] It is the geometric mean of the first seven months' rates (Central Bank of the Republic of Türkiye, 2023e).

[h] It is the average of the minimum wage determined twice in 2022 and 2023.

[i] TÜRK-İŞ—Confederation of Turkish Trade Unions (TÜRK-İŞ, 2023).

[j] TÜRKİYE KAMU-SEN —Confederation of Public Employees' Unions of Türkiye (TÜRKİYE KAMU-SEN, 2023); Consultation was held with the relevant organization's R&D specialist, and detailed information was obtained via email on July 5, 2023.

[k] 2017–2022 HLFSMDS of the TURKSTAT.

[l] 2017–2021 TURKSTAT Income and Living Conditions Survey Micro Dataset (ILCSMDS).

[m] Income information refers to the previous calendar year.

[n] Central Bank of the Republic of Türkiye (2023f).

[o] The calculations are for the period between January 1, 2023, and June 30, 2023.

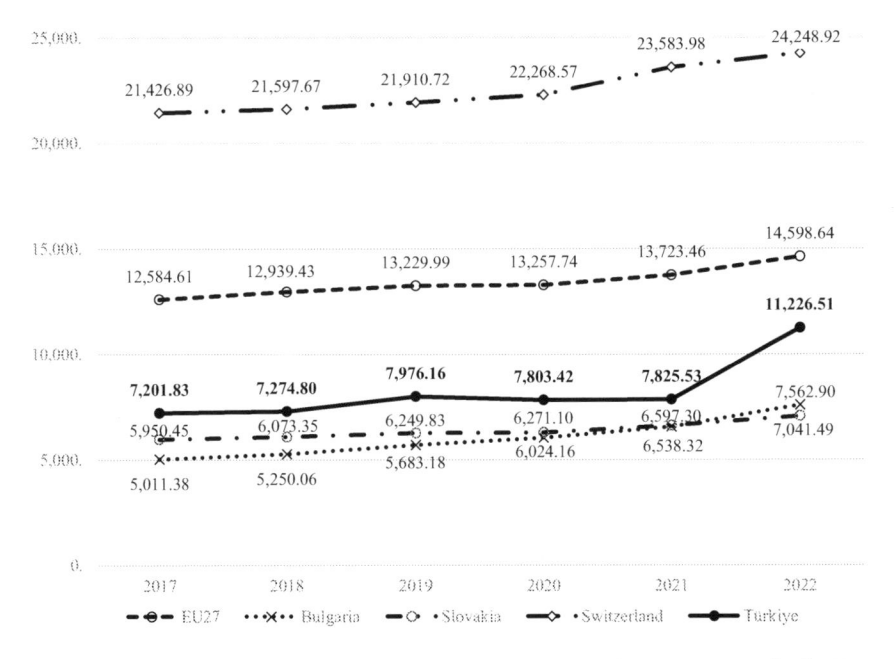

Figure 9.1 During the 2017–2021 Period—Annual—Purchasing Power Standard—Net Earnings—Single Person without Children Earning 50% of the Average Earning (Euro).

Source: Eurostat (2022a) Annual Net Earnings, June 7, 2023.

and professionals." In a compelling manner demonstrating the low female employment in Türkiye, it is evident that 5.35% of the total employed population (30,752,000 individuals) constitutes individuals from households consisting of four members, where both spouses work and have two children under the age of 18. Among the 20,144,000 RCEs, who declared their primary income, 5.13% are part of households where both spouses are RCEs and have two children under the age of 18.

For the year 2022, the income level of this household type in Türkiye corresponds to 86% of the EU-27 average. The substantial 64% increase (Figure 9.2) in the income level of couples with two children who earn 100% of the average income in 2022 compared to the previous year in Türkiye may be attributed to the conclusion of the pandemic and the rise in inflation and the minimum wage.

According to the 2022 HLFSMDS of the TURKSTAT, in households consisting of four members, including two children below the age of 18 and both spouses working as RCEs, the average nominal income from the primary job is TRY 9,562 for male RCEs and TRY 7,640 for female RCEs. Among RCEs in these households, 42.4% of women and 26.6% of men earn wages up to the level of TRY 5,500, which is the minimum wage for the second half of 2022. Gender-based wage

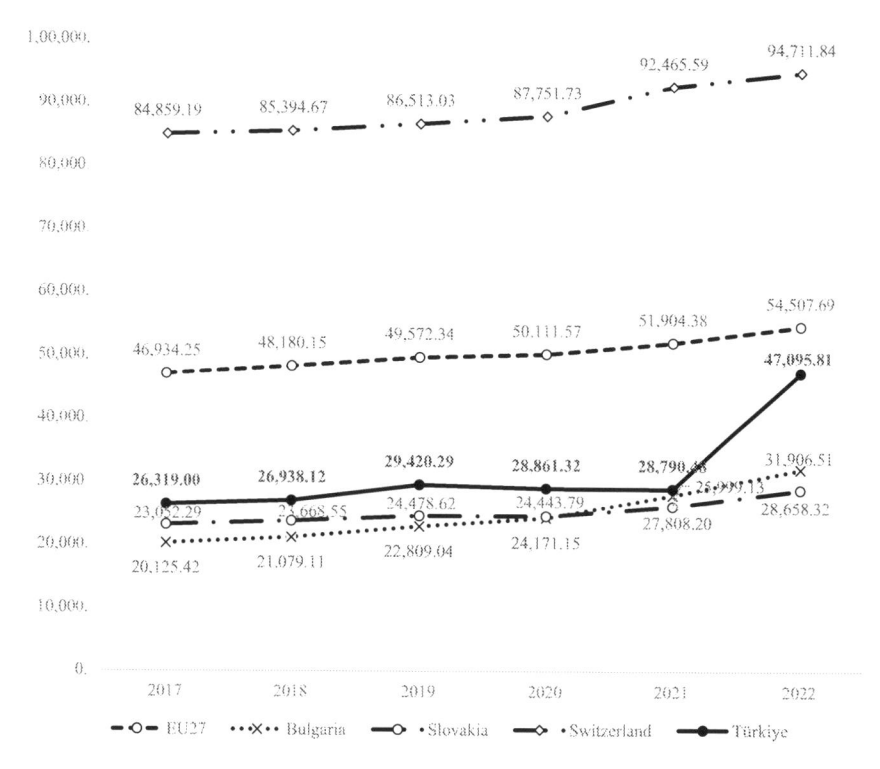

Figure 9.2 During the 2017–2021 Period—Annual—Purchasing Power Standard—Net Earnings—Two-Earner Couple with Two Children, Both Earning 100% of the Average Earning (Euro).

Source: Eurostat (2022a) Annual Net Earnings, June 6, 2023.

disparity among RCEs living in these households becomes more distinct based on whether they work in the public or private sector. The average wage for male RCEs in the private sector is TRY 8,433, and for female RCEs is TRY 5,921; in the public sector, the average wage for male RCEs is TRY 11,234, while for female RCEs it is TRY 9,746. The data indicates that the wage gap, compared to "single-person households," increases unfavorably for women residing in households where there are two children below the age of 18 and both spouses work as RCEs.

From 2017 to 2022, other EU candidate countries have been successful in reducing poverty and social exclusion risks among women aged 16 and above, as illustrated in Figure 9.3. One of the primary reasons for Türkiye's inability to achieve similar success, during the same period, is the attachment of median income to the minimum wage, both in general and particularly among women, as indicated in Table 9.1. According to official data, in Türkiye, from 2017 to 2022, the minimum wage is above the relative poverty threshold. However, according to the TÜRK-İŞ, from 2017 to 2023, the minimum wage levels for a single-person household were below both the hunger and poverty thresholds.[2]

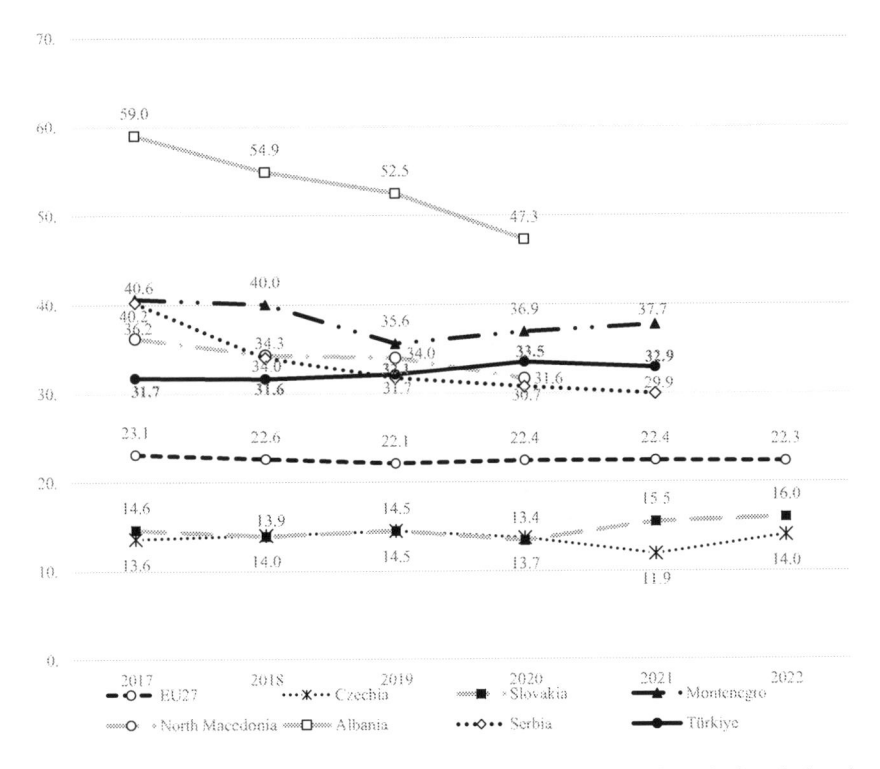

Figure 9.3 Females Aged 16 and Over at Risk of Poverty or Social Exclusion during the 2017–2021 Period—Annual—Percent.

Source: Eurostat (2022b) Living Conditions and Welfare Statistics, July 7, 2023.

According to the TÜRKİYE KAMU-SEN, except for the year 2023 (with the latest data available in April), the minimum wage is below the hunger and poverty thresholds[3] for both single-person households and households with one working member. In the second half of 2023, Türkiye ranks 24th among 27 countries with a value of € 473.69 (Eurostat, 2023). According to a report by Eurofound (2022), in 2019, only 4% of employees in the European Union (EU) received wages around the minimum wage. In contrast, according to HLFSMDS, in Türkiye, around 26.1% of RCEs, with 25.2% being male and 28.1% female, earned wages around the minimum wage (between TRY 2,000 and TRY 2,023) in 2019. Another contributing factor is the low female labor force participation rate (35.8%) and employment rate (31.8%), coupled with a high rate of those not participating in the labor force (64.2%) (TURKSTAT, 2023), when compared to the EU, OECD, E7, or some Asian countries. The limited presence of women in the labor market complicates efforts to prevent female poverty and exclusion.

The optimistic scenario presented in Figure 9.4 for gender-based wage disparity in Türkiye, covering a single year, does not illustrate the disadvantaged conditions

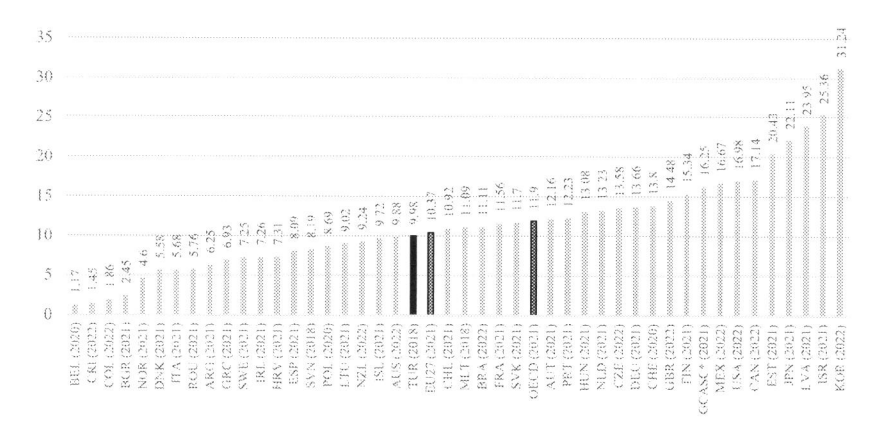

Figure 9.4 Gender Wage Gap, Employees, Percentage, 2022 or Latest Available, Yearly.
*Greek Cypriot Administration of Southern Cyprus.

Source: OECD (2022) Gender Wage Gap, July 17, 2023.

for women in terms of wages. However, according to the ILCSMDS data for the years 2017–2021, under both the OECD definition (30–40 hours per week) and the Turkish Labor Law (Article 63: 31–45 hours per week), the wages of full-time employed female RCEs are lower than those of men (Figure 9.5). The data is in line with the findings of Miyoshi (2008) in Japan, which indicated that the length of full-time work had a significant impact on the wage disparity between women and men.

According to the ILCSMDS, the fact that the wage gap between men and women who work full time for 31–45 hours per week is higher than those working 30–40 hours per week indicates that, as the working hours of RCEs increase, the wage gap also increases (Figure 9.5). The phenomenon of female wages being lower than male wages under both the OECD and the Turkish Labor Law frameworks might be attributed to conditions that cannot be explained solely by individual and job-related characteristics, such as gender-biased perspectives (Blinder, 1973; Heckman, 1976, 1979; Heckman & Macrudy, 1980; Oaxaca, 1973).

During the period of 2017–2023 in Türkiye, a significant relationship was found between women's relative poverty and the gender wage gap determined by the OECD approach ($r = 0.90$, $p = 0.037$). There was no significant relationship observed between the OECD approach and inflation ($r = 0.30$, $p = 0.624$), as well as between the OECD approach and policy interest rate ($r = 0.70$, $p = 0.188$). Similarly, considering the Turkish Labor Law No. 4857, no significant relationship was found between inflation ($r = -0.00$, $p = 1$) and policy interest rate ($r = 0.30$, $p = 0.624$). Additionally, no significant relationships were identified between policy interest rates and other indicators (except for gender-specific relative poverty rates), as presented in Table 9.1.

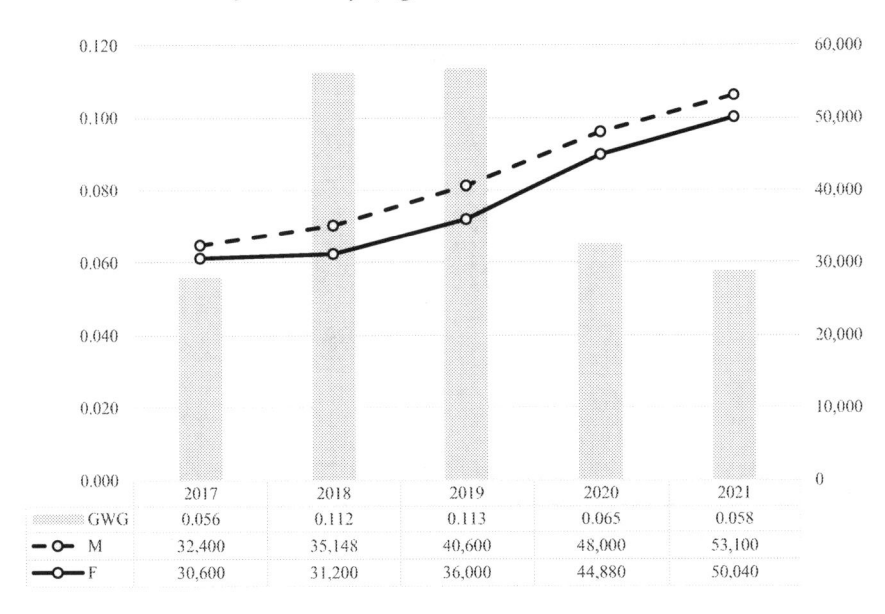

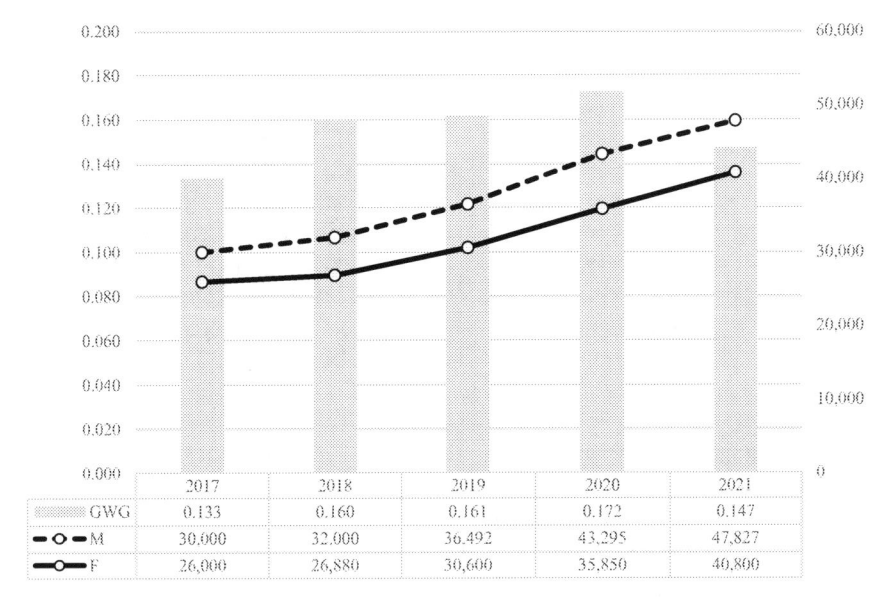

Figure 9.5 Median Wages and Wage Gap by Gender for RCEs and Full-Time (31–45 Hours per Week) Workers in Türkiye during the Period of 2017–2021; According to the OECD Approach (30–40 Hours per Week) and Labor Law No. 4857. *Calculated from the ILCSMDS Data of the TURKSTAT Covering the Years 2017–2022.

Materials and methods

Dataset and method

In Türkiye, for the purpose of identifying the factors influencing the wages of women working as RCEs, the HLFSMDS of the TURKSTAT was utilized. The HLFSMDS compiles information about the structure of the labor force, including details about economic activity, occupation (or job held), employment status, and working hours for the employed individual, as well as information about job search duration and desired occupation (or job) for the unemployed individual. This dataset is made available to researchers upon request by the TURKSTAT to be used in various analytical endeavors, including econometric modeling and data mining (TURKSTAT, 2022).

In the study, the "How much was your total net cash income from your main job last month? (in TRY)" question answered by the RCEs was utilized to create the "income level," which was taken as the dependent variable. The minimum wage was determined twice in 2022, in January and July. The dependent variable, income level, was categorized into four groups based on the average of the minimum wage for the two periods: up to TRY 4,877, between TRY 4,878 and TRY 9,754, between TRY 9,755 and TRY 14,631, and at least TRY 14,632.

In the study, individual and "job"-related characteristics, including completed age group, marital status, the highest level of education completed (education level), region of residence, occupation according to the ISCO-08 (International Standard Classification of Occupations) classification, the industry of employment according to the NaceRev2 classification (sector), size of the workplace (scale), workplace status, continuity of employment, registration status with the Social Security Institution, employment status, and usual weekly working hours in the main job (working hours), were taken as independent variables. While some of the independent variables were used as provided in the Micro Dataset, others were reorganized according to the purpose of the study. All independent variables are categorical variables measured on a nominal or ordinal scale.

The focus of the study is women working as RCEs. To make comparisons concerning women, the data of male RCEs and the outcomes of the developed model were utilized. However, among RCEs, those who did not earn any income from their primary occupation in the previous month were excluded. The TURKSTAT recommends applying weighting to the sample data to achieve representative values for the population. As a result, the analyses were conducted using the weights provided by the Micro Dataset. Accordingly, the study incorporates information from a total of 20,144,000 RCEs, comprising 6,610,000 women and 13,534,000 men. The variables employed in the study, the categories within these variables, and the ratios of women and male RCEs within each category are presented in Table 9.2.

Due to the ordinal nature of the income level variable, an ordinal logistic regression model was planned to be used to examine the factors influencing the wages of female RCEs. The ordinal logistic regression model is employed when the

Table 9.2 Distribution of Variables in the Models by Gender

Variable	Category	Female (%) (6,610 Thousand People)	Male (%) (13,534 Thousand People)
Income level	At most TRY 4,877	40.1	30.0
	TRY 4,878–TRY 9,754	44.5	52.0
	TRY 9,755–TRY 14,631	11.2	12.5
	At least TRY 14,632	4.2	5.5
Age group	15–24	14.9	14.4
	25–34	31.6	29.4
	35–44	30.1	29.5
	45–54	17.8	19.5
	55+	5.5	7.2
Marital status	Married	59.1	65.5
	Single	40.9	34.5
Education level	University and above	34.7	21.4
	At most primary education	31.9	40.8
	General high school	12.5	14.6
	Vocational or technical high school	9.3	14.7
	Vocational school	11.6	8.4
Region of residence	Istanbul	26.2	23.1
	Marmara	16.5	16.4
	Aegean	14.1	12.9
	Mediterranean	11.9	12.0
	Western and central Anatolia	13.9	15.2
	Black sea	7.1	7.1
	Eastern and southeastern anatolia	10.2	13.2
Sector	Service	76.6	60.2
	Agriculture	1.7	1.8
	Industry	20.6	30.7
	Construction	1.1	7.3
Scale	Micro	28.1	25.6
	Small	32.7	31.2
	Medium	23.4	24.2
	Large	15.6	18.8
	Don't know, but less than 10	0.1	0.2
Job	Skilled agricultural workers, unskilled workers, etc.	15.7	14.2
	Managers and professionals	28.2	16.9
	Technicians, technologists, and assistant professionals	8.3	8.2
	Office workers	13.0	8.5
	Service and sales workers	25.4	19.4
	Artisans and related workers	4.5	17.5
	Plant and machine operators and assemblers	5.0	15.3
Workplace status	Public	25.1	21.5
	Private	74.9	78.5

(*Continued*)

Table 9.2 (Continued)

Variable	Category	Female (%) (6,610 Thousand People)	Male (%) (13,534 Thousand People)
Continuity	Temporary, daily, and seasonal work	5.9	7.0
	Permanent	94.1	93.0
Registration	Not registered	13.6	8.7
	Registered	86.4	91.3
Employment status	Regular	88.9	95.6
	Irregular	11.1	4.4
Working hours	31–45 hours	49.6	45.0
	Up to 30 hours	12.3	4.9
	More than 45 hours	38.1	50.1

dependent variable has more than two ordered categories (Alpar, 2013). In fact, this model is a generalized form of binary logistic regression (Liu, 2016). For the predictions obtained from the ordinal logistic regression model to be valid, the assumption of parallel lines needs to be satisfied. According to this assumption, only one regression coefficient is estimated for each independent variable instead of multiple coefficients, assuming that coefficients are the same across all categories of the dependent variable (Liu, 2016; Şerbetçi, 2012). According to this assumption, the relationship between independent variables and the dependent variable does not vary across different categories of the dependent variable (Kleinbaum & Klein, 2010).

An ordinal logistic regression model was constructed using the variables provided in Table 9.2 to determine the factors influencing the wages of female RCEs. The results obtained using SPSS 29 indicated that the assumption of parallel lines in the model was not met ($\chi^2 = 437.494$, $df = 68$, $p = 0.000$). The same assumption of parallel lines was also not met in the ordinal logistic regression model created for male RCEs, which was constructed for comparison with female RCEs ($\chi^2 = 523.515$, $df = 68$, $p = 0.000$).

Generalized ordinal logistic regression model

When the assumption of parallel lines is not met in the ordinal logistic regression model, it is recommended to consider using the Partial Proportional Odds Model or the GOLRM (Liu, 2016; Mert, 2006; Peterson & Harrel, 1990). The GOLRM allows for flexibility in the assumption of parallel lines, allowing the coefficients of independent variables to vary across categories of the dependent variable. The programs developed by Fu (1998) and Williams (2006) have made the implementation of GOLRM much more straightforward (Liu, 2016; Williams, 2016).

In the GOLRM, as the transition probabilities from one level of the dependent variable to another level are assumed to be different, the model estimations are made for each level of the dependent variable (Hayat & Sözen Özden, 2021).

For a dependent variable with M ordinal categories, the GOLRM can be expressed as

$$P\left(Y_i > j\right) = \frac{exp\left(\alpha_j + \beta_1 X_{1i} + \beta_2 X_{2i} + \cdots + \beta_p X_{pi}\right)}{1 + exp\left(\alpha_j + \beta_1 X_{1i} + \beta_2 X_{2i} + \cdots + \beta_p X_{pi}\right)}, \quad j = 1, 2, \ldots, \left(M - 1\right)$$

$$(9.1)$$

Here, $X_1, X_2, \ldots, X_p$ represent the p independent variables, and Y represents the dependent variable. α_j represents the intercepts or cut points, while $\beta_1, \beta_2, \ldots, \beta_p$ denote the logistic coefficients or slopes to be estimated for the independent variables (Williams, 2006, 2016). A positive logit coefficient indicates that an individual is more likely to be in a higher category rather than in a lower category of the dependent variable (Liu & Koirala, 2012).

In the GOLRM, odds ratios can be obtained alongside the coefficients, allowing for interpretation. Additionally, even if the assumption of parallel lines is not met, some of the independent variables may still satisfy this assumption. To examine the assumption of parallelism in the constructed model, the "Likelihood Ratio Test" or "Wald Test" can be applied. Moreover, through the Wald Test, independent variables or categories that satisfy the parallelism assumption can be identified (Aydos & Toker, 2021). Variables that satisfy the assumption of parallelism in the GOLRM will have the same coefficient for different categories of the dependent variable.

There are a few studies in Türkiye employing the GOLRM for labor-related analyses: Kaya et al. (2020) conducted a study using the HLFSMDS dataset of the TURKSTAT to investigate the potential factors affecting personal income distribution in the TRA1 sub-region of Türkiye, where income inequality is the highest; Çakır (2021) identified factors influencing individuals' weekly working hours using the Household Budget Survey data of the TURKSTAT; Aydos and Toker (2021) examined youth unemployment by education levels using the HLFSMDS data of the TURKSTAT; Bozali and Uğur (2022) measured gender-based earnings inequality using the ILCSMDS of the TURKSTAT; and Yamak et al. (2023) analyzed factors influencing the duration of unemployment for unemployed individuals using the HLFSMDS data of the TURKSTAT. However, these studies were not specifically focused on using the GOLRM to determine the factors influencing female wages.

Findings

To investigate the factors influencing the wages of women working as RCEs in Türkiye, a GOLRM was constructed using the "gologit2" command in STATA, based on the information of 6,610,000 RCE women who reported their income in the 2022 HLFSMDS. The results of the model are presented in Table 9.3. In the GOLRM, since the transition probabilities from one level of the dependent

Table 9.3 GOLRM Results for Women Working as RCEs

Income Level (Y): If it is up to TRY 4,877, then Y = 1; If it is between TRY 4,878 and TRY 9,754, then Y = 2; If it is between TRY 9,755 and TRY 14,631, then Y = 3; If it is at least TRY 14,632, then Y = 4

	Y > 1 vs Y ≤ 1			Y > 2 vs Y ≤ 2			Y > 3 vs Y ≤ 3		
	β SE (β)	OR SE(OR)	p Value	β SE(β)	OR SE (OR)	p Value	β SE (β)	OR SE (OR)	p Value
Age group (RC[a]: 15–24)									
25–34	0.392 (0.092)	1.480 (0.136)	0.000						
35–44	0.621 (0.100)	1.862 (0.185)	0.000						
45–54	0.612 (0.119)	1.844 (0.220)	0.000	1.084 (0.143)	2.957 (0.424)	0.000	1.192 (0.189)	3.294 (0.623)	0.000
55+	0.623 (0.182)	1.864 (0.340)	0.001	1.164 (0.239)	3.204 (0.766)	0.000	1.631 (0.290)	5.111 (1.480)	0.000
Marital status (RC: married)									
Single	−0.074 (0.061)	0.928 (0.057)	0.227						
Education level (RC: university and above)									
At most primary education	−1.165 (0.127)	0.312 (0.040)	0.000	−2.965 (0.409)	0.052 (0.021)	0.000	−3.911 (1.510)	0.020 (0.030)	0.010
General high school	−0.682 (0.123)	0.506 (0.062)	0.000	−1.584 (0.231)	0.205 (0.047)	0.000	−1.867 (0.447)	0.155 (0.069)	0.000
Vocational or technical high school	−0.658 (0.129)	0.518 (0.067)	0.000	−1.260 (0.227)	0.284 (0.064)	0.000	−1.708 (0.515)	0.181 (0.093)	0.001
Vocational school	−0.578 (0.116)	0.561 (0.065)	0.000	−1.014 (0.145)	0.363 (0.053)	0.000	−1.421 (0.321)	0.241 (0.077)	0.000

(Continued)

Table 9.3 (Continued)

Income Level (Y): If it is up to TRY 4,877, then Y = 1; If it is between TRY 4,878 and TRY 9,754, then Y = 2; If it is between TRY 9,755 and TRY 14,631, then Y = 3; If it is at least TRY 14,632, then Y = 4

	Y > 1 vs Y ≤ 1			Y > 2 vs Y ≤ 2			Y > 3 vs Y ≤ 3		
	β SE (β)	OR SE(OR)	p Value	β SE(β)	OR SE (OR)	p Value	β SE (β)	OR SE (OR)	p Value
Region (RC: İstanbul)									
Marmara	−0.435 (0.083)	0.648 (0.054)	0.000						
Aegean	−0.436 (0.087)	0.647 (0.056)	0.000						
Mediterranean	−0.566 (0.095)	0.568 (0.054)	0.000						
Western and Central Anatolia	−0.376 (0.087)	0.686 (0.060)	0.000						
Black Sea	−0.496 (0.114)	0.609 (0.069)	0.000						
Eastern and Southeastern Anatolia	−0.650 (0.107)	0.522 (0.056)	0.000						
Sector (RC: service)									
Agriculture	1.160 (0.342)	3.189 (1.091)	0.001						
Industry	0.115 (0.087)	1.121 (0.097)	0.186						
Construction	−0.125 (0.240)	0.883 (0.212)	0.603						

Scale (RC: micro)

Small	0.263	1.301	0.001						
	(0.081)	(0.105)							
Medium	0.467	1.595	0.000						
	(0.089)	(0.142)							
Large	0.729	2.073	0.000	1.048	2.853	0.000	1.254	3.505	0.000
	(0.116)	(0.240)		(0.122)	(0.347)		(0.152)	(0.533)	
Don't know, but less than 10	−0.234	0.792	0.774						
	(0.813)	(0.643)							

Job (RC: skilled agricultural workers, unskilled workers, etc.)

Managers, professionals	0.796	2.216	0.000	2.291	9.883	0.000	4.955	141.825	0.032
	(0.145)	(0.322)		(0.337)	(3.328)		(2.308)	(327.400)	
Technicians, technologists, and assistant professionals	0.470	1.600	0.001	1.680	5.365	0.000	3.922	50.503	0.091
	(0.147)	(0.235)		(0.346)	(1.856)		(2.318)	(117.055)	
Office workers	0.183	1.201	0.147	1.130	3.095	0.001	3.229	25.245	0.164
	(0.126)	(0.152)		(0.344)	(1.064)		(2.319)	(58.539)	
Service and sales workers	0.171	1.187	0.117	0.973	2.645	0.006	3.988	53.945	0.085
	(0.109)	(0.130)		(0.354)	(0.936)		(2.318)	(125.033)	
Artisans and related workers	0.024	1.025	0.872						
	(0.151)	(0.155)							
Plant and machine operators and assemblers	0.079	1.082	0.585						
	(0.144)	(0.156)							

(Continued)

Table 9.3 (Continued)

Income Level (Y): If it is up to TRY 4,877, then Y = 1; If it is between TRY 4,878 and TRY 9,754, then Y = 2; If it is between TRY 9,755 and TRY 14,631, then Y = 3; If it is at least TRY 14,632, then Y = 4

	Y > 1 vs Y ≤ 1			Y > 2 vs Y ≤ 2			Y > 3 vs Y ≤ 3		
	β SE (β)	OR SE(OR)	p Value	β SE(β)	OR SE (OR)	p Value	β SE (β)	OR SE (OR)	p Value
Workplace status (RC: public)									
Public	−1.603 (0.120)	0.201 (0.024)	0.000	−1.035 (0.097)	0.355 (0.035)	0.000	0.206 (0.142)	1.228 (0.174)	0.146
Continuity (RC: temporary, daily, seasonal work)									
Permanent	1.767 (0.167)	5.856 (0.977)	0.000						
Registration (RC: not registered)									
Registered	1.411 (0.172)	4.100 (0.706)	0.000						
Employment status (RC: regular)									
Irregular	−0.901 (0.199)	0.406 (0.081)	0.000	0.538 (0.447)	1.712 (0.766)	0.229	−0.046 (0.886)	0.955 (0.846)	0.959
Working hours (RC: 31–45 hours)									
Up to 30 hours	−1.368 (0.199)	0.255 (0.032)	0.000	−0.598 (0.120)	0.550 (0.066)	0.000	−1.916 (0.332)	0.147 (0.049)	0.000
More than 45 hours	−0.151 (0.064)	0.860 (0.116)	0.019						
Constant	−0.973 (0.306)	0.378 (0.116)	0.001	−5.737 (0.434)	0.003 (0.001)	0.000	−10.665 (2.327)	0.000 (0.000)	0.000

[a] RC, reference category.

variable to another level are different, separate model estimates were made for each level of the dependent variable. The dependent variable consists of four categories, necessitating the estimation of three different models. Table 9.3 provides coefficients, odds ratios, and p-values for the categories of independent variables for each model. Since categories that satisfy the parallel lines, assumption share the same coefficients and odds ratios, they are presented in the first column only. Categories that do not satisfy the parallel lines assumption, thus having different coefficients in each model, are presented separately in each column. The model developed for women working as RCEs is statistically significant

$\chi^2 = 4,283.069$, $p = 0.000$, *Pseudo* $R^2 = 0.293$, $AIC = 1,451.21$, $BIC = 11,016.99$.

According to the results obtained from the model created for women working as RCEs (Table 9.3).

Women working as RCEs in the 15–24 age group are 1.480 times more likely to earn a higher wage compared to those in the 25–34 age group, and 1.862 times more likely compared to those in the 35–44 age group. When compared to female RCEs in the 15–24 age group, those in the 45–54 age group are 1.844 times more likely to earn more than TRY 4,877, 2.957 times more likely to earn more than TRY 9,754, and 3.294 times more likely to earn more than TRY 14,631. For those aged 55 and above, the odds ratios are 1.864, 3.204, and 5.111, respectively. The likelihood of female RCEs earning higher wages increases with age. This can be attributed to career advancement leading to higher earnings as individuals progress in their careers.

- Marital status of female RCEs does not have a statistically significant effect on their wages.
- All categories of education levels have a statistically significant impact on wages. The reference category, "university and above graduates," has a higher likelihood of earning higher wages compared to all other education levels. Moreover, this likelihood increases further as wages rise across all other education categories, supporting the findings of Topalhan and Yeşilkaya (2017), Gustafsson and Jacobsson (1985), and Nikulin and Wolszczak-Derlacz (2022).
- Istanbul, where approximately 20% of the Turkish population resides, is a region of significant importance to the country due to its trade and export capacity, which leads to a higher likelihood of female RCEs earning higher wages. Compared to female RCEs in other regions, those in Istanbul have a likelihood of earning higher wages that is at least 1.54 times higher and can be as much as 1.92 times higher. In Istanbul, 75% of female RCEs work in the service sector, and 25.6% of all female RCEs in the service sector are employed in Istanbul. Female RCEs working in the service sector in the Istanbul region earn an average wage of TRY 7,530, which is higher than the average wage of all female RCEs in the service sector (TRY 6,650).
- In the analysis where the service sector is the reference category, the coefficients obtained for the industrial and construction sectors were found to be statistically insignificant. When compared to the reference category of the service sector, female RCEs working in the agricultural sector have a remarkably higher

likelihood of earning wages that is 3.189 times higher. The reason for this result could be attributed to the low proportion of female RCEs working in the agricultural sector (1.7%) and consequently the small number of observations in the sample. In fact, around 89% of women working in the agricultural sector are either unpaid family workers or self-employed, which may reflect a gender-biased perspective or the informal nature of women's employment in this sector.

- The wage levels of female RCEs increase as the scale of the workplace/business[4] grows: The likelihood of earning higher wages for female RCEs working in micro-scale enterprises is 1.301 times higher compared to those working in small-scale enterprises, and it is 1.595 times higher in medium-scale enterprises. However, the parallel lines assumption is not satisfied for the last category, which is large-scale enterprises. The odds ratios obtained from the models are 2.073, 2.853, and 3.505, respectively. All female RCEs working in large-scale enterprises are registered and work regularly,[5] with 87.5% of them being in permanent employment. In this context, the higher wages of female RCEs in large-scale enterprises are related to the characteristics of these "jobs" within these enterprises.
- The occupations of female RCEs were grouped according to the ISCO-08 of the HLFSMDS, and a reference category was created by combining "unskilled workers" with "skilled workers in agriculture, forestry, and fisheries." Compared to the reference category, the odds ratios for "managers and professional workers" indicate that the likelihood of female RCEs earning more than TRY 4,877 is 2.216 times higher, that the likelihood of earning more than TRY 9,754 is 9.883 times higher, and that the likelihood of earning more than TRY 14,631 is 141.825 times higher. The same odds ratios for "technicians, technologists, and assistant professionals" are 1.600, 5.365, and 50.503 (which is only significant at the 0.10 level), respectively. The coefficients for "office workers" and "service and sales workers," which do not satisfy the parallel lines assumption, were found to be statistically significant only in the second model. Compared to the reference category, the likelihood of "office workers" earning more than TRY 9,754 is 3.095 times higher, and the likelihood of "service and sales workers" earning more than TRY 9,754 is 2.645 times higher. The coefficients for the other categories of the occupation variable were not found to be statistically significant.
- Female RCEs in the public sector are 4.975 times more likely than those in the private sector to earn more than TRY 4,877, and 2.817 times more likely to earn more than TRY 9,754. The coefficients estimated for those earning more than TRY 14,631 compared to those earning at most TRY 14,631 were not found to be statistically significant. Across all education levels and occupational groups, female RCEs in the public sector tend to have higher wage levels compared to those in the private sector.
- Female RCEs working in permanent positions are 5.856 times more likely to earn higher wages compared to those working in temporary positions (including trial periods), daily jobs, or seasonal jobs. Among female RCEs in permanent positions, 35.9% hold at least a bachelor's degree. On the other hand, 57.8% of

those holding temporary positions completed primary education at most. The average wage of female RCEs in permanent positions is more than twice that of those in temporary positions (TRY 6,607 and TRY 3,077, respectively). These findings align with the literature, demonstrating that as a woman's educational level increases, the likelihood of working in higher-paying and stable positions also increases.

– Female RCEs registered with the Social Security Institution are 4.100 times more likely to work in higher-paying jobs compared to those who are not registered. Unregistered female RCEs (earning TRY 2,780) can receive approximately 40% of the average wage of registered female RCEs (TRY 6,972).

– Female RCEs working in regular positions are 2.463 times more likely to earn more than TRY 4,877 compared to those working in irregular positions, with the highest probability of earning over TRY 4,877. The coefficients in the last two models are statistically insignificant. In the study by Güneş (2011), it was observed that having a regular income for women reduced their poverty.

– Female RCEs working full time, 31–45 hours per week, are 1.163 times more likely to earn higher wages compared to those working more than 45 hours per week (overtime workers). When compared to those working a maximum of 30 hours per week, female RCEs working 31–45 hours are 3.922 times more likely to earn over TRY 4,877, 1.818 times more likely to earn over TRY 9,754, and 6.803 times more likely to earn over TRY 14,631. According to the data, female RCEs have a higher likelihood of earning lower wages when working part-time or engaging in overtime work compared to those working 31–45 hours per week.

The results of the model created with the data of 13,534,000 male RCEs who reported their income in the 2022 HLFSMDS are presented in Table 9.A1, which can be found in the annex. The model created for male RCEs is statistically significant ($\chi^2 = 7,228.90$, $p = 0.000$, $Pseudo\ R^2 = 0.238$, $AIC = 23,269.60$, $BIC = 24,013.84$). Findings related to the male model have been included in this section, and only discrepancies that significantly differ from the female model were discussed in the results section.

Conclusion

In this study, the relationship between women's wages and various interest rates was searched since the beginning of the new discourses on interest. in this context, the study examined the trend of women's wages during the period 2017–2023, considering factors such as inflation rates, different interest rates, minimum wage, and hunger and poverty thresholds. Additionally, this study empirically analyzed the impact of individual and job-related characteristics on women's wages in Türkiye using the 2022 HLFSMDS of the TURKSTAT. The individual characteristics of female RCEs (age group, marital status, education level, and region of residence) and job-related characteristics (sector, workplace scale, occupation, workplace status, continuity, registration status, employment status, and weekly working hours) obtained from the HLFSMDS were used as independent variables. The dependent variable was the wage level determined by multiples of the minimum wage. The study employed the GOLRM to examine the effects of the independent variables on the wage level.

The individual characteristics determining the wage level of female RCEs included "increasing age, higher education level", particularly holding positions in the occupation categories of "managers and professionals" and "technicians, technologists, and associate professionals," and residing in the "Istanbul region". Marital status did not have a significant impact on the wage level. Among the job-related characteristics, variables such as workplace scale, working in the public sector, and having a continuous, registered, and full-time job were effective in increasing the wage level.

In the GOLRM model created for male RCEs, all variables had at least one category which was statistically significant. Unlike the female model, factors such as marital status, working in artistic and related occupations, and working in skilled agricultural, forestry, and fishery occupations as well as plant and machine operators and assemblers contributed to the increase in wage levels. The significance of marital status as a variable affecting the wages of male RCEs can be attributed to a gender-biased perspective that traditionally views men as the primary breadwinners of the household. For male RCEs, working in a registered job was significant in the first model, where the wages of those earning more than the minimum wage were compared with those earning the minimum wage. In the male model, overtime work did not have a significant impact on wage levels. All these findings support the Dual Labor Market Theory, which suggests that individuals employed in good jobs tend to have higher wages (Doeringer & Piore, 1970).

It can be stated that wages in Türkiye are influenced by the country's unique economic policies. During the years 2017–2021, policy interest rates and inflation rates exhibited similar trends of increase and decrease. However, after the year 2021, policy interest rates have decreased while inflation has increased dramatically. Due to the rise in inflation, the minimum wage has approximately doubled in the years 2022 and 2023, an unprecedented trend in the past 20 years. This situation directly impacts the wages of RCEs who predominantly earn the minimum wage. In the current circumstances, the main question is whether, in the continued conditions of high inflation rates and the depreciation of the TRY, the minimum wage will revert to affecting general wage practices. Furthermore, it remains to be seen whether the wage gap between men and women will persist even in low-paying jobs, in line with the findings of Deshpande et al. (2018) in the context of India.

In conclusion, the data indicates that inflation has an observable impact on wages in Türkiye. However, to clearly observe the effects of implementing the recent trend of reducing policy interest rates (started to rise again since June 23, 2023) on wages, more extensive data covering a longer period is needed.

In future studies, conducting a micro-level analysis of women's wages with detailed subcategorized variables could contribute to identifying the most effective and efficient policies for social policymakers.

Appendix

Table 9.A1 GOLRM Results for Men Working as RCEs

Income Level (Y): If it is up to TRY 4,877, then Y = 1; If it is between TRY 4,878 and TRY 9,754, then Y = 2; If it is between TRY 9,755 and TRY 14,631, then Y = 3; If it is at least TRY 14,632, then Y = 4.

	Y > 1 vs Y ≤ 1			Y > 2 vs Y ≤ 2			Y > 3 vs Y ≤ 3		
	β SE (β)	OR SE (OR)	p Value	β SE (β)	OR SE (OR)	p Value	β SE (β)	OR SE (OR)	p Value
Age group (RC: 15–24)									
25–34	0.367 (0.067)	1.444 (0.096)	0.000	0.716 (0.092)	2.045 (0.189)	0.000	0.850 (0.122)	2.340 (0.285)	0.000
35–44	0.495 (0.077)	1.641 (0.127)	0.000	0.962 (0.102)	2.618 (0.268)	0.000	1.182 (0.135)	3.262 (0.440)	0.000
45–54	0.561 (0.086)	1.753 (0.150)	0.000						
55+	0.298 (0.106)	1.347 (0.143)	0.005	0.827 (0.137)	2.286 (0.313)	0.000	0.991 (0.197)	2.694 (0.531)	0.000
Marital status (RC: married)									
Single	−0.204 (0.057)	0.815 (0.046)	0.000	−0.435 (0.071)	0.647 (0.047)	0.000	−0.357 (0.106)	0.700 (0.074)	0.000
Education level (RC: university and above)									
At most primary education	−1.110 (0.085)	0.329 (0.028)	0.000	−1.886 (0.107)	0.152 (0.016)	0.000	−2.377 (0.244)	0.093 (0.023)	0.000
General high school	−0.790 (0.090)	0.454 (0.041)	0.000	1.237 (0.099)	0.290 (0.029)	0.000	−1.423 (0.188)	0.241 (0.045)	0.000
Vocational or technical high school	−0.725 (0.091)	0.484 (0.044)	0.000	−0.999 (0.094)	0.368 (0.035)	0.000	−1.419 (0.188)	0.242 (0.046)	0.000
Vocational school	−0.554 (0.075)	0.574 (0.043)							

(Continued)

Table 9.A1 (Continued)

Income Level (Y): If it is up to TRY 4,877, then Y = 1; If it is between TRY 4,878 and TRY 9,754, then Y = 2; If it is between TRY 9,755 and TRY 14,631, then Y = 3; If it is at least TRY 14,632, then Y = 4.

	Y > 1 vs Y ≤ 1			Y > 2 vs Y ≤ 2			Y > 3 vs Y ≤ 3		
	β SE (β)	OR SE (OR)	p Value	β SE (β)	OR SE (OR)	p Value	β SE (β)	OR SE (OR)	p Value
Marmara	−0.212 (0.059)	0.809 (0.047)	0.000						
Aegean	−0.451 (0.062)	0.637 (0.040)	0.000						
Mediterranean	−0.549 (0.064)	0.578 (0.037)	0.000						
Western and central Anatolia	−0.326 (0.059)	0.722 (0.043)	0.000						
Black Sea	−0.461 (0.077)	0.631 (0.049)	0.000						
Eastern and southeastern Anatolia	−0.704 (0.065)	0.494 (0.032)	0.000						
Sector (RC: service)									
Agriculture	0.326 (0.174)	1.385 (0.241)	0.000						
Industry	0.035 (0.050)	1.035 (0.052)	0.486						
Construction	0.380 (0.088)	1.463 (0.129)	0.000	0.066 (0.157)	1.068 (0.167)	0.673	−0.405 (0.280)	0.667 (0.187)	0.148
Scale (RC: micro)									
Small	0.287 (0.057)	1.333 (0.075)	0.000	0.730 (0.107)	2.074 (0.221)	0.000	0.716 (0.189)	2.047 (0.387)	0.000
Medium	0.603 (0.067)	1.827 (0.123)	0.000	1.100 (0.107)	3.004 (0.322)	0.000	1.096 (0.186)	2.991 (0.557)	0.000
Large	0.912 (0.079)	2.488 (0.197)	0.000	1.552 (0.110)	4.720 (0.517)	0.000	1.655 (0.185)	5.231 (0.966)	0.000
Don't know but less than 10	0.500 (0.439)	1.649 (0.724)	0.255						

Job (RC: skilled agricultural workers, unskilled workers, etc.)

Managers and professionals	1.128 (0.118)	3.088 (0.364)	0.000	2.503 (0.172)	12.218 (2.095)	0.000	3.476 (0.564)	33.320 (18.225)	0.000
Technicians, technologists, and assistant professionals	0.747 (0.109)	2.111 (0.230)	0.000	1.655 (0.175)	5.233 (0.917)	0.000	2.372 (0.569)	10.715 (6.099)	0.000
Office workers	0.233 (0.097)	1.263 (0.123)	0.016	0.983 (0.181)	2.673 (0.483)	0.000	1.307 (0.590)	3.695 (2.181)	0.027
Service and sales workers	0.148 (0.075)	1.159 (0.087)	0.048	1.143 (0.171)	3.137 (0.536)	0.000	1.846 (0.573)	6.336 (3.632)	0.001
Artisans and related workers	0.281 (0.073)	1.324 (0.097)	0.000	1.101 (0.178)	3.008 (0.537)	0.000	1.346 (0.598)	3.842 (2.297)	0.024
Plant and machine operators and assemblers	0.260 (0.075)	1.297 (0.097)	0.000	0.942 (0.177)	2.566 (0.453)	0.000	1.187 (0.601)	3.277 (1.968)	0.048
Workplace status (RC: public)									
Public	−1.296 (0.088)	0.274 (0.024)	0.000	−1.123 (0.067)	0.325 (0.022)	0.000	−0.015 (0.094)	0.985 (0.093)	0.874
Continuity (RC: temporary, daily, seasonal work)									
Permanent	0.821 (0.091)	2.274 (0.206)	0.000						
Registration (RC: not registered)									
Registered	0.755 (0.079)	2.128 (0.169)	0.000	0.384 (0.240)	1.468 (0.352)	0.110	−0.168 (0.366)	0.840 (0.309)	0.647
Employment status (RC: regular)									
Irregular	0.028 (0.117)	1.028 (0.120)	0.812	0.729 (0.290)	2.072 (0.601)	0.012	1.227 (0.436)	3.411 (1.487)	0.005
Working hours (RC: 31–45 hours)									
Up to 30 hours	−1.596 (0.122)	0.203 (0.025)	0.000	−1.129 (0.138)	0.323 (0.044)	0.000	−1.732 (0.269)	0.177 (0.048)	0.000
More than 45 hours	−0.076 (0.041)	0.927 (0.038)	0.062						
Constant	0.742 (0.185)	2.100 (0.388)	0.000	−3.574 (0.325)	0.028 (0.009)	0.000	−6.316 (0.701)	0.002 (0.001)	0.000

Notes

1 In examining the relationships between all variables, the Spearman correlation coefficient was employed.
2 The hunger threshold represents the monthly expenditure required for a healthy, balanced, and adequate diet for a family of four. On the contrary, the poverty threshold encompasses the total amount necessary for monthly expenditures on food, clothing, housing (rent, electricity, water, fuel), transportation, education, healthcare, and other essential needs (TÜRK-İŞ, 2023).
3 The hunger threshold refers to the total expenditure covering the cost of food and other essentials necessary for a worker to fulfill their basic needs and obtain the required caloric intake to sustain their well-being and ability to work. On the contrary, the poverty threshold represents the minimum amount required for a family of four, with at least one wage earner, to sustain their basic needs without relying on external support. (This information was obtained through consultation with the confederation's Research and Development specialist on August 3, 2023.)
4 The scales were determined according to Article 5 of the Regulation on the Definition, Qualifications, and Classification of Small- and Medium-Sized Enterprises.
5 In the HLFSMDS, the question regarding workplace status is asked to employees in the private sector, while it is assumed that employees in the public sector work in a regular workplace.

Bibliography

Aksoy, N., Felek, Ş., Yayla, N., Çeviş, İ. 2019. "Türkiye'de Kadın İstihdamı ve Etkileyen Faktörler", *Journal of Management and Economics Research*, Vol.17, No.3, 146–163.
Aldan, A. 2021. "Rising Female Labor Force Participation and Gender Wage Gap: Evidence from Turkey", *Social Indicators Research: An International and Interdisciplinary Journal for Quality-of-Life Measurement*, Springer, Vol.155, No.3, 865–884.
Alpar, R. 2013. Çok Değişkenli İstatistiksel Yöntemler, Detay Yayıncılık, Ankara.
Altan, A. 2021. "Rising Female Labor Force Participation and Gender Wage Gap: Evidence from Turkey", *Social Indicators Research*, Vol.155, 865–884.
Arslan, G. 2021. "Türkiye'de Kadın İstihdamının Görünümü: Kadın İstihdamı ile FBGSYH, Enflasyon Oranı ve Kadın İşgücü Oranı Arasındaki Eştümleşme İlişkisinin Araştırılması", *Uluslararası Sosyal ve Ekonomik Çalışmalar Dergisi*, Vol.2, No.2, 1–19.
Aydos, M., Toker, Ç.D. 2021. "Eğitim Seviyelerine Göre Genç İşsizliğinin Ekonometrik Analizi: Türkiye Örneği", İzmir İktisat Dergisi, Vol.36, No.1, 109–126.
Ayvaz Kızılgöl, Ö. 2012. "Kadınların İşgücüne Katılımının Belirleyicileri: Ekonometrik Bir Analiz", *Doğuş Üniversitesi Dergisi*, Vol.13, No.1, 88–101.
Batu Ağırkaya, M. 2022. "E7 Ülkelerinde İnsani Gelişmişlik Endeksi: Kadın Faktörü", *Uluslararası İktisadi ve İdari İncelemeler Dergisi*, Vol.35, 61–84.
Blinder, A.S. 1973. "Wage Discrimination: Reduced Form and Structural Estimates", *The Journal of Human Resources*, Vol.8, No.4, 436–455.
Bozali, N., Uğur, M.S. 2022. "Türkiye'de Cinsiyetler Arası Kazanç Eşitsizliğinin Ölçülmesi", *Anadolu Üniversitesi İktisadi ve İdari Bilimler Fakültesi Dergisi*, Vol.23, No.3, 229–251.
Çağlayan Akay, E., Kömüryakan, F. 2023. "Gender Wage Gap among Couples and the Role of Parenthood across the Wage Distribution in Turkey", *Journal of Family and Economic Issues*, Published online: 24 April 2023, https://doi.org/10.1007/s10834-023-09901-3.
Çakır, N.Z. 2021. "Bireylerin Haftalık Çalışma Saatlerini Etkileyen Faktörlerin Genelleştirilmiş Sıralı Logit Modeli ile Analizi", *Biga İktisadi ve İdari Bilimler Fakültesi Dergisi*, Vol.2, No.3, 281–291.

Çelik Uğuz, S., Topbaş, F. 2016. "Turizmde Kadın İstihdamı ve Ücret Ayrımcılığı: Karşılaştırmalı Bir Analiz", *Anatolia: Turizm Araştırmaları Dergisi*, Vol.27, No.1, 62–78.

Central Bank of the Republic of Türkiye. 2023a. Fiyat Endeksi (Tüketici Fiyatları), https://www.tcmb.gov.tr/wps/wcm/connect/TR/TCMB+TR/Main+Menu/Istatistikler/Enflasyon+Verileri/Tuketici+Fiyatlari, 2023-07-03.

Central Bank of the Republic of Türkiye. 2023b. Politika Faizi, https://www.tcmb.gov.tr/wps/wcm/connect/TR/TCMB+TR/Main+Menu/Temel+Faaliyetler/Para+Politikasi/Merkez+Bankasi+Faiz+Oranlari/1+Hafta+Repo, 2023-07-03.

Central Bank of the Republic of Türkiye. 2023c. Bankalarca Açılan Mevduatlara Uygulanan Ağırlıklı Ortalama Faiz Oranları (Aylık-Stok), https://evds2.tcmb.gov.tr/index.php?/evds/portlet/lrcsQFWXtqo%3D/tr, 2023-07-03.

Central Bank of the Republic of Türkiye. 2023d. Kredili Mevduat Hesabı Faiz Oranları, https://evds2.tcmb.gov.tr/index.php?/evds/portlet/K24NEG9DQ1s%3D/tr, 2023-07-03.

Central Bank of the Republic of Türkiye. 2023e. Bankaların Kredi Kartı Faiz Oranları, https://www.tcmb.gov.tr/wps/wcm/connect/TR/TCMB+TR/Main+Menu/Istatistikler/Faiz+Istatistikleri, 2023-07-03.

Central Bank of the Republic of Türkiye. 2023f. Electronic Data Delivery System, https://evds2.tcmb.gov.tr/index.php?/evds/serieMarket, 2023-08-15.

Cergibozan, Y., Özcan, Y. 2012. "Türkiye İçin Bölgelere Göre Ücret Ayrıştırma Analizi: Ekonometrik Yaklaşım", *Kırklareli Üniversitesi İktisadi ve İdari Bilimler Fakültesi Dergisi*, Vol.1, No.1, 27–48.

Deshpande, A., Goel D., Khanna S. 2018. "Bad Karma or Discrimination? Male–Female Wage Gaps Among Salaried Workers in India", *World Development*, Vol.102, 331–344.

Doeringer, P.B., Piore M.J. 1970. *Internal Labor Markets and Manpower Analysis*, USA Department of Labor, Eric.

Doğan, B. 2022. "Cinsiyet Farkına Dayalı Ücret Farklılaşması ve Yoksulluğun Kadınlaşması: Türkiye Örneği", *Yayımlanmamış Doktora Tezi, Bursa Uludağ Üniversitesi*, 196 pages.

Duman, A. 2019. "Türkiye'de Emeğin Değişen Payı ve Gelir Dağılımı", Çalışma ve Toplum, Vol.60, No.1, 349–370.

Duruoğlu, T. 2007. "Emek Piyasasında Cinsiyetçi Ücret Ayrımı: Bursa Organize Sanayi Bölgesinde Bir Araştırma", *İletişim Kuram ve Araştırma Dergisi*, Vol.24 Kış-Bahar, 61–17, http://www.irfanerdogan.com/dergiweb2008/24/4.pdf, 2023-a04-07.

Eraslan, V. 2012. "Türkiye İşgücü Piyasasında Ücret Seviyesinde Cinsiyet Ayrımcılığı: Blinder-Oaxaca Ayrıştırma Yöntemi", İstanbul Üniversitesi İktisat Fakültesi Mecmuası, Vol.62, No.1, 231–248.

Erdem Karahanoğlu, G., Kumaş, H. 2022. "Türkiye'de İyi ve Kötü İşler: Genç Çalışanlar Üzerinden Bir Analiz", *Sosyoekonomi*, Vol.30, No.51, 427–447.

Erdoğan, E., Yeşilyurt, C. 2022. "Cinsiyete Dayalı Ücret Ayrımcılığının ISCO Meslek Gruplarına Göre Analizi", İstatistik Araştırma Dergisi, Vol.12, No.1, 16–38.

Eurofound. 2022. *Minimum Wages in 2022: Annual Review, Minimum Wages in the EU Series*, Publications Office of the European Union, Luxembourg.

Eurostat. 2022a. *Labour Market Database*, Annual Net Earnings, https://ec.europa.eu/eurostat/databrowser/view/earn_nt_net/default/table?lang=en, 2023-07-06.

Eurostat. 2022b. *Living Conditions and Welfare Statistics, Persons at Risk of Poverty or Social Exclusion by Age and Sex*, https://ec.europa.eu/eurostat/databrowser/view/ILC_PEPS01N/default/table?lang=en&category=livcon.ilc.ilc_pe.ilc_peps, 2023-07-07.

Eurostat. 2023. *Minimum Wages*, July 2023 and July 2013 (Levels, in € per Month and Average Annual Growth, in %). png, https://ec.europa.eu/eurostat/statistics-explained/index.php?title=File:Minimum_wages,_July_2023_and_July_2013_(levels,_in_%E2%82%AC_per_month_and_average_annual_growth,_in_%25)_.png, 2023-07-05.

Fu, V. 1998. "Estimating Generalized Ordered Logit Models", *Stata Technical Bulletin*, Vol.44, 27–30.

Gültekin, M. 2022. "Türkiye'de Ücretli ve Ücretsiz Emek Ekseninde Kadınlarla Erkeklerin Hem Kendi İçlerindeki Hem de Kendi Aralarındaki Eşitsizlikler", *Fe Dergi*, Vol.14, No.2, 33–55.

Güneş, F. 2011. "Farklı Emek Kategorileri Açısından Kadın Yoksulluğu", Çalışma ve Toplum, Vol.2, No.29, 217–248.

Gustafsson, S., Jacobsson, R. 1985. "Trends in Female Labor-Force Participation in Sweden", *Journal of Economics*, Vol.3, No.1, 256–274.

Halaçlı, B., Karaalp Orhan, H.S. 2022. "Cinsiyete Dayalı Ücret Eşitsizliği: İşveren Yönlü Bir Analiz", *Erciyes Üniversitesi İktisadi ve İdari Bilimler Fakültesi Dergisi*, Vol.61, 65–90.

Hayat, E.-Sözen Özden, A. 2021. "Genelleştirilmiş Sıralı Lojistik Regresyon Analizi ile Bireylerin Mutluluk Düzeylerine Etki Eden Faktörlerin Belirlenmesi", *OPUS–Uluslararası Toplum Araştırmaları Dergisi*, Vol.18, No.40, 2288–2316.

Heckman, J.J. 1976. "The Common Structure of Statistical Models of Truncation, Sample Selection, and Limited Development Variables and A Simple Estimator for Such Model", *Annals of Economic and Social Measurement*, Vol.5, No.4, 475–492.

Heckman, J.J. 1979. "Sample Selection Bias as a Specification Error", *Econometrica*, Vol.47, No.1, 153–161.

Heckman, J.J., Macurdy, T.E. 1980. "A Life Cycle Model of Female Labor Supply", *Review of Economic Studies*, Vol.47, No.1, 47–74.

İlkkaracan, I., Selim, R. 2007. "The Gender Wage Gap in the Turkish Labor Market", *Labour*, Vol.21, No.3, 563–593.

ILO. 2022. World Employment and Social Outlook- Trends 2022, https://www.ilo.org/wcmsp5/groups/public/---dgreports/---dcomm/---publ/documents/publication/wcms_834081.pdf, 2023-04-07.

Karamızrak, B. 2019. "Türkiye'de Enflasyon, İşsizlik ve Büyüme'nin Asgari Ücret Üzerindeki Etkisinin Ekonometrik Analizi", *Akdeniz Üniversitesi Sosyal Bilimler Enstitüsü Dergisi*, Vol.6, 88–102.

Kaya, G., Selim, R. 2018. "The Gender Wage Inequality in Turkey", *Pressacademia Procedia*, Vol.7, 408–413.

Kaya, V., Çelik, A.K., Kutlu, M. 2020. "Personal Income Distribution in Turkey: A Generalized Ordered Logit Analysis", *Economic Journal of Emerging Markets*, Vol.12, No.2, 138–150.

Kılıç, D., Öztürk, S. 2014. "Türkiye'de Kadınların İşgücüne Katılımı Önündeki Engeller ve Çözüm Yolları: Bir Ampirik Uygulama", *Amme İdaresi Dergisi*, Vol.47, No.1, 107–130.

Kılınç, N. 2020. "İşgücü Piyasasında Toplumsal Cinsiyet Eşitsizliği ve Gelir Dağılımı", Yayımlanmamış Doktora Tezi, Hacettepe Üniversitesi, 230 pages.

Kleinbaum D.G., Klein, M. 2010. *Logistic Regression: A Self-Learning Text*, Springer, New York.

Kumaş, H., Çağlar, A. 2011. "Türkiye'de Kadın Eksik İstihdamını Belirleyen Faktörler: TÜİK 2009 Hanehalkı İşgücü Anketi Ham Verileri ile Cinsiyete Dayalı Bir Karşılaştırma", Çalışma ve Toplum, Vol.2, No.29, 249–289.

Kumaş, H., Çağlar A. 2017. "Tabakalı İşgücü Piyasası Teorisine Göre Türkiye'de Özel-Hizmet Sektöründe İstihdamın Kalitesi", *İŞGÜÇ Endüstri İlişkileri ve İnsan Kaynakları Dergisi*, Vol.19, No.1, 49–86.

Liu, X. 2016. *Applied Ordinal Logistic Regression Using Stata: From Single-Level to Multilevel Modeling*, Sage Publications Inc., Los Angeles.

Liu, X., Koirala, H. 2012 "Ordinal Regression Analysis: Using Generalized Ordinal Logistic Regression Models to Estimate Educational Data", *Journal of Modern Applied Statistical Methods*, Vol.11, No.1, 242–254.

Mert, M. 2006. *SPSS, STATA Yatay Kesit Veri Analizi Bilgisayar Uygulamaları*, Detay Yayıncılık, Ankara.

Miyoshi, K. 2008. "Male–Female Wage Differentials in Japan", *Japan and the World Economy*, Vol.20, 479–496.

Neef, T., Robilliard, A.S. 2021. "Half the Sky? The Female Labor Income Share in a Global Perspective", World Inequality Lab—Working Paper N° 2021/22, https://wid. world/news-article/half-the-sky-the-female-labor-income-share-in-a-global-perspective/, 2023-04-08.

Nikulin, D., Wolszczak-Derlacz, J. 2022. "GVC Involvement and the Gender Wage Gap: Micro-Evidence on European Countries", *Structural Change and Economic Dynamics*, Vol.63, 268–282.

Oaxaca, R. 1973. "Male-Female Differentials in Urban Labor Markets", *International Economic Review*, Vol.14, No.3, 693–709.

OECD. 2022. "Gender Wage Gap", https://data.oecd.org/earnwage/gender-wage-gap.htm 2023-07-17.

Onuk, P. 2017. "Ücret Eşitsizliği ve Ücretin Sosyoekonomik Belirleyenleri: İstanbul Örneği", Çalışma ve Toplum, Vol.2, No.53, 703–720.

Özer, M., Biçerli, K. 2003. "Türkiye'de Kadın İşgücünün Panel Veri Analizi", *Sosyal Bilimler Dergisi*, Vol.14, No.2, 55–85.

Peterson, B., Harrell, F. E. Jr. 1990. "Partial Proportional Odds Models for Ordinal Response Variables", *Applied Statistics*, Vol.39, No.2, 205–217.

Sayar Özkan, G., Özkan, B. 2010. "Kadın Çalışanlara Yönelik Ücret Ayrımcılığı ve Kadın Ücretlerinin Belirleyicilerine Yönelik Bir Araştırma", *Çalışma ve Toplum*, Vol.1, No.24, 91–104.

Şentürk, İ., Demir, Ö. 2022. "Türkiye'de Cinsiyete Dayalı Ücret Eşitsizliği: Üç-Parçalı Blinder-Oaxaca Ayrıştırması", *Uluslararası Yönetim İktisat ve İşletme Dergisi*, Vol.18, No.1, 153–181.

Şerbetçi, A. 2012. "Sıralı Lojistik Regresyon Analizi ile İstatistik ve Ekonometri Derslerinde Başarıyı Etkileyen Faktörlerin Belirlenmesi: Atatürk Üniversitesi İktisadi ve İdari Bilimler Fakültesi Öğrencileri Üzerine Bir Uygulama", Yayımlanmamış Yüksek Lisans Tezi, Atatürk Üniversitesi, 64 pages.

Tansel, A. 2002. Economic Development and Female Labor Force Participation in Turkey: Time-Series Evidence and Cross-Province Estimates, METU/ERC Working Paper, No:01/05, https://erc.metu.edu.tr/en/system/files/menu/series01/0105.pdf, 2023-04-07.

Tansel, A. 2005. "Public–Private Employment Choice, Wage Differentials and Gender in Turkey", *Economic Development and Cultural Change*, Vol.53, No.2, 453–477.

Tatoğlu, T. 2022. "Drivers of Low Female Labor Force Participation in Türkiye", BBVA Research Working Paper, No:22/13, https://www.bbvaresearch.com/wp-content/uploads/2022/12/WP_22_13_Drivers_of_Low_Female_Labor_Force_Participation_in_ Turkiye.pdf 2023-04-07, 2023-07-10.

Topalhan, T., Yeşilkaya, F. 2017. "Kadın Yoksulluğunu Etkileyen Faktörlerin Panel Veri Analizi ile Belirlenmesi", *KARATAHTA İş Yazıları Dergisi*, Vol.9, 55–82.

Tunalı, H., Göksu, Y.D. 2018. "Türkiye'de Kadınların İşgücüne Katılımının Belirleyicileri Üzerine Ekonometrik Bir Analiz", *Uluslararası Ekonomik Araştırmalar Dergisi*, Vol.4, No.1, 29–45.

TÜRK-İŞ. 2023. Açlık&Yoksulluk Sınırı, https://www.turkis.org.tr/category/aclik-yoksulluk/, 2023-07-04.

TÜRKİYE KAMU-SEN. 2023. Asgari Geçim İndeksi, https://www.kamusen.org.tr/?tksTag=asgari%20ge%C3%A7im%20endeksi, 2023-07-04.

TURKSTAT. 2017, 2018, 2019, 2020, 2021. Income and Living Conditions Survey Micro Data Set.

TURKSTAT. 2017, 2018, 2019, 2020, 2021, 2022. Household Labour Force Survey Micro Data Set.

TURKSTAT. 2022. İşgücü İstatistikleri Mikro Veri Seti, TÜİK, Yayın No:4692, Ankara.

TURKSTAT. 2023. "İşgücü İstatistikleri", https://data.tuik.gov.tr/Kategori/GetKategori?p=istihdam-issizlik-ve-ucret-108&dil=1, 2023-07-27.

Tütüncü, A., Zengin H. 2020. "E7 Ülkelerinde Kadın İstihdami ve Ekonomik Büyüme Arasındaki İlişki", *Uluslararası Yönetim İktisat ve İşletme Dergisi*, Vol.16, No.1, 1–16.

Williams, R. 2006. "Generalized Ordered Logit/Partial Proportional Odds Models for Ordinal Dependent Variables", *The Stata Journal*, Vol.6, No.1, 58–82.

Williams, R. 2016. "Understanding and Interpreting Generalized Ordered Logit Models", *The Journal of Mathematical Sociology*, Vol.40, No.1, 7–20.

World Economic Forum. 2023. Global Gender Gap Report 2003 Insight Report June Report 2023, Geneva: Switzerland, https://www3.weforum.org/docs/WEF_GGGR_2023.pdf, 2023-07-05.

Yalçın, E.C., Bayram Arlı, N., Aytaç, S., Başol, O., Aydemir, M. 2019. "Türkiye'de Emek Piyasalarında Cinsiyete Dayalı Ücret Ayrımcılığı: IBBS Düzey1'e Göre Farklılıklar", *Kocaeli Üniversitesi Sosyal Bilimler Dergisi*, Vol.38, 293–314.

Yamak, N., Abdioğlu, Z., Doğan, S. 2023. "İşsizlik Süresine Etkide Bulunan Faktörler: Türkiye için Mikro Veri Analizi", *Sosyal Güvenlik Dergisi (Journal of Social Security)*, Vol.13, No.1, 1–14.

Zeren, F., Kılınç, S. 2018. "Kadınların İşgücüne Katılım Oranı, Ekonomik Büyüme, İşsizlik Oranı ve Kentleşme Oranı Arasındaki Saklı Koentegrasyon İlişkisinin Araştırılması", *Yönetim Bilimleri Dergisi*, Vol.15, No.30, 87–103.

Index

Printed in the United States
by Baker & Taylor Publisher Services